THE ROAD TO BARBAROSSA

THE ROAD
TO
BARBAROSSA

THE ROAD TO BARBAROSSA

SOVIET-GERMAN RELATIONS, 1917–1941

NORMAN RIDLEY

FRONTLINE
BOOKS

ff

First published in Great Britain in 2023 by
FRONTLINE BOOKS
an imprint of Pen & Sword Books Ltd,
47 Church Street, Barnsley, S. Yorkshire, S70 2AS

ISBN: 978-1-39906-882-6

CIP data records for this title are available from the British Library

For more information on our books, please visit
www.frontline-books.com, email info@frontline-books.com
or write to us at the above address.

Printed and bound by CPI Group (UK) Ltd, Croydon, CR0 4YY
Typeset by Concept, Huddersfield, West Yorkshire
Pen & Sword Books Ltd incorporates the imprints of Pen & Sword
Archaeology, Atlas, Aviation, Battleground, Discovery,
Family History, History, Maritime, Military, Naval, Politics,
Social History, Transport, True Crime, Claymore Press,
Frontline Books, Praetorian Press,
Seaforth Publishing and White Owl

For a complete list of Pen and Sword titles please contact
PEN & SWORD LTD
47 Church Street, Barnsley, South Yorkshire, S70 2AS, England
E-mail: enquiries@pen-and-sword.co.uk

Or

PEN AND SWORD BOOKS
1950 Lawrence Rd, Havertown, PA 19083, USA
E-mail: Uspen-and-sword@casematepublishers.com

CONTENTS

LIST OF PLATES

1. Signing the truce between the Central Powers and Soviet Russia on 15 December 1917 in Brest-Litovsk.

2. Kapp Putsch conspirators under arrest 1921.

3. Enver Pasha.

4. Karl Radek.

5. Carden-Loyd tankette of the type used at the secret Russian Kama facility where the German Panzer I was developed.

6. Soldiers training at the Soviet-German Tomka chemical weapons facility.

7. Junkers aircraft manufacturing plant at Fili 1923.

8. German communist anti-Fascist demonstrators.

9. Ernst Thalman addressing a communist rally in the Berlin Lustgarten 1931.

10. Hans von Seeckt and Adolf Hitler.

11. Soviet Foreign Minister Molotov and German Foreign Minister von Ribbentrop after signing the Molotov-Ribbentrop Pact on 26 August 1939.

12. Molotov and Ribbentrop's signatures.

13. German and Soviet commanders meet in Poland, September 1939.

14. German troops burn a Russian village during Operation Barbarossa.

15. German troops hang Russian civilians during Operation Barbarossa.

16. Soviet prisoners of war captured by German forces during Operation Barbarossa.

LIST OF PLATES

INTRODUCTION

European history is littered with long-running sagas of rivalries, treaties, alliances and betrayals between neighbouring peoples striving for dominance over each other or sometimes just fighting for survival in the face of aggression. In this rich litany of war, peace and everything in between, Russian-German relations between 1917 and 1941 stand out as following the most improbable and unexpected trajectory of all. From the chaos of the First World War where the two nations had fought each other to a standstill there emerged two societies whose diametrically-opposed ideologies clashed in bloody and brutal street battles but whose governments and military establishments were able to meet on a different plane, where political expediency saw cooperation and eventual alliance before their armies once again fell upon each other, destroying the lives of countless millions of their soldiers and civilians in cataclysmic battles all across the great East European plains from Moscow to Stalingrad.

Cooperation between Russia and Germany had been a feature from as early as the Middle Ages, when the Hanseatic League of Merchant Guilds in market towns throughout northern and central Europe produced the first signs of wealth in Russia and brought her into the orbit of European trade. Based on German models, towns such as Riga, Mitau, Reval and Kiev would go on to introduce their own democratic conceptions with the first inklings of a Bill of Rights. Relations were developed to mutual benefit with no necessity for conflict with Germany just so long as German, Russian and Austrian ambitions in the Balkans did not conflict beyond the point where the talking stopped. Diplomacy at the time was essentially conducted between monarchs where personal friendships and relationships held sway.

Peaceful coexistence, however, often fell victim to rival ambitions and in 1761, long before Germany had even been created as a nation state, Russian troops had overrun Prussia, occupied Berlin and humbled Frederick the Great but the sudden enthronement of the extremely pro-Prussian Peter III in Russia saw him make peace and agree a formal alliance with Frederick. With growing wealth and aspiration, in a few short years, the two countries had joined with Austria to rise up to vie with each other for domination of Northern and Eastern Europe and like 'two gangsters . . . with a weaker confederate [divided up] the rich haul of loot [Poland]'.[1] An independent Poland had for years acted as a buffer state and kept the Russians and Prussians apart with relatively harmonious foreign policies but, with Poland gone from the map, they stood face to face across a common frontier where familiarity bred not only contempt but outright hostility.

The outbreak of the French Revolution distracted them momentarily from glaring at each other over a disputed border and then the rise of Napoleon saw the establishment of the Grand Duchy of Warsaw which Russia viewed as a move towards the creation of an independent Poland and a direct threat to its interests in the Baltic region. The diplomatic spat between Russia and France soon escalated into armed conflict with Napoleon's march on Moscow in 1812 and then when Prussia joined forces with Russia to drive Napoleon back across Eastern Europe, it was very much as the junior partner living in Russia's shadow and remained so until Bismarck unified Germany around the political and military power of Prussia. The vigorous new nation saw Prussian military tradition allied to the industrial powerhouse of the Ruhr and was soon strong enough to assert itself as an international force by negotiating with Russia to arrive at the Black Sea Agreement of 1871 and the secret Reinsurance Treaty of 1887. Friendship between the two nations was of paramount importance not only for security reasons but also fundamentally for the German concept of *Weltmacht* (world power) which envisaged Germany and Russia as the dominant powers in Eastern Europe. After Bismarck, however, German foreign policy bifurcated between those who saw Russia as an ally and those who had ambitions for German aggrandisement at Russia's expense. The 'Greater Germany' faction became dominant, which eroded the structure of alliance so painstakingly developed by Bismarck and led to a slow decline in German-Russian relations.

At the outbreak of the First World War, because of the Franco-Russian Agreement which had been in place since 1894, German military strategy was based almost entirely on the Schlieffen Plan which envisaged war on two fronts. The plan was to strike quickly in the West and achieve an early victory, allowing German forces to then turn and face Russia in the East. Russia was militarily weak and vulnerable after the Russo-Japanese War and diplomatic isolation in the six decades before 1914 had sapped the nation's moral strength.

In the opening months of the war, the Imperial Russian Army attempted to invade eastern Prussia, only to be beaten back at the Second Battle of Tannenberg, suffering the almost complete destruction of the Russian Second Army and the suicide of its commander General Alexander Samsonov. The Germans had become bogged down in trench warfare in the West but were still able to transfer sufficient troops to the Eastern Front in 1915 and, although they failed to take Warsaw, were able, together with Austro-Hungarian armies, to advance into Galicia and Poland after which the Russian Tsar Nicholas II took personal control of his country's war effort. The combat then followed a similar pattern to that on the Western Front where trench warfare had resulted in a stalemate. After the revolution of February 1917, the Tsar was forced to abdicate and a Russian Provisional Government was established under Alexander Kerensky.

Chapter 1

THE BOLSHEVIK REVOLUTION

By 1917, just as on the Western Front, both Germany and Russia had become enmired in the stalemate and slaughter of trench warfare. In Russia, the large numbers of war casualties and food shortages in the major cities had stirred up civil unrest and fomented the February Revolution that forced Tsar Nicholas II to abdicate. Following on from that, the rising tide of communist Bolshevik opposition to the Provisional Government saw support for the war effort against Germany dissipate further and transmute instead into internal strife. The Russian Army in its exhausted state, emaciated by massive desertions and faced with the threat of Bolshevik power in the northern and central regions, showed itself powerless to prevent the country collapsing into full-scale revolution.

After the Russian Revolution in 1917, the German military strategist Carl Adolf Maximilian Hoffmann, who would go on to conduct the peace negotiations at Brest-Litovsk, held firmly to the belief that Europe could not have peace unless the Bolsheviks were overthrown and stable conditions restored in Russia through intervention by a combination of the Western Powers and Germany. The immediate problem, as he saw it, was the territories of Poland and Lithuania, whose striving for statehood was reliant on German support as buffer states against Russia. Ambitious to create new states with maximum territorial boundaries, the two were, in 1918, showing disturbing ambitions to expand east into a bitterly divided Russia with its crumbling army and collapsed administration. Hoffmann argued that to help the nascent states compete for territory would incur Bolshevik wrath and to deny them help would encourage the Russians to drive west and retake lands lost during the war. For him the only solution for Germany was

1

to crush the Bolsheviks, restore Tsarist power in Russia and declare an immediate cessation of hostilities in Eastern Europe.

The new Russian leader Vladimir Lenin, however, did not see it this way. His solution certainly was to take Russia out of the war but as a functioning Bolshevist state. He signed a 'Decree on Peace' on 8 November 1917 calling upon all the belligerent nations and their governments to start immediate negotiations for peace and proposed an immediate withdrawal of Russian forces from the war. His situation was desperate because, as Soviet General Posokhow said at the end of November, 'the [Red] army just doesn't exist'.[1] Time was of the essence since not only were the Germans still menacing them but there was also pressure rising on the new Bolshevik government as anti-Soviet factions in the Ukraine saw their chance to rise up and break free from Russian domination, and worst of all civil war threatened at home. In February 1918, German forces were on the point of breaking through the feeble Russian defences at Petrograd and crushing the revolution before it could draw breath and that left Lenin with peace negotiations as the only means of survival, but the Western Allies would countenance no talk of peace on any front until Germany was defeated. The only recourse for Lenin was now to make a separate peace with Germany but that would free up German troops to move onto the Western Front and as such would be interpreted by the Western Allies as a hostile act, giving them an excuse to bring military action against Bolshevist Russia which they now saw as a new and immediate threat to Western democracy. Nevertheless, on 15 December 1917 an armistice was signed between Soviet Russia and the Central Powers (Germany, Austria-Hungary, Bulgaria and the Ottoman Empire) and peace talks began at Brest-Litovsk a week later. In a moment of unique drama, representatives of the most revolutionary regime ever known, whose clothes 'reeked of dungeons', sat down and negotiated an agreement with the extreme reactionary military caste of German nobility.[2]

Faced with danger on all sides, Leon Trotsky (Lev Davidovich Bronstein), as Soviet Commissar for Foreign Affairs, had wasted no time in replacing the exhausted and unreliable Russian army with a new revolutionary force that was formally established in January 1918. With decrees of equality of rights for all soldiers and command restructuring, the old Tsarist order was being swept away. However, he was not able to give credibility immediately to this new army as a force capable of influencing foreign affairs, which left the Soviets with a very weak negotiating position at Brest-Litovsk.

Germany had been desperate to free up its troops for redeployment in support of their planned Spring Offensive on the Western Front but the German General Staff also saw a chance to exploit Russian weakness and force the embattled Bolsheviks to hand over to them control of those states, such as Courland, Livonia and Estonia, where Germanic culture flourished. Annexation of the rich wheat fields of the Ukraine, too, seemed within reach to alleviate the food shortages in Germany and on the fighting fronts but German diplomatic delegates at the peace talks did not share the military's optimism and saw annexation of the disputed territories as being burdensome from an administrative perspective. They preferred instead to use the threat of occupation of these lands as a bargaining chip to be exchanged for territorial concessions in the West when the war ground to its inevitable end in peace talks with the Western Allies.

At the second meeting of the German-Russian peace negotiators on 18 January 1918, Hoffmann presented the German peace demands whereby the Germans would withdraw in return for independent states being established in the former Russian territories of Poland and Lithuania. To the intense frustration of the Germans, the Russian delegate, Leon Trotsky, procrastinated and turned negotiations into 'a debating society'.[3] While the Germans spoke the language of diplomacy and concentrated on territorial claims and strategic and economic advantage, the Bolsheviks devoted their efforts to propaganda in favour of proletarian emancipation and 'world revolution' in the name of communism. For Trotsky, arguing over territorial control was of no consequence when measured against the opportunities afforded by the rising tide of popular revolution.

Meanwhile, on 9 February, Germany became frustrated with Trotsky's machinations, concluded a separate peace treaty with the Ukraine and resumed hostilities with Russia. The Red Army crumbled under the renewed pressure, forcing a more conciliatory stance but still Trotsky, who preferred confrontation over compromise[4] and thinking that he could exploit Germany's desperation for a treaty to free up troops, responded by declaring an end to the war but refused to accept Germany's terms in what became his 'No War – No Peace' position to terminate hostilities without formal capitulation. German diplomats were nonplussed by this manoeuvre and seemed willing to accept Trotsky's terms, but the German General Staff was affronted by this impertinent refusal to acknowledge their clear superiority and intensified the German assault on Petrograd. Russian defences around the city disintegrated as its troops dissipated, as one German general described it, 'like thin clouds before a gale'. Lenin contested Trotsky's position and persuaded the Politburo to vote for compromise. The Germans restated their demands, insisting on immediate agreement, and with Trotsky powerless to resist any further the Brest-Litovsk Treaty was agreed on 3 March 1918 and signed by Russia and the Central Powers, Polish representatives having been excluded from the talks. It is worth noting that the Russian delegation included a woman, Anastasia Bizenko (Bitsenko), representing Russia's Socialist Revolutionary Party. Days afterwards, Trotsky, who was no diplomat, heaved 'a sigh of relief'[5] when he was replaced by Chicherin and was able to turn his attention to reorganising the Red Army.

Georgy Vasilyevich Chicherin was a classically educated career diplomat fluent in a number of European languages. Born into one of Russia's noble families, he was extremely wealthy but used his resources to finance revolutionary movements. He spent many years in exile from Russia, returning in 1917 to join Lenin's government. He had a keen understanding of the Soviet Union's extremely precarious position as a socialist republic surrounded by capitalist enemies.

The terms of the Brest-Litovsk Treaty were a massive humiliation for Russia. Under the treaty, the state of war between Russia and the Central Powers would cease, Russia would demobilise its army ceding Russian Poland, Lithuania, Courland, Livonia and Estonia to Germany and Ardahan, Kars and Batum to Turkey. In addition, Russia was forced to recognise the independence of Finland, Ukraine and Georgia. Reparation payments of six billion marks were demanded in gold and goods. Russia lost a third of its agricultural land, more than three-quarters of its coal mines and lost access to the Black Sea ports. Despite its draconian terms, the treaty was an essential step for Russia, giving it breathing space to confront its many problems, not least of which was a civil war with the White Russian reactionary forces of monarchists, capitalists and social democrats that had to be resolved in order to consolidate the revolution. Without the treaty it is doubtful if the Bolshevik revolution could have been successful and the whole history of Europe and the world would have been quite different. In a sense, Germany had given the Soviets a lifeline and was fundamentally the saviour of communism in Russia, the irony of which cannot be overstated given that one of the messianic motivations and underlying philosophy of Nazism would be its destruction.

It is interesting to look at the conclusions in a 1918 report of the Committee on Public Information in Washington. It said:

> The treaty of Brest-Litovsk was a betrayal of the Russian people by the German agents, Lenin and Trotsky; that a German-picked commander was chosen to defend Petrograd against the Germans; that German officers have been secretly received by the Bolshevik Government as

military advisers, as spies upon the embassies of Russia's allies, as officers in the Russian army, and as directors of the Bolshevik military, foreign, and domestic policy. They show, in short, that the present Bolshevik Government is not a Russian government at all, but a German government acting solely in the interests of Germany and betraying the Russian people, as it betrays Russia's natural allies, for the benefit of the Imperial German Government alone.

A number of documents quoted in the report are of particular interest and show the extent to which the German government dominated the new Soviet government at this time.

19 November 1917 from the German General Staff Central Division to the Council of People's Commissars signed by O. Rausch:

This is to advise you that the following persons have been put at the disposal of the Russian Government as military advisers: Maj. Erich, Maj. Bode, Maj. Sass, Maj. Zimmerman, Maj. Anders, Lieut. Haase, Lieut. Klein, Lieut. Breitz. These officers will choose a cadre of the most suitable officers from the list of our prisoners, who will likewise be at the disposal of the Russian Government, as was agreed at the conference in Stockholm.

12 January 1918 from the German Intelligence Bureau to the People's Commissar of Foreign Affairs signed by Agasfer on behalf of Rausch:

By the order of the local department of the German General Staff, the Intelligence Department has reported the names and the characteristics of the main candidates for the re-election of the Central Executive Committee. The General Staff orders us to insist on the election of the following persons: Trotsky, Lenin, Zinovieff, Kameneff, Joffe, Sverdlov, Lunacharsky, Kollontai, Fabrizius, Martov, Steklov, Golman, Frunze, Lander, Milk, Preobrajenski, Sollers, Studer, Golberg, Avanesov, Volodarsky, Raskolnikov, Stuchka, Peters, and Neubut. Please inform the president of the council of the General Staff's wish.

The following documents are examples of the way in which the German Imperial Bank financed the Bolshevik revolution.

28 December 1917 Resolution of the Reichsbank concerning the Rhine-Westphalian Industrial Syndicate and Handelstag.

- The purchase is permitted of all Russian securities and dividend bearing paper by the representatives of the German banks.

- After the conclusion of separate peace, on the expiration of 90 days, there are re-established all the shares of private railway companies, metallurgical industries, oil companies, and chemical pharmaceutical works.
- There are banished and for five years from date of signing peace are not to be allowed English, French, and American capitals in the following industries: Coal, metallurgical, machine building, oil, chemical, and pharmaceutical.
- In the question of development in Russia of coal, oil, and metallurgical branches of industry there is to be established a supreme advisory organ consisting of 10 Russian specialists, 10 from the German industrial organisations and the German and Austrian banks.
- The Russian Government must not interfere in the region of questions connected with the transfer to the benefit of Germany of two mining districts in Poland, Dombroski and Olkishski, and to Austria of the oil region in Galicia.
- Private banks in Russia arise only with the consent and according to the plan of the Union of German and Austrian Banks.

8 January 1918 from the Reichsbank (very secret) to the People's Commissar of Foreign Affairs signed by G. von Schanz:

Notification has to-day been received by me from Stockholm that 50,000,000 roubles of gold has been transferred to be put at the disposal of the representatives of the People's Commissars. This credit has been supplied to the Russian Government in order to cover the cost of the keep of the Red Guards and agitators in the country. The Imperial Government considers it appropriate to remind the Council of People's Commissars of the necessity of increasing their propaganda in the country, as the antagonistic attitude of the south of Russia and Siberia to the existing Government in Russia is troubling the German Government. It is of great importance to send experienced men everywhere in order to set up a uniform government.

11 January 1918 from the Reichsbank to the Chairman of the Council of People's Commissars signed by G. von Schanz:

The industrial and commercial organisations in Germany interested in trade relations with Russia have addressed themselves to me in a letter, including several guiding indications. Permit me to bring them to your attention . . . The conflict of the Russian revolution with the Russian capitalists absolutely does not interest German manufacturing circles, in so far as the question does not concern industry as such. You can destroy the Russian capitalists as far as you please, but it would by no means be possible to permit the destruction of Russian enterprises.

For the Germans, with their negotiated access to Ukrainian wheat and Romanian oilfields, there was a momentary rekindling of enthusiasm for the war as their territorial gains under Brest-Litovsk were lauded to the German population. When Austria-Hungary grabbed the lion's share of the spoils, however, German optimism waned. Not only that but the necessity for German occupying troops to remain in the Baltic States, Ukraine, Romania and Finland to supress communist movements meant that very few of the million men who should have been transferred to the Western Front were ever redeployed there.

The consequences for the German political landscape were no less extreme than in Russia as the flames of communist revolutionary fervour were fanned by the thousands of released prisoners of war, swamped by Soviet propaganda, returning to a German homeland crushed by food shortages and war weariness. Hundreds of thousands of German soldiers stationed in Russia were returning home with many of them imbued with communist ideas and demanding unprecedented reforms such as 'soldier's councils' and the right to elect officers. Worn out through fighting, they had mingled with Soviet soldiers after the treaty was signed and been subjected to communist propaganda to the point where Hoffmann declared that he 'did not dare to transfer certain [eastern divisions most heavily influenced] to the west[ern front]'.[6] Not only did the treaty save the revolution in Russia, it almost led to a communist state being created in Germany. Officers tried to preserve order in units that had come under Bolshevik influence by forming *Vertrauensträte* (councils of trusted soldiers) to counter the influence of communist propaganda. On the other hand, however, many returning war-hardened veterans went the other way and joined armed right-wing organisations such as the Iron Division. The German General Staff gave full approval to President Friedrich Ebert's fragile government in his stance to 'fight against Bolshevism'.[7]

In Russia, Trotsky had given up his role as Commissar for Foreign Affairs to become Commissar for War under the aegis of which he set about the formidable task of creating a new Red Army but time was not on his side. The Russian Civil War was gathering momentum and Russia's former allies were circling like vultures to pick at the carcass of the Tsarist state. Naturally, resistance to change within the old Imperial army, notwithstanding its failures, led to 'continued friction and conflict' given that Trotsky's new force would be a political entity designed to serve 'the dictatorship of the proletariat' and be 'imbued with the ideas of the workers' and peasants' revolution'.[8]

To overcome immediate manpower shortages in the army, recruits were drawn from POW camps to form International Battalions, but this strategy was particularly ill-founded and produced little more than 'ill-clad, ill-equipped and mutinously-disposed [units]'.[9] Trotsky was a firebrand politician, not a soldier, and he saw the Red Army as the embodiment of revolution with its primary role as the defender of the nation and not as a vehicle to export communism abroad. With no military background, he became fascinated by the bonds between fighting men and the complexities of running an army. He forced through the revolutionary changes required to build his new army by creating a centralised military and political machine but along the way made the first of what would become a legion of enemies. One of his most serious errors had been his peremptory decision to disarm the Czechoslovak Legion of former POWs on the Trans-Siberian railway in February 1918. This force had just defeated the Germans at the Battle of Bakhmach as the Brest-Litovsk talks were taking place. Trotsky was unwilling to see these men, fully armed and flushed with victory, return to Russia where they might join up with anti-government forces. What started out as an attempt at containment of these troops actually had the precise effect that Trotsky had been trying to avoid. They resisted all attempts to disarm them and went on to link up with White forces in Siberia and join the counter-revolution against the Bolsheviks. To meet the challenges facing the Red Army Trotsky then made another unpopular decision when he resolved to bring back officers of the old Imperial army to take up command roles in November 1918.

After the signing of the Treaty of Brest-Litovsk, Germany and Russia ceased all official hostilities towards each other and saw that now they actually had something in common. They had both become defeated pariah states, scorned, vilified and punished by the West. Riven internally by factional conflicts and facing dangers across their borders, they saw that they had good reason to turn to each other for support despite their fundamentally opposing political values. Indeed, some in Germany saw communism in Russia as no more than a transient phase within the country and its demise would be accelerated by reconstruction of its economic life with the help of German finance. Redirecting Russia back onto the road of capitalism would revitalise the German economy and create a huge new market for its products. The fundamental problem with this scenario, however, was that both countries were broke and it would take some time and effort to create the foundation for economic recovery in either.

All Western nations saw the potential for trade with Russia as a means of stimulating their economies but none were so well placed as Germany. At the All-Russian Congress of Soviets, the Minister of Trade Leonid Krasin said:

> None of the western European countries has such experience of working with Russia or such profound and exact knowledge of all conditions in our country as Germany. Hundreds of thousands of Germans used to live in Russia before the war; many of them are complete masters of the Russian language and have the most extensive personal connections throughout the length and breadth of Russia. Finally, our whole civilisation, in particular our technical development, industry, and trade, have been based for decades past mainly on work done in partnership with Germany, and it is easier for the Russian industrialist, merchant, and even worker to get on with the German than with any other foreigner.[10]

German militarism had been humbled by defeat but had not been stripped of its innate sense of worth and it had retained ambition which it allied to cunning in pursuit of its own survival in the finest Bismarckian traditions. The main architect of this unlikely liaison between the two countries was the Prussian General Hans von Seeckt, described as 'a typical representative of the reactionary Junker-caste of Germany'.[11] He had been the creator of the Reichswehr (combined German armed forces after 1919) and untiring champion of the German military establishment who was to become one of the dominant forces of the Weimar Republic.

The Treaty of Versailles, signed on 28 June 1919, officially ended the state of war between Germany and the Allied Powers. It effectively negated the Treaty of Brest-Litovsk and put severe restrictions on German military strength. From the moment the treaty was signed it became von Seeckt's all-consuming ambition to circumvent its restrictions and see Germany once again become self-reliant militarily. Article 231 of the Treaty of Versailles stated: 'Germany admitted its responsibility for the damage which it has done to the governments of unions, and united to them and their citizens in consequence of the war which was tied to them by aggression from German side.'

Very soon afterwards German nationalists began to criticise this declaration. The Treaty had placed a list of fundamental restrictions on Germany including depriving it of the right to use resources which still belonged to it as well as stripping it of its colonies. Germany lost its strategic industrial regions and was forced to pay massive reparations to the victorious Allies. All this resulted in unemployment, inflation and a drastic fall in living standards. It was Versailles above all else that would drive Germany and Russia into each other's arms.

Johannes 'Hans' Friedrich Leopold von Seeckt had been born in Schleswig in 1866 and although his family had become impoverished, his father was a general in the German army and Hans had grown up to be a dyed-in-the-wool aristocrat. He had fondness for few outside his class and little tolerance of dissenting views. He had joined the army in 1885 and within four years had been elevated to the General Staff. During the First World War he had reserved most of his vitriol for his Austro-Hungarian allies whose officer class he found intolerable and who in turn had loathed his Prussian arrogance. On the other hand, he found France also to be beyond the pale with its democratic ideals that were anathema to the whole basis of his Junker status and prestige.

At the outbreak of the First World War he had been Chief of Staff of the German III Corps in Belgium and France. He cemented his reputation in January 1915 when he defeated the French at Soissons. In March 1915 he was transferred to the Eastern Front as Chief of Staff of the Eleventh Army under General von Mackensen where he laid out the plans for the German offensive against the Russians at Gorlice in Galicia, one of the greatest German victories of the war. In the autumn of 1915 Bulgaria entered the war on the side of the Central Powers, seeking revenge for the defeat in the Second Balkan War in 1913. On 6 October 1915 he led the attack against Serbia and held his ground against a Russian counter-attack in the Brusilov offensive. Two years later, in December 1917, von Seeckt was sent to Turkey as Chief of Staff of the Ottoman field army, where his leadership prevented the collapse of the Turkish army. As a result of his postings in the East, von Seeckt avoided being tarnished with the failed German strategy on the Western Front.[12]

His views of the world led him to believe that Germany, because of her geographical position, was wedded more to the politics of the East rather than the West. The danger, as he saw it, was that the Western Powers would force Germany into an alliance with them that would put it at the forefront of a military campaign to crush the new communist government in Russia. German industrialists were keen to take up an anti-Russian stance but von Seeckt was firmly opposed to the idea since 'the future understanding with Greater Russia was to be the permanent target of Germany's foreign policy,' he wrote in 1920, 'it was inappropriate to antagonize Russia's new masters'[13] and he was totally against intervention in the Russo-Polish dispute on the side of Poland. He shuddered at the thought of German troops fighting under

French or Polish control. 'What do we win,' he wrote,' if we achieve victory over the Bolsheviks?'[14] Only if the Red Army appeared at the German frontier would he look upon it as a foe in which case he would oppose it with all means at his disposal. He would even tease the Western Allies with such a prospect when Tukhachevsky's Russian forces later stood at the gates of Warsaw. The sight of Bolsheviks taking over Poland, he hoped, might cause the Allies to take a more lenient approach to German rearmament but, coming so soon after Versailles, the French especially were in no mood to scale back their opposition to any such move. It was, however, a sound plan which saw much success with secret deals struck with Russia before the Allied fear of Bolshevism finally saw them acquiesce to German rearmament.

Von Seeckt's creation, the Reichswehr, was a professional volunteer force more formidable even than most conscript armies but lacked, under the baleful gaze of Allied scrutiny, the means or freedom to develop professionally. It did, however, in von Seeckt's eyes, have a distinct advantage in that a smaller army was easier and cheaper to fit out with modern equipment and weaponry, especially given Germany's dire financial situation, and a defeated army was much easier to persuade to change its ways. As a result the Reichswehr under his command was well-trained and well-equipped. Of necessity, he was forced to abandon the previous German army doctrine of massed troops and heavy artillery but his experiences had shown that small, well-trained and mobile forces could overcome a numerically stronger opponent and for this training was the key. His philosophy might be summed up as 'mobility over mass' but the limit of 100,000 men imposed upon the army at Versailles was leaving Germany open to danger both externally and internally. The problem in the future, as von Seeckt saw it, was to expand the armed forces rapidly in time of war and still retain a high level of skill and competence, especially with technically advanced equipment. Adolf Hitler would later describe von Seeckt as the master of the professional army but not the conscript army. In addition, von Seeckt had ambitions to create a militia, a sort of extended national service, to defend the country against any aggression. The restrictions on armed forces, however, had serious consequences when Russia's defeat at the hands of the Poles had given Poland the time and energy to stand up to the Germans during the battles surrounding the plebiscite in Upper Silesia. It had been a humiliation for von Seeckt when he had been unable to send in Reichswehr units and had to leave the fighting to paramilitaries whose unreliability and unruliness had been exposed in the Kapp Putsch.

While he was always ready to give the impression to the Western Allies that Germany would be a willing partner in the struggle against Bolshevism, von Seeckt also saw the power of the Soviet state as an important factor capable of bolstering Germany's position in the great game of European diplomacy. It was essentially the balancing of these two elements and, perhaps more importantly, the lack of alternatives that initially led von Seeckt to look upon Russia, which had not signed up to Versailles, as probably the only country that would collaborate with him in developing a modern German army outside the confines of the Treaty but there were formidable hurdles to overcome before that could become a reality.

For the moment, though, Russia, riven by internal strife, did not present itself as a particularly desirable partner. Its loss of prestige and influence had left Poland with a free hand in Upper Silesia where it took advantage of the opportunity to challenge Germany over the border demarcation. That is something it would not normally have done had Germany been able to rely on Russian support in a region overrun with a ragtag of irregular militias and paramilitary groups such as the one led by Wolfgang Kapp who would later launch a coup against the German government. Unable to contain these groups, Germany had been forced into the humiliation of seeing troops of the Western Allies called into maintain order during a plebiscite. Faced with a continuation of this indignity, von Seeckt saw some sort of alliance with Russia as the only way of stabilising Eastern Europe against Polish aggression and Western interference. This was echoed in Moscow where Lenin called Germany 'the most advanced country with the exception of America' and saw that, because of Versailles, it would be 'pushed into alliance with Russia'.[15]

Opposition to collusion with Russia came, not least, from within von Seeckt's own ranks, where Generals Hoffmann and Groener, who had witnessed the effects of Bolshevik propaganda on German troops during the war, could not be convinced that the answer lay in the East but they, like von Seeckt, admired the fighting spirit of the Russian armed forces even though they deplored their politics. There was also the particularly attractive prospect of using Russia as a manufacturing base for otherwise embargoed military equipment but that would obviously involve sharing new developments with what had sometimes been, and might yet be again, a formidable enemy. The political situation in Germany however, with its troublesome undercurrents of communist agitation, denied von Seeckt a legitimate pathway to explore the potential for cooperation with the very Bolshevist regime that was so blatantly trying to undermine the German state with its financing of the *Kommunistische Partei Deutschlands* (KPD – German Communist Party). Collaboration between Germany and Russia in military affairs was nothing new, however. Even before the First World War the German Krupp works had benefitted from Russian artillery experts advising them on development of German guns, especially large-calibre ones. A firing range near St. Petersburg had been used as a testing ground but the German government preferred to deal with the British and it took all of Krupp's economic clout to persuade them to support the Russian venture. There was, however, one possible ally right under von Seeckt's nose in the form of the Russian intellectual and political heavyweight Karl Berngardovich Radek. A close ally of Trotsky, Radek was currently in custody in Germany for inciting Bolshevik insurrection and it was he who would go on to play a pivotal role in the next phase of cooperation.

Back in Russia, Lenin's new Bolshevist regime was struggling to survive its infancy in the face of almost universal condemnation and internal opposition. Inside the country many rival factions were at each other's throats. Civil war had broken out in December 1917 but there was no clear divide between the two sides. The Red Army of the Bolsheviks was up against the White Army but a number of rival militant socialist forces opposed both. From the international community, thirteen foreign nations had sent troops to oppose the Red Army while Germany, Austria-Hungary and the Ottoman Empire took advantage by nibbling away at Russia's borders, hoping to regain lost territory. Despite all opposition, the Red Army's fronts held through the summer of 1918 and began the following year in relative control of the centre of the country but in March 1919, the White Army launched a major offensive. The Red Army, led by Mikhail Tukhachevsky and Mikhail Frunze, was just able to hold its ground and managed to turn the tables and assumed the offensive itself in May.

Mikhail Nikolayevich Tukhachevsky had been born in the Safonovsky District into an aristocratic but impoverished family. Fighting in the Imperial army, he had been captured by the Germans in February 1915 and imprisoned in Ingolstadt in Bavaria, at one point sharing a cell with the future French general Charles de Gaulle. He was eventually able to escape and returned to Russia in October 1917 just in time for the revolution. Singled out by Trotsky as a potential leader for his 'strategic talents and tactical abilities of a conspicuously high order',[16] he was given command of the Russian First Army facing the Czechs. During the Civil War he was to play a major role in the defence of Moscow which led to further promotion. At the age of 23, he would go on to lead the Russian troops in the war against Poland. On the personal level, there is much evidence to show that Tukhachevsky was virulently anti-Semitic and given to irrational extreme pagan beliefs.

Mikhail Vasilyevich Frunze was born in Pishpek, Kyrgystan. For his part in the 1905 Russian Revolution he was sentenced to death by the Tsarist regime but had his sentence commuted to hard labour. When the 1917 revolution came, he was put in charge of the Minsk civilian militia. After success against White forces in the Civil War, Trotsky gave him command of the whole Eastern Front where he found the troops in 'a parlous state verging on mutiny'. It says much for his abilities to overcome such inauspicious beginnings that he was to achieve a number of significant victories at Omsk, Turkestan and in the Crimea.

By the autumn the White armies had retreated to the south and east. With the Whites dispatched, Frunze turned his attention to the urgent task of considered how the Red Army was to be modernised. With war activity, both externally and internally much reduced, his first priority was to release the majority of the more than five million men under arms for industry. For the retained forces Frunze then proposed the creation of a cadre system comprised of elite officers with an emphasis on technological knowledge, training in mobility and personal initiative. It did not go unnoticed that this was exactly the kind of military that von Seeckt was developing in Germany. Unlike von Seeckt, however, Frunze lacked trained, professional officers who were also doctrinally acceptable to their political masters but perhaps the most pressing issue which could not be immediately addressed was the paucity of modern military equipment. Isolated as it was, Trotsky's new army was denied access to technological developments that were taking place in Western Europe.

Despite the numerous small conflicts that raged all across Eastern Europe, the signing of the Versailles Treaty saw a certain degree of closure for the signatories. It marked both an ending and a beginning and a time for all countries to take stock. Almost immediately after signing, Britain was ready to admit the failure of its intervention policy in support of White Russian forces against what was now undisputed Bolshevik control of Russia. Facing the reality of that situation meant entering into a dialogue to come to a diplomatic and economic understanding so that countries could move on. While many in the West expected Lenin's reign to be short-lived and advised a cautious approach, others chose to end the economic blockade and promote trade links through a – notionally – non-political organisation, the Russian Cooperative Societies. The Russians were happy to respond positively in a matter of only a few days but made it clear that it continued to view the British government as hostile. Negotiations unsurprisingly progressed at a snail's pace with both the French and Italian governments refusing point-blank to take part. Their scepticism proved well-founded when the Russian delegation under Leonid Krasin was brought under tight political control which meant that effectively Britain was dealing not with Russian industry per se but directly with the Russian government; a fact that it went to great pains to conceal. Lord Curzon, the British Foreign Secretary, however, was confident that Britain held the whip hand in all negotiations and said; 'We know from a great variety of sources that the Russian government is threatened with complete economic disaster, and that it is ready to pay almost any price [for assistance] . . . We can hardly contemplate coming to its rescue without exacting a price for it.'[17] That price was the cessation of Bolshevik agitation in the countries of the British Empire. Having presupposed that Russia had no alternative but come to terms it came as a shock to Curzon to find that this was not the case and that there was no softening of the Moscow line politically.

Krasin met with the British Prime Minister David Lloyd George directly, but serious issues soon surfaced. There was the question of pre-revolutionary debts to international creditors and the validity of the Russians using gold seized from the Imperial State Bank, and other assets such as confiscated White Russian valuables, to pay these debts and to finance future trade deals. Russia bluntly refused to acknowledge responsibility for meeting Tsarist debts and Britain agreed that, for the purposes of concluding trade deals, only British debt needed to be considered. Alongside commercial arrangements a prisoner exchange was negotiated, and an official armistice agreed.

The man destined to play a major role in Soviet-German relations and the one to whom von Seeckt turned was the prisoner Radek who had been born Karol Sobelsohn in Lemberg (Lviv) in the Ukraine in 1885 moving to Germany in 1907 where he joined the *Sozialdemokratische Partei Deutschlands* (SPD – German Social Democratic Party). When war broke out, he moved to Switzerland and worked with the exiled Lenin, eventually riding with him on the 'closed train' that took the communist leader to Russia in 1917 to launch the revolution there. Radek had also been a member of the Russian delegation at the Brest-Litovsk negotiations where he was described by the German journalist Wilhelm Herzog as having a 'lively and ever-active mind . . . feverishly at work. His brain [was] filled with Germanic romanticism . . . rich in irony and energy . . . [he had] an immense historical culture and a very clear knowledge of world political relations.' At that time

Moscow had high hopes of Germany quickly following it down the path of communist insurrection as the country staggered under the weight of military defeat but reactionary forces there proved stronger than the Tsarists had been in Russia. In December 1918, Radek entered Germany illegally with a mission to harness what Moscow saw as an irrepressible revolutionary zeal and drive the German communists to power. While there may have been justification for Moscow's initial optimism, it had not fully appreciated the residual German military strength under von Seeckt who, aided by the splits within the German communist movement, systematically and ruthlessly smashed the poorly organised Spartacist uprising of February 1919 with his *Freikorps* units using machine guns and artillery.

The Spartacists, named after the Roman slave Spartacus who led a revolt in 73 BC, had been founded in 1915 by Rosa Luxemburg and Karl Liebknecht and had strong ties to Radek since that time and through him had a direct line to Lenin. Radek had tried to enter Germany in December 1918 as part of a five-man Soviet delegation to the Reich Congress of Councils but was refused entry. Nothing daunted, he tried again but this time disguised as an Austrian prisoner of war and was on hand to help in the founding of the KPD. It is not known to what extent Radek spoke for Moscow at this time but he argued strongly but unsuccessfully against direct action against the German government. His view was that the KPD was not an effective party and had an insufficient groundswell of support. When, against his counsel, the revolt was launched prematurely and revolutionary councils were set up in many major cities, his warnings proved to be prescient as the military authorities were able to restore control quickly. Radek, Luxemburg and Liebknecht were hunted down with a reward of 10,000 marks being offered to anyone who gave information leading to Radek's arrest. He was eventually arrested on 17 February while attending a meeting of the Red Soldiers' League and incarcerated under military protective custody in Berlin's Moabit Prison.[18]

At this point Germany briefly offered itself to the Western Allies as a bulwark against Bolshevism in return for more lenient armistice terms but its advances were rebuffed and when the drastic terms of the Versailles Treaty were made clear Germany reversed its policy and turned away from its attempts to court the West and began to consider instead a military concordat with Russia. This was by no means straightforward given that German troops under General Gustav Adolf Joachim Rüdiger Graf von der Goltz were still fighting alongside White Russian monarchist against the Red Army in Latvia. The Western Allies, however, brought pressure to bear and insisted that Goltz pull back from Estonia to avoid the whole of the Baltic becoming enflamed when the emphasis was now on achieving some sort of stability in Eastern Europe. Von Seeckt was in complete agreement with the Allies on the issue and reined Goltz in, but German industrialists continued to fund the Baltic operations, hoping to break the communists and open up their Russian markets once more.

Chapter 2

THE RUSSO-POLISH WAR

The four years of world war ended with the armistice declared on 11 November 1918 and left Eastern European international borders in flux. Once-powerful empires had crumbled, and new states were being created. The Western Allies tried to bring order by decree but on the ground, it was military might that held sway. While politicians grappled with the problem of re-drawing the map of all the lands from the Baltic to the Black Sea, militias of many nations disputed territories that had become uncoupled as the Austro-Hungarian and the Russian Empires evaporated.

In February 1919, the febrile state of East European politics gave way when the Polish leader Jósef Piłsudski saw an opportunity to expand the frontier of the newly reformed Polish state eastwards into areas with large Polish-speaking populations but currently without strong legitimate administrations. At this time, areas ceded by Germany to Russia by the Treaty of Brest-Litovsk were being vacated by German forces and being occupied by Russian troops. It was inevitable that Polish and Russian ambitions would collide in those areas now characterised by the fragility of their constitution and fluidity of borders, even though the Red Army was still heavily involved in the Russian Civil War. The Poles quickly advanced into Lithuania and Belarus, also occupying much of western Ukraine. An arrogant Piłsudski was contemptuous of Russian strength as he easily took Kiev in April 1920 but the Russians had not been defeated, they had merely withdrawn in order to launch effective counter-attacks. The first turning point of the whole war came in early July when a massive Russian offensive was launched along the Smolensk-Brest axis to surround the Polish forces near the Lithuanian and Prussian border. By 7 July the Polish forces were in full retreat along the entire front with Russian forces taking

Minsk on 11 July and Vilnius three days later. As a result, the Poles were pushed all the way back to Warsaw.

The British government delivered an ultimatum to the Soviets demanding that they halt their offensive and accept a temporary border with Poland until a permanent one could be established by negotiation, otherwise the British and French would assist Poland with all means available. The Soviets rejected all British mediation and declared a willingness to negotiate only directly with Poland. Piłsudski was rapidly losing the support of the Polish government who now dispatched a delegation to Moscow to ask for armistice talks. The Soviet peace terms, apparently approved of by Britain, amounted to a complete Polish surrender. France, however, was appalled by the imminent collapse of the Polish state and declared its moral, political and material support for Poland in its fight for independence.

Trotsky preached reconciliation given the heavy human and economic costs of the war for Russia that was crippling the economy and preventing recovery that he believed would best be achieved with German cooperation. Russia and Germany, he said, held strong hands to play in the game of international trade. Russian grain and German technology were essential to the Western Powers in their post-war reconstruction which was the only hope of creating European stability. Attempting to turn the war into a Polish proletarian revolution, he said, would risk intense opposition within the country, not to mention foreign intervention. Lenin overruled Trotsky and rejected calls for mediation, urging Russian forces to take Warsaw.

The Russian advance on Warsaw had aroused consternation in Berlin as it brought Russian troops closer to German borders, energising the communist factions and creating instability inside the country but that fear was countered by the prospect of Poland's defeat opening up the possibility of the restoration of the Reich's former eastern territories. There was also the alternative option of taking Poland's side and turning the tide of its fortunes and even pressing on to bring down the Bolshevist regime altogether, which would also create opportunities to advance German territorial ambitions. For the Soviets the throwing back of Polish forces and the anticipated taking of Warsaw opened up the tantalising prospect of getting within touching distance of the German Spartacist insurrection, which, with the support of a Russian army on Germany's border, could bring about a government in Germany that might be able to precipitate a pan-European communist revolution.

The formal Russian policy towards Germany at this time, however, was confused by deep divisions within its leadership over strategy. While Trotsky called for Russia to focus internally and consolidate the revolution at home, Lenin wanted to exploit the war with Poland as a revolutionary crusade to inflame the whole of Poland in a class war in which Germany could play no substantive part. That, in turn, would ignite revolution in Germany which had come closer due to the Kapp Putsch of March 1920, but many saw the sovietisation of Poland as unrealistic given its intrinsically reactionary establishment. Chicherin, the Russian Commissar for Foreign Affairs, preferred a third route of pursuing economic cooperation with Germany but soon realised that it was too much under the sway of the other Western Powers to respond positively. There could be no help from Germany in the fight against Poland, he concluded.

All Russian and German preconceptions rested on the assumption that Poland was about to fall to the Russians but on 8 August, when Tukhachevsky launched his attack against Warsaw, it was halted at Radzymin and the Poles counter-attacked under General Sikorski. When Piłsudski's forces struck in support, the Russians were forced to retreat. Within ten days much of the Russian force at Warsaw had been captured or had fled. Semyon Budyonny's cavalry tried to hold the Russian line but failed as the Poles continued to force all remaining Russian forces to fall back and Moscow was forced to sue for peace against the vehement protestations of Piłsudski who wanted to continue the fight. An armistice was agreed in October and the Treaty of Riga was signed on 18 March 1921. As Piłsudski feared, as part of the agreement Poland was forced to recognise Russian control of the Ukraine and Belarus.

On 5 March the chairman of the Council of People's Commissars of the Ukraine, Rakovsky, informed the Ministry of Foreign Affairs in Berlin that Radek, still incarcerated in Germany, had been appointed as the Ukrainian Ambassador to Germany.[1] The British and French did not like the idea of Radek operating inside Germany and wanted him expelled but the German Foreign Minister Ulrich von Brockdorff-Rantzau refused to allow it. Just before Radek's trial was about to begin, however, the Russians arrested a number of Germans and held them as hostages which appears to have persuaded the Germans to change their minds and, on 26 June, they offered to send him back to Russia in exchange for the hostages but before that could be arranged Radek was to play a new role in Soviet-German relations. Despite evidently having friends in high places both in Russia and Germany, he was becoming increasingly anxious about his safety in Moabit prison and feared assassination. In a letter to the journalist Alfons Paquet, he asked for a meeting with Major Carl von Schubert, the former military attaché in Moscow, with whom, despite calling him a 'vulgar Anglophile', he had been involved during Lenin's journey from Switzerland to Russia in 1917 and through whom he was able to negotiate his relocation to less perilous quarters. He was eventually also given the special privilege of being allowed to receive visitors, one of whom was the German industrialist and future Foreign Minister Walter Rathenau. The identity and frequency of visits soon led to his prison cell being referred to with some levity as his 'political salon'. Between them Radek and Rathenau had arranged for a semi-official 'Industrial Commission' to visit Russia for the purposes of investigating possible trade links, but the Germans returned from Moscow with dented hopes and a dim view of economic conditions there.[2]

The range and variety of callers to talk to Radek was impressive. Two such visitors were ex-Turkish ministers living in exile in Berlin. Talaat Pasha and Enver Pasha had been members of the Young Turk government. Enver was a personal friend of von Seeckt whom he had come to know while von Seeckt was Chief of Staff of the Turkish Army during the First World War. Both Turks had been complicit in the Armenian Genocide and had been tried and condemned to death in absentia by a Turkish court for 'plunging the country into war without a legitimate reason, forced deportation of Armenians and leaving the country without permission'. Now living in Germany, Enver was part of a Russian plan to rebuild a Russian-Turkish front against the British and was a natural choice for Radek when looking for an emissary to communicate with Moscow. Enver would later be killed by Russian cavalry during the Turkish War of Independence on 4 August 1922 and Talaat Pasha was assassinated in Berlin in 1921 by Soghomon Tehlirian. At his trial in June 1921, the 'undersized swarthy pale-faced' student claimed that he had killed Talaat to avenge the murder of his Armenian family. On hearing the evidence of Johannes Lepsius, a German Protestant missionary, the judge directed the jury to free Tehlirian if they believed him to have acted out of 'inner turmoil'. In less than an hour the jury found him not guilty.[3]

While von Seeckt communicated with Radek on a number of matters through emissaries, he baulked at actually meeting him in person. For a man in his position, whose troops had crushed the Spartacist uprising, it was a political step too far to contemplate. Enver's first attempt to reach Moscow under cover of the Turkish Red Crescent ended in farce. A British colonel, R.B. Ward, the Assistant British Commissioner for the Baltic Provinces stationed at Kovno (Lithuania), sent a report to the Chief of the British Military Mission in Berlin saying that they had captured a German monoplane of new and interesting construction that had evidently been built by the Junkers Flugzeugwerke A.G.

Dessau. The aircraft had flown from Berlin on 10 October under the authority of the German Ministry of War en route to Moscow but had made two forced landings before arriving at Königsberg on the 13th and then, in poor weather, it was forced to land at Abeli on the 15th. All the following occupants were arrested; Hans Hesse, a pilot employed by the Junkers Flugzeugwerke A.G., Paul Maruscyk, a mechanic also employed by the Junkers Flugzeugwerke A.G., Abraham Frankl, a Russian Jew believed to be the interpreter, Dr Dmitri Nicola, alias Sayd Emin, a Christian Turk, native of Bulgaria, recently staying in Berlin, who stated that he was a chemist by profession and now working for the Turkish Red Crescent, and Mohammed Ali Sami, a Turkish subject recently staying in Berlin, native of Constantinople who claimed to be the Chief of the Turkish Red Crescent in Russia.

Documents taken from Frankl showed that the mission was to establish the Soviet attitude to patents and patent law, to investigate the possibility of aircraft manufacture using German engineers particularly in relation to security, to investigate the demand in Russia for the sale of aircraft, to investigate the possibility of opening up air routes across Russia to the Far East and rail links to the Siberian fur trade, to ensure that any arrangements would survive a change of government (presumably in either country) and to inquire if the aircraft could be sold rather than have it return to Germany.

The British were not willing to allow the aircraft to break the Russian blockade and the men were taken into custody by the Lithuanian authorities. They were only released when von Seeckt sent Major Fritz Tschunke to negotiate on their behalf. Tschunke's report of the incident mentions two hooded men being brought to him by heavily armed Lithuanian guards. One of the men he recognised as Enver Pasha who was able to give some details of their mission. Enver said that he had a price on his head and was in fear of his life. Tschunke organised a daring escape during which Enver had to leap from an aircraft as it was taking off from a military airfield. The whole incident shows the extent to which plans were already advanced for Soviet-German cooperation and the extent to which von Seeckt was involved.

On the military side, the Germans were anxious to use Radek to explore the possibility of German-Soviet rapprochement, having been instrumental in arranging for Viktor Kopp to negotiate a German-Russian prisoner exchange in November 1919. Kopp, who had also at one time been a prisoner in Germany but was now an unofficial Russian delegate, was a close ally of Trotsky. He arrived in Berlin to negotiate the POW issues but was, at the same time, able to clandestinely conduct subversive activities with German communists as well as discuss trade matters with the *Auswärtiges Amt* (German Foreign Office) and make important contacts with the military. One of these contacts was von Seeckt who had established a highly secret Task Group Russia (*Sondergruppe R*), the purpose of which was to explore the prospects of military-industrial collaboration, led by Oskar Ritter von Niedermayer, under whose aegis Fritz Tschunke, Carl von Schubert, von Schleicher and General Otto Hasse met with Kopp, Krasin, Radek and others. Von Niedermayer, had been educated in Russia, was a close confidant of von Seeckt. He would later be involved in plots to assassinate Hitler but survived the Second World War only to disappear while in Soviet custody some time in 1948.[4]

At the same time, Herr Albrecht, a representative of the Allgemeine Elektrizitäts Gesellschaft (AEG), had gone to Moscow to look at industrial conditions there and, while he had been enthusiastically received, reported back that they were uninspiring. Britain was naturally interested in keeping a close eye on developments and when General Malcolm, a member of the British embassy in Berlin, wrote that whilst 'all classes in Germany are looking towards Russia for one reason or another . . . communication is much too difficult to make any practical steps possible [at this time]', they seemed to have taken the view that any liaison between Germany and Russia was unlikely.[5]

Kopp had initially been welcomed in Berlin just at the time that Germany had refused to take part in the Allied blockade of Soviet Russia. Lenin, however, could see no future in talks and instructed Kopp to break off all contact with the German government. This may have been no more than a cosmetic gesture to misdirect international scrutiny because talks certainly did not end. Kopp was secretly authorised to offer Germany all territories lost to Poland at Versailles in exchange for military cooperation against that country which was seen by both Germany and Russia as the real enemy.

In reality, this had already begun on a very informal and ad hoc basis during the Russo-Polish War so it was not exactly a revolutionary development. Von Seeckt arranged for General von Reibnitz, who had distanced himself from the fierce anti-Bolshevist faction in Germany, to look for common ground in a German-Russian military front against Poland and here again was evidence of the way Radek was treated in that this conversation took place at von Reibnitz's apartment in the presence of the chief of AEG Electrics, Feliks Deutsch. Later, Admiral Hintze, an ex-German naval attaché in Moscow, also met Radek but by this time Radek had been released from prison and was living more comfortably under house arrest with easy access to communications with Moscow although he was by no means a formal representative of the Russian government at this time.

Kopp, with Radek, developed the idea of forging economic ties with Germany, still an industrial giant with technical expertise second only to the US, and won the support of Rathenau who eyed Russia as a huge potential market for German goods. As Germany had not joined the economic blockade of Russia, Rathenau was able to establish an 'Industrial Commission' to investigate the potential of German-Russian trade links. He was of the opinion that the Allies would wage an economic war 'to the death' against Germany, requiring new markets and sources of raw materials to compensate for the loss of Germany's extensive pre-war trade with the Allies and their dependencies. He reasoned that this would oblige Germany to seek a close relationship with, or in his view economic domination of, her neighbours in Central Europe and above all with Russia, which he regarded as a semi-colonial, agrarian region which naturally complemented the industrial society of Germany.[6] For Rathenau, economic cooperation with Russia was vital to pre-empt the Western states from beating them to it.

On 10 January 1920, Radek met high-ranking German officials to discuss the reconstruction of Russian industry with German financial and technical assistance. To allay fears and in accordance with Trotsky's personal stance, he told the German representatives, Deutsch and the German Foreign Minister Walter Simons, that Russia had no intention of forcing Bolshevism on Germany. With a general understanding of a way forward, Radek was released and was due to return to Russia on the same aircraft as Enver but cried off at the last minute, fearing some sort of attack when his flight was mentioned in an intercepted telegram written by the head of Polish counterespionage, Ignaz Berner.[7] Kopp remained in Berlin to continue negotiations which now included the prospect of direct collaboration between the armed forces of both countries. Von Seeckt had boldly predicted a Russian victory in the war with Poland and, despite events conspiring against him on that front, still lauded the achievements of the new Red Army and its Chief of Staff P.P. Lebedev. In Russia itself Chicherin, Lenin's man, took charge of the secret negotiations with Germany.

It was at the time of Radek's repatriation that the Western Allies, Britain in particular, started pressing for war crimes charges to be brought against the German Kaiser Wilhelm II who had fled to Holland. The procedure for this had been embodied in Article 227 of the Treaty of Versailles and the charges included 'a supreme offence against international morality and the sanctity of treaties'. A number of other German military personnel were indicted for war crimes, but a compromise saw them tried by German courts and most were found not guilty. Von Seeckt vowed to challenge the threat to the Kaiser with 'every means in [my] power',[8] even if it meant reopening hostilities in the West and invading Poland in support of the Russians. Allied enthusiasm to pursue the Kaiser soon waned which meant that von Seeckt never had his bluff called on that count but it had, nonetheless, intensified his ambition to seek closer ties with Russia. Furthermore, his belligerent stance had won over to his side of the argument two powerful German leaders in Baron von Maltzan, head of the Eastern Department of the *Auswärtiges Amt*, and Brockdorff-Rantzau, the former Foreign Minister. This emboldened von Seeckt to despatch the ultra-conservative and monarchist ex-Secret Service chief Colonel Walter Nicolai to Moscow as part of *Sondergruppe R* to explore the prospect of building of aircraft factories in Russia. Nicolai was a fluent Russian speaker and had been head of the German High Command Intelligence service since 1913 during which time he had employed the famous exotic dancer Mata Hari whom he was to betray to a French firing squad. He would later be kidnapped and executed by Soviet agents after the Second World War. Nicolai's mission found favour in Moscow and was followed by that of Generals von Hammerstein and von Schleicher. Talks on economic ties would bear fruit with a trade agreement signed on 8 May 1921. While it was clear that wide irreconcilable differences would remain as long as Russia was ruled by the communists, there had been a perceptible thaw in relations during the two years since Brest-Litovsk. There was a ray of hope when Krasin professed himself to be an advocate of a more moderate form of Bolshevism, a sort of state capitalism which had gained some support in Moscow. There was a significant degree of hope that there would be a reintroduction of trade and a closer approximation to the capitalism of the Western World. The economic situation of Russia was so grave and Bolshevik economic doctrine considered to be so unworkable by the German capitalists that they believed that eventually the Bolsheviks, in order to remain in power, would be compelled to fully restore a capitalist economy.

In a letter of 20 January 1920, von Seeckt wrote:

Only in firm cooperation with a Great Russia does Germany have a chance of regaining her position as a world power. England and France fear the combination of the two land powers and attempt to prevent it with all their means – hence we have to seek it with all our strength . . . It is quite immaterial whether we like or dislike the new Russia and its

internal structure . . . we have to come to terms with Soviet Russia – we
have no alternative.

On a separate level, Enver Pasha had succeeded on his second attempt
to reach Moscow but this time he had gone overland. He was invited
to a congress in Tiflis in the Soviet Union and was accompanied by von
Seeckt's former adjutant, Rittmeister Ernst Kostring. They travelled
through British-occupied East Prussia to the Lithuanian border.[9] Once
in Moscow, Enver was encouraged by the enthusiasm Russia showed
for military cooperation with Germany. He met military leaders of
Trotsky's circle, six days after Tukhachevsky had been driven back from
the gates of Warsaw which encouraged the Russians to be attentive to
offers of cooperation. The Russians expressed a willingness to meet
German representatives and to recognise the old German frontier
of 1914 on condition that Germany would provide Enver's Turkish
groups with weapons so that they could make life uncomfortable for
British forces in Turkey, Persia and Afghanistan. It is worth noting that
the Russian conditions indicate they believed that Germany still had
large stores of weapons and had not been fully disarmed to the extent
demanded by Versailles.

Enver reported to von Seeckt that there was a powerful faction within
the Soviet leadership headed by Trotsky, although crucially having
little sway inside the Politburo, eager for an agreement with Germany
and Turkey. This faction was willing to cooperate on the condition that
Germany agreed to sell arms to Russia whose stocks of weapons and
ammunition was running perilously low. Russian ambitions, however,
were far from limited to guns, with Trotsky's sights set on much wider
cooperation. The war with Poland was seriously impacting Bolshevik
plans for the economic reconstruction of Russia and his ambition was
to harness German cooperation to rebuild the Russian economy.

In contrast to Lenin's views, there was a strong Russian body of
opinion that saw German assistance against the Poles and their
Western Allies as both necessary and possible. The Russian overtures to
Germany were designed to secure its aid against the Poles in exchange
for the return to Germany of territories lost to Poland in 1919, and at
the establishment of a broad German-Soviet political and economic
alliance against the West. It is likely that the moves for negotiations
with Germany were instigated by independent groups within the
Soviet leadership opposed to Lenin.

On 7 February 1920 a Soviet agent had arrived in Berlin to meet
the Foreign Minister Hermann Müller and proposed a German-Soviet

alliance in terms akin to those made to Enver. The Versailles Treaty would be repudiated and Germany's old eastern borders restored. In return Russia would expect significant German economic assistance and, with Turkey, the three powers would create a formidable military and economic powerhouse. The official German response was to reject the proposals, fearing that any such move would risk military intervention by the Western Powers and further misery for Germany. Müller, however, was sufficiently convinced to urge support for Russia, which he believed could turn the tide of war and defeat Poland leaving Germany with the prospect of occupying Polish territory after a Russian victory.

Kopp inquired of von Maltzan whether Germany would send troops or permit the transit of French troops to aid the Poles against Russia. Von Maltzan thought this unlikely. Kopp then suggested cooperation between Soviet and German forces in joint action against Poland which von Maltzan again thought illusory and rounded off the meeting by refusing to recognise Kopp, who was really only Trotsky's man, as a representative of the Soviet state. Kopp, however, did not remain idle. In a letter to the *Auswärtiges Amt* he expressed a desire 'to establish closer economic, political, and cultural connections with the German people as soon as possible'[10] but the *Auswärtiges Amt* remained cool towards him. Not so von Seeckt whom he met along with his aide, Major von Niedermayer, possibly Hermann Müller and German armament manufacturers to discuss German assistance in the production of war materiel in Russia. Von Seeckt reiterated that he would oppose any attempt by France to send military aid to the Poles overland through German territory.

The German Foreign Minister, Simons, was not prepared to discuss Kopp's proposition given that the Spa Conference, called to discuss German disarmament, coal shipments to the Allies and war reparations, was about to begin and he was not prepared to prejudice relations with the Western Powers but he did not reject Kopp's ideas out of hand. He told Kopp that he had taken his views under consideration with satisfaction and that he hoped 'present conditions will soon make possible the realisation of mutual desires'.[11] The Spa Conference took place in July 1920 between the Supreme War Council that coordinated the military strategies of Britain, France, Italy, the USA and Japan, and the government of the Weimar Republic. The Allies' rejection of German requests for concessions at Spa, however, had the effect of increased German hostility toward the West and encouraged them to turn elsewhere for a sympathetic hearing.

Days after the end of the conference, Kopp pressed Simons and von Maltzan for further negotiations and a 'quick clarification of German-Russian relations'. He again offered the establishment of a common Russo-German border and the settlement of the Polish Corridor problem to Germany's satisfaction. It appears that an undocumented agreement was reached in private over the dismemberment of Poland. As a result, the following day the *Auswärtiges Amt* proposed that Germany declare neutrality in the Russo-Polish War and barred the shipment of arms to Poland.

Simon now thought that 'the resumption of normal relations between Germany and Russia should be officially discussed' and Germany should take advantage of the 'enormously developing economy [the rebuilding of which was] a labour in which we would do well [to join]' but first demanded an apology for the assassination of the German ambassador to Moscow, Wilhelm von Mirbach, in 1918.[12] In both, he had the full support of von Seeckt. A Foreign Ministry spokesman went further and said that Germany could not initiate the annexation of the now-Polish territories because of fear of Western countermeasures, but these former areas of the Reich, once 'liberated' by the Soviets, should declare their independence from Poland on the basis of the right of self-determination. Von Seeckt sent orders for an eventual occupation of the Danzig Corridor. The Supreme Command of the Red Army had directed as early as 10 July that the borders of Germany be scrupulously respected, ostensibly to protect the Soviet right flank from a German response but, in reality, they were part of Trotsky's deal with von Seeckt to dismember Poland. It was this development that Lenin saw as an attempt by the German government to switch allegiances at the last minute and caused him to call off Kopp's negotiations in July. With Warsaw about to fall and the Red Army poised to reach the German border, he believed his position was strong and saw no benefit in further discussions with Germany.

Chicherin expressed satisfaction in the German position but, taking Lenin's line, pointedly asked why it had taken them so long to respond to Russian overtures and bluntly dismissed any possibility of an apology for von Mirbach's assassination. His cool response to the other issues was that they would take some time to formulate since they would have to be discussed at length by the Soviet Politburo. The issue of German annexation of Polish territory was also revisited and revised with the official Soviet position now that borders would have to be dictated by 'ethnographic factors', not historical ones. Von Maltzan was 'seriously disappointed' by this turn of events. Clearly Chicherin and Kopp did not have the same agenda, not least over the von Mirbach issue which Kopp seemed willing to concede. Chicherin was bullish in reminding Germany that Brest-Litovsk had been annulled at Versailles and no historic demands could be allowed to interfere with current negotiations. He warned Kopp that the Politburo had 'finally and categorically' rejected any concessions with regard to von Mirbach. Kopp was clearly feeling the pressure of acting almost on his own initiative in trying to advance the Trotsky line of economic cooperation with Germany over the Leninist policy of the export of communism.

Trotsky had a much more nuanced view of international politics than had Lenin. He well understood its complexities and perceived that France, not Britain, was the main supporter of Poland and the driving force behind the Polish decision to attack Russia in the first place. He was also aware of internal divisions over policy toward Russia within Britain and Germany which could be exploited to the advantage of the Soviet state. Lenin controlled the Politburo, however, and it was not until the tide had turned in the war with Poland that he came round to accepting Trotsky's arguments.

The idea of defeat for Poland in the war had never been acceptable to Britain and extra military aid sent to Poland at the last minute saw the Russians driven back from the Vistula and Poland eventually prevail, forcing the armistice signed at Riga on 18 March 1921. The British Secretary of State for the Colonies, Winston Churchill, was totally against any sort of deal with Russia and laid out his objections in a note of 16 November, the content of which ensured that there would be no lasting thaw in British-Russian relations. In particular, he criticised the payment of Russian debts using money acquired by 'naked robbery', an inevitable trade imbalance given the lack of Russian markets for British goods and total absence of good faith by communists who 'regarded [duping] non-communists as a virtue and a duty'.[13] This obdurate stance from the heart of the British government further encouraged Moscow to look favourably on overtures which had been playing on German strings since before Versailles.

The Polish victory put an end to plans for the country being divided up but a start had been made by the Russians and Germans to work together militarily on some level which fed into the wider scenario of economic cooperation. Both sides were cautious and careful not to over-commit initially but when talks proved to be amicable a significant barrier had been broken down. For Russia, Germany was the least hostile of all the world's major powers, which counted for something while Western forces were still on Russian soil and Western money was financing the continuing counter-revolution within its borders. The formation of an independent Poland and the signing of the Treaty of Riga in March 1921, which ended the Russo-Polish War, had also stripped Russia of territory. Russian technical deficiencies had ensured its eventual defeat by French and British-equipped Polish forces and whilst rapprochement with Germany might not have seemed a politically attractive move in the long term, it was certainly expedient under the circumstances.

Chapter 3

EARLY TANK WARFARE DOCTRINE

German aid to the Bolsheviks had been in evidence since before the signing of the Treaty of Brest-Litovsk and whilst it may have been low-key and limited in scope, it created the precedent that was to lead to a truly spectacular development in covert armaments manufacture. German finance had been channelled to Lenin even before the October Revolution as a means of bringing about an end to hostilities on the Eastern Front. In early 1918 German banks invested considerable amounts in Soviet industry with a concomitant investment of expertise and skilled labour. This was halted temporarily but resumed after Brest-Litovsk. In a supplementary treaty signed on 27 August 1918, Russia not only granted Germany additional economic rights on its territory but obtained pledges that German troops would intervene to expel Allied forces from its territory. These arrangements, however, would became obsolete after the German surrender to the Western Allies in November.

Now that there was a renewed appetite for military cooperation between Russia and Germany it is worth looking at how each of them was responding to changing technology. Russian experience of the First World War was limited to the Eastern Front but Germany had seen a much more technologically-driven evolution of battlefield tactics in the West. This had manifested itself most strikingly with the introduction of tanks. When the British tank burst onto the First World War battlefield in 1916 it had caused panic among even the toughest infantrymen and British commanders, momentarily, thought they had found the way to break out of the stalemate of trench warfare. Unfortunately for them, although this revolutionary fighting machine seemed unstoppable, the complexities of a completely new technology meant that initial efforts were less than successful. The tanks were slow (2–3 mph), noisy, clumsy and prone to frequent breakdowns. After only a very short time, the ponderous giants had become easy prey for artillery. Even when they could achieve higher speeds, their flimsy armour offered little protection.

The Germans were less inclined to produce their own tanks, preferring instead to concentrate on heavier and heavier artillery and new battlefield tactics that placed emphasis on concentration of force to smash through at a single point and gave low-level commanders freedom to use their initiative to rapidly exploit situations. When some analysts argued that tanks could play an important part in any such strategy, others pointed to the way in which, even where the British tanks had broken through, German artillery had driven them back with relative ease.

That did not, however, blunt German enthusiasm completely and they came up with their own design, the A7V, first deployed in March 1918 but produced on a very small scale. It was heavier and better armed than those of its adversaries but crucially it was slower and less manoeuvrable. When three of five called to action along the St. Quentin Canal suffered mechanical failure before they could fire a single shot it was clear that they were no better than the British or new French machines. The German High Command took the view that however questionable might be the tank's future contribution to warfare it was still very necessary to investigate its potential and it was in this light that Chief of the General Staff, Erich Ludendorff, wrote his 'Guide for the Development of Armoured Vehicle Assault Units' in January 1918. Interestingly, right from the first, the Germans saw tanks as a weapon to be deployed in cooperation with infantry but under separate command as specialised armoured units. There was sufficient enthusiasm for the idea of tanks, even if the reality of them had been thus far less than encouraging, for the German High Command to plan for expansion of their armoured units as effective replacements for cavalry but all that planning ceased abruptly with the signing of the Treaty of Versailles and its stipulation that all German manufacture of tanks was absolutely forbidden in perpetuity.

On the Eastern Front, the Russians had possessed no tanks and the Germans had not deployed any of theirs, which left the Russian commanders having to analyse their impact and potential from a distance. It was no surprise when all they could come up with was a re-hash of what the combatants on the Western Front had come up with. Trotsky, who had been appointed Commissar for War, was a keen advocate of progress through science and he was never afraid of new ideas, which opened the door for the tank to enter Red Army doctrine. It was on the side of the Whites, however, that the first British-supplied tanks appeared on the battlefields of Eastern Europe. Unfortunately for them the Whites were an uncoordinated melange of various opposition groups and, although supported by British and French forces in the Baltic, offered only sporadic resistance to the Red Army that mopped them up, capturing most of the machines in the process at Rostov and Novocherkassk. As more tanks, now superfluous to British and French requirements after the armistice, flowed in to the Whites, so they inevitably ended up with the Reds who started using those that were still operational against the troops of those countries that had made them.

These tanks were used again in the war against Poland where Polish troops had managed to establish a defensive line against Tukhachevsky's advancing army. They broke through at Ziabka in concert with artillery but generally there were too few and offered tactical advantage in only a small number of situations to be taken too seriously by the Red Army High Command. On the plains of Eastern Europe where the battlefield was fluid and constantly moving, slow-moving tanks had a great deal of trouble keeping up with the action. The fact, also, that tanks required skilled and trained mechanics to maintain them was a factor in relegating them to be of little more than a battlefield curiosity. Only after six months was a unit established to give basic training but even then it struggled to find recruits with sufficient education or aptitude.

It was now necessary also to start looking seriously at what role the tank would play in a post-war army. The Russians produced a guide; *Instructions for the Employment of Tanks in the Worker-Peasant Red Army.* Again it added little to what had already been written about tank operations on the Western Front. Overall the tank was viewed as being slow, dependent on trained crews, dependent on fuel supply and of limited manoeuvrability on anything other than a flat surface. Crews generally hated them because they shuddered constantly, had foul air inside and could not shoot accurately. While the natural role for tanks was to replace cavalry, the comparison between serving in a tank and serving on a fine horse with all the pageantry, skill, prestige and tradition that entailed was obvious. It was necessary to either transfer unwilling troops from the highly-trained cavalry units with all the required tactical knowledge or train completely new infantry recruits who had no understanding of reconnaissance or mobile warfare.

Much as the Germans had done before them, the Russians saw tanks operating as separate units within a combined force under a

35

single command but when they created eleven such units the state of readiness of the tanks meant that only five were operational, the others being laid up for maintenance or repair. Tank commanders were not discouraged by the limitations of the tank in practice and came to have faith that with technical innovation and development of better machines their role would evolve and become increasingly more important. In preparation for the advent of newer machines, theorists began to explore doctrine.

In Germany, similar ideas were also on the table but the difference was that they had no machines to try them out in practice. After the withdrawal from the battlefield and the humiliation of Versailles, von Seeckt had more pressing problems than how to deploy tanks. His priority was to revive morale and resuscitate the German armed forces before the country was carved up by the several hostile powers on its borders that would not hesitate to pounce if Germany could not build up a defensive capability quickly. To him the Reichswehr was the embodiment of German nationhood and its only guarantee of security. Fundamental to military efficiency was doctrine and the first conclusion to emerge from a detailed analysis of the German effort during the war was that there was nothing wrong with their own. It had been the peculiar circumstances of the Western Front battlefield that had defeated them, not doctrine.

For von Seeckt, offense was still the key to victory and ultimately to survival. In another war, the German armed forces would retain the initiative through freedom of movement and would not allow themselves to become bogged down in a war of position again, although how to ensure that was far from clear. The British were concentrating their effort on new technology such as tanks but the Germans did not have that luxury and so for the moment concentrated on tactics to break down strong defences by the employment of concentrated effort. This, together with the Versailles restrictions, effectively made the study of tank warfare little more than a theoretical exercise of little interest. There were, however, a small number of officers assigned to keeping abreast of developments in other countries. One report that landed on von Seeckt's desk foresaw tanks being used in combination with infantry and aircraft but bearing the brunt of the assault to break through the enemy line and create a safe passage for infantry. This was markedly similar to Soviet conclusions although there is no evidence to suggest that there was any collusion. It was, in fact, little more than an elaboration of tactics that had been used for centuries in battlefields across Europe and was based on firm principles of cavalry, infantry and artillery that had been developed over that time. What mechanisation would bring to modern war was speed of action but what must not be forgotten, said von Seeckt, was that it was not only the machine but the fighting spirit and morale of the men that was and would continue to be the deciding factor in war.

After the Treaty of Riga was signed, Lenin's government turned inward to tackle the immediate problems of the economy and food production in particular. As a consequence, military matters slipped down the agenda. Defeat at the hands of the Poles had not left either the Red Army or its leaders with much to shout about and had in fact exacerbated the situation by draining the nation of morale and belief in its government. Although Poland had won the war, it also had exhausted itself militarily and posed no ongoing threat of aggressive action. This, together with the stripping out of German arms at Versailles, lifted all immediate threats to Russia and allowed Lenin to order massive demobilisation. This time of relative peace at last gave Trotsky precious time to make important decisions about how his new revolutionary army would develop. As part of his programme, he authorised an investigation into the production and deployment of tanks but there was little funding nor much enthusiasm from the officers.

Nevertheless Grigory Kotovsky, who had been given the job, showed willing and told Trotsky that 'as a type of weapon, by their combined characteristics and tactics, armoured units are highly distinctive and may not be likened to any other types of weapons'.[1] It was the first indication that tanks required special consideration as a distinct new weapon that required new doctrine and support facilities under a new directorate directly subordinate to the RVS (Military Council). This spawned an internecine war for control over tank development between the GVIU (Armour Directorate) and the AU (Artillery Directorate), neither of which was successful as Kotovsky was given the task of setting up a new armoured division. In the dire economic conditions, however, what little was done initially was done very ponderously until he was able to get authorisation for a 'Detached Training Auto-Tank Armour Brigade' made up of a large number of men but, unfortunately, only very few vehicles.

Kotovsky was a colourful character of Russo-Polish descent who had spent a number of years prior to the 1917 revolution as a bank robber. With a number of prison sentences behind him he was wounded and arrested for the last time in 1916 and condemned to death but escaped during the revolution to join the new Red Army. He would be killed in 1925 by his friend Seider Meyer after Meyer discovered that Kotovsky had been having an affair with his wife.

With little experience to call on and no tanks to train with, Kotovsky trawled Western publications for information about tank development and sources from which they might be able to purchase some given that Soviet factories had neither the technology nor the skills to make their own. Those tanks that had survived the Polish war were more often than not commandeered to act as tractors to plough the land. There was still no real idea of how tanks were to be deployed in action, other than vague assertions that they would assist the infantry, but at least one influential directorate argued that although they had not yet revolutionised warfare in the way some had predicted, their potential was limitless. There was a limiting factor, however; cost. To create a tank force of strategic importance meant new manufacturing tools, skilled labour and investment in research or the purchase of machines from abroad. The battle for funding was not helped by the power struggle that would develop between Josef Stalin and Leon Trotsky for leadership after Lenin; a battle that Stalin would win.

When cooperative ventures were discussed between Germany and the Soviet Union after 1924, tank development was to be one of the most important areas of collaboration and would prove to be a huge factor in the way that warfare developed during the Second World War. Ironically, it would be on the plains of Eastern Europe where much of the early German-Soviet research and development of tanks would take place that the greatest tank battle of the war would take place between the two of them at Kursk in 1943.

Chapter 4

THE GENOA CONFERENCE AND RAPALLO

On 10 April 1922, thirty-four countries attended a conference in Genoa, led by the British Prime Minister David Lloyd George, to resolve the major economic and political issues facing Europe and to deal with the pariah states of Germany and Russia. They looked for a strategy to rebuild the German economy and, at the same time, establish a working relationship between European capitalist economies and the new communist regime in Russia to resolve the issue of Tsarist debt. The British were sympathetic to German demands to be released from the burden of reparations but the French, who had suffered devastating losses in the war, feared that any relaxation would encourage a rapid resurgence of German political and military hegemony and refused point blank to even discuss revision of reparation payments, and international bankers refused to lend to Germany unless there was agreement on the issue of reparations. Lloyd George saw no reason to disagree publicly with the French position. The French President Raymond Poincaré successfully managed to sideline the issue of relaxation of German reparations and instead was able to focus the conference solely on the issue of Russian debt. Chicherin, who claimed to have come in the interests of peace and of the general reconstruction of the economic life of Europe, urged delegates to recognise the cost that Russia had borne in a war 'the profits from which went exclusively to the other side'.[1] He pleaded his case by saying that 'the problem of universal economic reconstruction is, in present conditions, so immense and comprehensive that it can only be solved if all countries, both European and non-European, sincerely desire to co-ordinate their efforts'. Western delegates dismissed Chicherin's arguments with some contempt and wanted only to discuss how Russia would pay its debts to them. This left the Soviet camp with few options.

In the months leading up to Genoa, many German firms such as Stinnes, Siemens und Halske, Thyssen, Haniel, the Hamburg-Amerika Line, Krupp, IG Farben, the Deutsche Bank and Borsig had explored links with the Soviets but only seven concessionary agreements had been concluded, none of which provided the level of access to Russia's raw materials or consumers which German commerce and industry wanted. The big German firms saw Russia as more or less as a colony whose carcass was there to be 'picked clean' but the project was stalled by the lack of finance available from within either country.[2] The industrialist Felix Deutsch did not necessarily see the lack of Russian cash as an obstacle since 'wealth could be extracted' in a variety of other ways. He certainly did not see the end goal of cooperation as the rebuilding of Russian industry but as a mechanism for exploiting Russia's vast raw material resources. Russian peasants were seen as relatively wealthy but lacking every article of everyday necessity which for German manufacturers was a goldmine opportunity for exports.

Russian grain exports were well below expected levels and gold reserves were rapidly disappearing. There was no indication of how Russia might make financial contributions to any future cooperative ventures. Germany saw the answer in tapping US and other Western financial markets. Germany's weakness was forcing her to seek help from its competitors but only in this way could the massive amounts of capital that were required be found. The British government gave encouraging but non-specific replies and simply indicated that it would not stand in the way of private investment flowing to German-Soviet ventures.[3] Proposed projects included the complete rebuilding of the Soviet railway system to connect regions where raw materials were found. Only in this way, argued the Germans, could they rebuild an economy capable of paying the vast reparations debt that had been heaped upon it at Versailles and developed in such a way as to keep German exports away from areas where they might compete with established Western trade.

The Russians saw this 'consortium' approach as a capitalist threat to their communist system. If Russia became too indebted to the West then they would inevitably come under concerted pressure to emulate their economic models. Radek saw it as a back door to dictatorship of the Russian economy by Western governments. Chicherin saw it as of vital concern to smash the consortium idea and his method was to detach Germany from the other Western Powers. As a carrot, Lenin made significant concessions to Krupp but wielded the stick by getting

Radek to make vague threats of cancelled orders or putting punitive import duties on German manufactured goods. As an ace up his sleeve he hinted at Russia making a deal with Britain and France, leaving Germany out in the cold. German industrialists thought the threats genuine and called for immediate clarification and a clear understanding with Russia. Moritz Schlesinger, the *Auswärtiges Amt* economic expert on Soviet matters, spent months going to and fro between Berlin and Moscow with Rathenau's support to test the feasibility of several projects. The irony was that even if Germany broke away from the consortium and forged a bilateral deal with Russia it could only set about restructuring Russian industry with Western capital.

Despite a violent struggle against Bolshevism still raging on the streets of Germany, aside from the main conference the leader of the Russian delegation Chicherin secretly met the German Chancellor Dr Karl Joseph Wirth and Rathenau at the nearby town of Rapallo. They now tried to build on the foundations that had been laid during the previous months, the Germans trying to show that their approach to a bilateral agreement was essentially different from the rapacious intentions of Britain and France. Wirth along with von Maltzan had been amongst the most ardent advocates of cooperation with the Soviets but they had to tread carefully because there were many in the German government, such as Rathenau and Ebert, who were cautious about alienating Western opinion. For this reason they had agreed a secret *Waffenbrüderschaft* (brotherhood of arms) in 1921 to promote *Ostpolitik* and work towards a closer relationship with the Soviet Union in the form of a treaty. The Russian delegates had stopped over at Berlin for four days as they journeyed to Genoa and it was clear that on the main issues around both economic and political cooperation they were deadlocked and the prospects of an agreement seemed far off.[4]

The Soviet delegation to the Genoa Conference were accommodated some 30km from Genoa in the Hotel Imperial in Rapallo with the attention of 200 Italian mounted police and a sizable force of undercover *Cheka* operatives. Despite this, the connecting road to Genoa, in Chicherin's somewhat paranoid opinion, was 'a long road especially convenient for assassination'.[5] It was, however, the separation of the Soviet delegation from the main talks that would lead to their eventual breakdown.

German hopes seemed crushed at the Genoa Conference on 15 March when the London Memorandum was presented, reaffirming Russian rights to claim compensation against Germany for war damage. German objections were brushed aside by Britain and France with the arrogance of the victor. The Soviet delegate Adolph Joffe, the ex-Ambassador to Berlin, confided to Rathenau and von Maltzan that the Soviets were holding secret meetings with Lloyd George in Genoa. Rathenau seemed unconcerned and unconvinced by this revelation, having tried and failed three times to get private meetings with Lloyd George during the previous week. Joffe's warning, however, resonated with a previous note Wirth had got from the Italian delegate Amedeo Giannini informing him that talks between the Soviets, British and French were ongoing, amicable and productive.

Taken together, these two messages, as well as the location of the German delegation at Rapallo, suggested that the Germans were being marginalised in negotiations and appeared to leave their strategy in ruins. Later that night, however, von Maltzan received a telephone call from Chicherin who wanted a meeting early the next morning in Rapallo. When von Maltzan confronted Chicherin with rumours of secret Russian talks with the British and French, Chicherin denied all knowledge of them and urged von Maltzan to ignore the rumours and meet him. It was unclear to von Maltzan, who had been wakened to take the call, what sort of game the Soviets were playing so he stalled and said that it might be difficult to change pre-arranged plans on what would be Easter Sunday but after getting assurances that the Soviets were willing to make significant concessions to Germany he agreed to the meeting. Not sure how to prepare for the meeting, von Maltzan went immediately to see Rathenau whom he found pacing his hotel room in pyjamas with a 'haggard look and eyes staring out of his head'.[6] Rathenau's response was that he would tell the whole story of Chicherin's telephone conversation to Lloyd George, hoping to curry favour and bring everything out into the open, but when he tried to arrange a meeting early the next morning through the British delegation's hotel, he was again rebuffed with a contemptuous reply that 'the gentleman [Lloyd George] has gone out of town for the day'.[7] Von Maltzan was now knocking on an open door and found no difficulty in persuaded Rathenau to meet Chicherin.

Little progress was made when the two men met during the morning with neither side showing much enthusiasm for compromise and the Soviets being rather less forthcoming about improving relations than von Maltzan had been led to expect. When they adjourned for prior lunch appointments, Lloyd George had got wind of the meeting, possibly leaked to him by the Germans, and called the Germans' hotel asking for an urgent meeting with Rathenau. This was conveyed to Rathenau when he returned from his lunch appointment and the meeting reconvened in the afternoon, but it was obvious from their demeanour that the Soviets had heard about Lloyd George's call also.

They were much more conciliatory now and progress was swift, with the signing of an agreement late in the afternoon. This guaranteed mutual diplomatic recognition, the cancellation of war debts owed to each other and pledges to increase economic ties under the principle of 'most favoured nation'. Rapallo was a significant achievement for Russia, bringing its first official recognition as a world power. When news of the Rapallo Agreement leaked out it caused a furore. Lloyd George claimed that he had not been told about Chicherin's early-morning telephone call and demanded to know why he had not been told of the meeting at Rapallo. All other participating countries at Genoa signed a note to Wirth in protest at the Rapallo agreement and the Genoa Conference collapsed. The agreement itself, which promised a strategic partnership with long-term, primarily economic, prospects, now also provided a convenient diplomatic cover for secret military discussions between Germany and Russia. Von Seeckt was delighted with the treaty which he saw as the first step in the direction of an independent German policy in the international field. The only thing he feared was that President Ebert, who had already objected to the Wirth-Radek negotiations, would not support it.

The Rapallo Treaty provoked violent reactions, not least in Germany whose people had been taken completely by surprise and could not understand why their leaders had made a pact with a country whose government was actively trying to destroy theirs from within. Many Germans hated communism but for political and economic reasons supported Russo-German friendship, while others such as Hoffmann wanted to rid Russia of Bolshevism and re-establish a constitutional government. In spite of opposition the Reichstag approved the treaty and it was ratified on 4 July two months after the Soviets. Trotsky was effusive in his praise of the treaty which he saw as a 'model' agreement on which to build economic and military cooperation, but Chicherin and Radek saw it in terms of power politics and the first step in the road to bringing down the First World War victors from their high perch of superiority and further isolate Poland. Beyond the posturing and fabricated justification for the agreement, however, the most important development opportunity that Rapallo delivered for the Soviets was in terms of finance. Almost all of the Tsarist gold bullion that the Bolsheviks had taken control of in 1917 had been used up in war, propaganda and the international drive to export communism throughout the world. In 1922, the country most able to provide the country with credit with the least onerous conditions was Germany.

Poincaré was livid and called the Soviet-German accord a 'new principle of division [and] a serious obstacle to the re-establishment of an era of confidence and peace'.[8] He wanted to end the conference forthwith and persuaded Lloyd George to demand that the Germans abandon their deal with the Soviets. Wirth replied that the Rapallo agreement had entered into for 'compelling reasons' and Germany had 'establishing peace with one of the greatest belligerent powers under conditions excluding lasting dictatorship and rendering possible, on a fresh basis unencumbered by the past' and asked for the Soviet-German accord to be incorporated into the Genoa declaration.[9] There was broad agreement on this but only with stringent conditions applied to the Soviets, calling on them to 'refrain from stimulating revolution in other states, adopt a position of strict neutrality, recognise all Tsarist debts, and not pursue loss claims stemming from the civil war'. Naturally they refused and the conference was abandoned without agreement. Chicherin later sought to justify the Soviet action and berated the French in an interview in the *Observer* newspaper on 20 August in which he said that Russia needed the economic collaboration of other countries to counter the 'aggressive policy of French imperialism'.[10]

A number of other newspapers carried reports that Rapallo had included secret protocols around military-industrial collaboration. *The Times* carried an article quoting 'an authoritative quarter . . . tending to confirm' such an agreement. *The Chicago Daily Tribune* reporter David Darrah claimed that Rapallo had at least two secret protocols that 'obligated Germany to refuse to join the League of Nations without previous consultation with Moscow' and 'established consultative and cooperative staffs of the Reichswehr and the Red army'.[11] Immediately after the signing at Rapallo, Admiral Hintze led a small delegation to Moscow and at the same time Alexander Svechin took a Soviet mission to Berlin where discussions took place with Junkers executives Spalock and Sachsenberg around setting up an aircraft manufacturing plant at Fili. Radek was now able to meet von Seeckt in person and the Junkers contract was signed on 15 March. Nikolai Krestinsky and General Hasse were deep in discussions about financial support for cooperative ventures while von Seeckt reached preliminary commercial agreements with the Soviet delegate Frank Rosenblatt. All of these developments were conducted in the utmost secrecy. A provisional agreement was reached between the Red Army and the Reichswehr on 11 August 1922 whereby the Germans would gain experience in tactics, training and technical matters as well as the opportunity to study, under battle conditions, the use of weapons forbidden to them under Versailles. To this end they required training bases, freedom to conduct training and experimentation according to their own requirements, and full exchange of analysis of joint military ventures. The Soviets were to receive annual payments for the lease of facilities and full access to all German technical and administrative processes. They were keen to go ahead but first wanted von Seeckt's personal assurance that he had the full backing of the German government. Von Seeckt consulted Wirth, one of whose roles was Finance Minister, whose natural tendency was to look to the West but who had become worn down by constant rebuffs to overtures in that direction. He had come more and more under the influence of von Maltzan whose pro-Russian views were well known and before he could give von Seeckt the vital support he was looking for, he gave up his role in finance and the strategy faced collapse.

The situation was saved, however, when Niedermayer returned from Moscow with Radek in January 1922 and called for an urgent meeting with von Seeckt who agreed after getting advice from Wirth. The Soviets, said Radek, wanted Germany's help to rebuild and modernise their armament industry. He asked for immediate talks to begin between Soviet and German general staff officers and the distribution of German military literature to the Red Army. When von Seeckt hesitated, Radek reminded him that the Reichswehr was doing something similar, in terms of officer exchange at least, with the Western Allies but von Seeckt somewhat sheepishly explained that he was obliged to negotiate with the British, who favoured leniency in terms of applying the terms of Versailles, in order to gain support against the French who did not. The implication of Radek's appeal was that the Soviets were looking for an early opportunity to strike at Poland and win back territory lost at Riga.[12]

The majority in the German General Staff had supported von Seeckt's policy of rapprochement with the Soviet Union but there was still a significant body of opinion that regarded Bolshevism as the root of all evil and saw in the Rapallo Agreement the end of any ambitions for German territorial expansion in the East and a death-knell for the spirit of Brest-Litovsk. This feeling of an opportunity spurned, was somewhat supressed during the Weimar era, but came to find renewed vigour when the Nazis came to power and the short-lived Treaty of Brest-Litovsk would act as a template for German policy during the 1930s. Indeed in 1932, even before Adolf Hitler's rise to power, the German Economic Minister Hjalmar Schacht would extol the advantages of colonisation and 'expansion into Russia'. A little later on, Hitler, in a speech of 1936 that echoed the aspirations of 1918, would bring Brest-Litovsk storming back onto the agenda when he issued a blatant incitement to plunder by saying 'If the Urals and their incalculable wealth of raw materials, the rich forests of Siberia, and the unending cornfields of Ukraine lay within Germany . . . the country would swim in plenty'.[13]

The German company of Gesellschaft für Förderung gewerblicher Unternehmungen (GEFU) had been established with the support of Wirth and von Maltzan in 1921 and run by General Karl von Borries assisted by Tschunke. It was generously financed with its purpose to direct military-industrial relations with the Soviet Union and create a joint-venture company with its Soviet counterpart called Bersol (*Aktiengesellschaft*) and set up at Samara. Two headquarters were created: one in Berlin and one in Moscow. GEFU was designed to enable the Dessau aircraft manufacturer Junkers to produce aircraft and engines at Fili, to enable Stolzenberg to produce poison gas and to produce 300,000 artillery shells under the supervision of German engineers at Slatoust in the Urals, in the former Poutilov works in Leningrad and in Schlusselburg at Lake Ladoga. Krupp's interests in Russia at this time were consolidated in a Russo-German company called Manych while Blohm und Voss and the Albatros Werke were supplying artillery, submarine and aircraft technology.

On 17 April 1922, *The Wall Street Journal* reported that AEG had concluded a five-year deal with the Soviet Electro Trust for the electrification of Soviet industries. It also reported that Krupp hoped to establish a railway syndicate to lay down 1,500 miles of track in Siberia, Stinnes was considering constructing hotels and the Hamburg American Line wanted to restore its shipping facilities. The British *Observer* reported in September that Krupp was involved in a

> transaction which marks a notable step in the recent co-operation of Germany in the revival of industry in Russia. Messrs. Krupp have for some time been in negotiation with Dmitri Rubinstein, formerly a banker in Petrograd, and the friend of . . . the family of Putiloff, the owners of the famous armament works. These negotiations have . . . resulted in Messrs. Krupp acquiring a controlling interest in the Putiloff works, which have been taken over by their former owners from the Soviet government.[14]

On 2 July 1926, *The New York Times* reported that

> the Soviet Government has about completed purchase from Germany of the entire 'Rheinmetall' factory, one of Germany's largest plants for manufacture of locomotives and railroad rolling stock. . . . The deal is

being handled by the Ukrainian government, which intends to transport the works to Kharkov, 420 miles southwest of Moscow.

Aircraft production in the Soviet Union had begun in 1920 at the Duks plant in Moscow (Aviation Factory No. 1) producing Nieuports and Spads but they only managed two or three finished aircraft a month.[15] Productivity was marginally better at the Letchik factory in Petrograd (Aviation Factory No. 3). Manufacture was plagued by employment of unskilled labour and many component parts had to be manufactured in situ. Equipment was varied in quality, supplies of raw materials was sporadic and management dismal. The Gnome-Rhône engine assembly plant faced the gravest difficulties due to lack of metallurgical expertise. Some small-scale informal contacts with German manufacturers had been ongoing for a number of years and it was really this and French technical help that had prevented the complete shutdown of Soviet aircraft manufacture after the First World War.

Even before the Radek contacts and the Enver mission, von Maltzan had alluded in a letter to secret contacts between the German and Russian military during the Russo-Polish War.[16] Foreign Minister Rathenau, who would be assassinated on 24 June 1922 by right-wing extremists for his pro-Russian views, had learned about the secret military dealings with Russia, having been informed by Wirth, who was also the German acting Foreign Minister in the summer of 1921. It is likely that leading German diplomats knew about the secret negotiations but chose to feign ignorance so as not to risk embarrassment should the talks fail or become public knowledge. For the Russians it is very unlikely that such an initiative would be attempted without the full knowledge and approval of both Lenin and Trotsky. While building diplomatic relations with Soviet Russia gave Germany the opportunity to shape foreign policy according to its revisionist ambitions, Russia was relieved to see Germany separated from any move by the Western Powers to involve it in an anti-communist crusade.

The Treaty of Rapallo enabled von Seeckt to send each year to Russia a certain number of officers to act as instructors to the Red Army, and a further number to gain experience in the use of heavy artillery, tanks, armoured cars and other weapons forbidden to Germany under the Treaty of Versailles. From that time, the two General Staffs worked hand-in-hand to both modernise the Russian army and make a mockery of the Versailles Treaty. The chasm between pragmatic compromise and political philosophy, however, remained as wide as ever even up to the signing of the Locarno agreement in 1925 when

Gustav Stresemann, the German Foreign Minister, wrote in his diary: 'To celebrate a marriage with communist Russia would mean to go to bed with the killer of one's own fatherland.'

The first German chargé d'affaires to communist Russia, Professor A. Bernhardt Wiedenfeld, was told by von Maltzan that secret military talks were under way but he was to keep well away from them. He did, however, promise Chicherin, on the eve of Rapallo, that the proposals being put forward officially by Germany were far less than those that had been discussed secretly and which had been agreed to, indicating the gulf between what the politicians were discussing and what the military were actually doing. When Brockdorff-Rantzau was appointed as the first German ambassador to Moscow, however, he was determined to close the gap between the two and take some control of military negotiations. Initially an opponent of rapprochement, Brockdorff-Rantzau, although still 'fully aware of the dangers of Bolshevism', had veered into von Seeckt's camp after the 'vengeful and capacious enemies [of Germany]' had imposed the harsh terms of Versailles.[17]

Ulrich Karl Christian Graf von Brockdorff-Rantzau was of Prussian Junker stock and a member of the German aristocracy but he had distinct democratic leanings. A qualified lawyer, he had been appointed as Foreign Minister in 1919 and led the German delegation to the Versailles peace talks where he vehemently challenged accusations that Germany and Austria had been solely responsible for the war, a stance that angered the Western Allies, and when the final swingeing terms of the treaty were agreed, Brockdorff-Rantzau resigned in protest. He still had influence, however, and argued strongly against any move by Germany to play the other Great Powers off against each other. When he was appointed to the Moscow embassy in November 1922, his policy was to pursue rapprochement between Germany and the Soviet Union without sacrificing German links to the West. Von Seeckt was unhappy with the choice of ambassador, not having overcome his residual antipathy from earlier encounters, and feared that Brockdorff-Rantzau lacked the 'mettle' to represent the Reich with his 'defeatist attitude' and would oppose von Seeckt's ambitions for close military ties with the Soviets.[18] The two men exchanged a series of heated memoranda that went through Wirth's office but all three found common ground in their contempt for Poland.

Von Seeckt was right to be wary since Brockdorff-Rantzau's pragmatic assessment was that making any sort of military alliance with the Soviets could only aggravate relations with the West but he was mollified and eventually persuaded to take up his post in Moscow after assurances that he would be kept fully informed of any moves towards military alignment. Whether or not von Seeckt ever had any intention of sticking to that agreement or not is moot because when General Otto Hasse, Chief of the General Staff, led a delegation to Moscow, Brockdorff-Rantzau bitterly complained that he had not been officially informed about the visit and he was not privy to the discussions. Radek was also concerned about the undue haste being shown by the German military and let it be known that Hasse had actually committed Germany to a 'war of liberation' in discussions with the Soviet negotiator Arkady Rosengoltz and made the point in a written document that, now being in the hands of the Soviets, could prove to be very embarrassing if the Soviets ever chose to leak it. Von Seeckt himself had unashamedly declared that his ambition was to put the Reichswehr in a position where it could exploit the next international conflict and fight for Germany's 'freedom'.

Hasse failed to make any progress, however, partly because Trotsky fell ill and a second mission was led by Lieutenant Colonel Mentzel and Major Tschunke over which Brockdorff-Rantzau was determined to keep closer watch. Mentzel was contemptuous of Brockdorff-Rantzau's overbearing attitude and, like Hasse before him, saw no place for diplomats in military negotiations. Brockdorff-Rantzau enjoyed no better relations with Mentzel than he had with Hasse and was scathing about what few German proposals he was able to discover. The military, he thought, were far too eager to make concessions and failed to appreciate that, in his opinion, the Soviets needed the Germans more than the Germans needed them.[19] In Berlin there was general enthusiasm, with few concerns being raised about negotiations and financial arrangements were put in place to facilitate further talks.

Brockdorff-Rantzau tried to take more control of negotiations by inviting a Soviet delegation to Berlin, which was not appreciated by the Reichswehr but if news of the Berlin meeting were to leak out it would be no great trouble for him to depict it as the Soviets coming to Berlin with a begging bowl. He drafted a memorandum for German Chancellor Wilhelm Cuno, who was in office for only 264 days, in which he complained that, because of lax political control, the Reichswehr were conducting their own policy which was usually coloured by a general tendency to propose schemes that were far more advantageous to the Soviets than to Germany. He demanded that negotiations be conducted by political rather than military authorities. In particular he insisted that there should be German monopoly control of Soviet military firms receiving German aid. Furthermore, there should be no question of either a political or a military alliance but there should be an understanding about protection from Polish aggression, and by extension, since Poland was reliant on French military aid, from France also.

(At a conference of representatives of Soviet Republics in December 1922, the USSR [Union of Soviet Socialist Republics] was created and henceforth in this book, unless part of a direct quotation, Russia will now be referred to as the USSR or the Soviet Union.)

This clearly shows that Brockdorff-Rantzau was very much in favour of an informal military understanding with the Soviet Union but his grievances were primarily centred around the haste with which the German military were giving in to Soviet demands. He had long been concerned about an attack against Germany coming from the West, especially France, and saw the Soviet Union as the only country upon whom they could call if that turned out to be the case. In this context, help to build up Soviet military power was advantageous, but it should not be done to the extent of allowing them more military might than was necessary to keep a check on Poland whose containment was seen as a vital component of Germany strategy against Poland's ally France.

In January 1923, a Soviet commission came to Berlin to arrange for the purchase of armaments and a loan to finance it. The Germans baulked at the size of the request and asked for time to consider it. Their response was to send a return party to Moscow on 17 February with all of its members travelling under pseudonyms. General Hasse was Professor Heller, Kapitan von Wulfing was Direktor Wolf, Major von Plotho was Trigonometer Probs, Major Tschunke was Kaufmann Teichmann, Hauptmann Student got the name Kaufmann Sebach and Oberstleutnant Mentzel was Landmesser Moersbach. It was the first deputation that brought up the idea of the Soviets paying for German help with food and raw materials. They were met in Moscow by Arkady Rosengoltz, the State Commissioner for Finance, and Pavel Lebedev, the Red Army Chief of Staff, but the meetings did not go well with the Soviets requesting details of what sort of goods and services might be exchanged before talking about the mechanics of the deal. The Germans had not come prepared to go into details, expecting just to agree the principles of the exchange. Discussions went on late into the night and had to be halted when the translators became exhausted.

Things improved during the following days with the Germans pleasantly surprised at the industrial premises made available to them for military production. By the time the Germans returned home on 2 March a reasonable start had been made. A second mission arrived in Moscow on 25 April again led by Tschunke and Mentzel but again talks stalled over what exactly the two sides were prepared to discuss. The Soviets wanted to talk about how much the Germans would provide in monetary terms but the Germans wanted to have a better look at the manufacturing facilities before deciding what and how much they could manufacture. Like the first mission, things improved after the first couple of days and the Germans were taken to St. Petersburg to inspect factories there and later to shipyards on the Baltic. The Germans were impressed with Soviet technological facilities, especially those of the gun manufacturers in Tula, and were generally pleased with the cleanliness and efficiency of the factory workers but considered the Soviet negotiators to lack knowledge or deep understanding of financial and economic matters. Overall, the Germans decided that facilities in the Soviet Union were adequate but were a little concerned that some items they saw being produced were done in violation of Danish patents.[20] The Germans left to return home on 15 May.

These moves had not gone entirely unnoticed in the West but few diplomatic objections were raised. On 18 April 1923 *The New York Times* stated that 'American Secret Service Operators in Germany [had] discovered the existence of a giant plot on the part of the German government for the construction of an enormous airplane fleet ostensibly for Russia but available for a sudden onslaught against France.' German firms also provided the Soviet Union with 'enormous transports of . . . supplies required for the reconstruction and extension of all branches of industry in Russia. Industrial machinery that was shipped to the Soviet Union from Germany included mining equipment for use in the Ukrainian Nikopol manganese beds.'[21]

The next discussions took place in Berlin on 30 July when Soviet negotiators Rosengoltz and Krestinsky held talks with Brockdorff-Rantzau and Cuno in the utmost secrecy in private apartments. Here the agenda was a little wider and included military and political issues. Cuno asked for an understanding that the Soviet Union would come to Germany's aid in the event of an attack from Poland but Rosengoltz told him that Germany itself should do more to protect itself against the Poles and here was the rub, said Cuno. If Germany was to do that, even if it could under the constraints of Versailles, France would take any build-up of German arms as a provocation. What was required was some way of developing the necessary military means of pursuing a realistic defensive policy whilst giving the impression of passive acquiescence. Rosengoltz could see the merits of Cuno's argument and between them they agreed that the Soviet armaments industry would benefit from German investment and technical expertise while the Germans would take a share of the war materials produced. Further talks were planned in Moscow to be led on the German side by Brockdorff-Rantzau, feeling more than a little smug at his success. His main success had been to combine military and economic cooperation to tie the Soviets more closely to the deal but the main engine driving negotiations was the desire for closer military ties.

The next problem was finance. The initial estimate of 35 million Reichsmarks was now seen as quite insufficient and it was more than doubled to 75 million. It took the combined financial clout of the Reichsbank and industry to find that amount of funding and that, according to Reichsbank director Havenstein, 'seriously strained the resources of the Reich'.[22] All seemed to be going well, but Cuno had been replaced as Chancellor by Stresemann who told Brockdorff-Rantzau, on the eve of his return to Moscow, that both he and German President Ebert had grave misgivings about the military aspect of the negotiations. Brockdorff-Rantzau could not ignore such high-level opposition to his plans and was forced to tone down his enthusiasm when he met Radek in Moscow. The Soviets were not impressed with the sudden coolness on the German side and scaled back their commitment to German monopoly control of the new armament factories. To add weight to their argument, the Soviets claimed that they had opened negotiations with both Britain and France to purchase military aircraft. Brockdorff-Rantzau was starting to lose control of the situation and beginning to appreciate just how difficult it was going to be to do business with the Soviets.

He was not to know, however, the extent to which the Reichswehr had already been negotiating with the Soviets behind his back. A delegation had arrived in Moscow which included Direktor Eckhardt, Direktor Fritz Teichmann of GEFU, Direktor Freiherr von Hagen (Chemische Werke Stolzen-berg, Hamburg) and Professor Egon Graf. Protestations and demands that no agreements were to be entered into without Brockdorff-Rantzau's agreement were casually ignored. The Reichswehr had even gone so far as to establish their own headquarters in Moscow (*Zentrala Moskau – Z. Mo*). Colonel Hermann von der Lieth-Thomsen, who was nominal head of Z. *Mo*, had been invited to inspect a number of Soviet airfields and aircraft factories and, as a slap in the face to the diplomat, Brockdorff-Rantzau's preferred negotiator to lead the talks, Major Fischer, was overlooked in favour of Tschunke and Niedermayer (called Neumann when travelling in the Soviet Union), whom the ambassador considered to be 'a fantastic and unscrupulous adventurer'.[23] The Reichswehr professed absolute confidence in their man, however, and got their way.

Panicked by the Reichswehr's underhand tactics and Stresemann's objections, Brockdorff-Rantzau again tried to scale back German commitments to the Soviets by appealing to Stresemann to cut off funding to the Reichswehr and limit all investment in the Soviet Union to industries of a non-military nature but whose factories might be converted to armaments production at some future date. When the scale of what the Reichswehr had already committed to became apparent to Brockdorff-Rantzau, however, he was shocked by the 'careless and catastrophic' nature of deals already struck and realised that to change tack now would seriously endanger political relations with the Soviets.[24] Niedermayer was just as concerned as the ambassador and tried to build bridges by saying that all decisions had been taken on instructions from his superiors and the main players Mentzel, Tshunke and Eckhardt were now trying to distance themselves from the affair. Only Stresemann and von Seeckt had the necessary clout to save the situation. Brockdorff-Rantzau suggested that since agreements could not be broken without catastrophic political consequences, the best thing was to alter the details so that the military nature of collaboration might be gradually converted into an economic one. It was a pious hope, however. Things had gone too far for that and back home, Stresemann was causing more confusion by looking west to build his legacy as Foreign Minister.

As if it had not been sufficiently febrile and contentious right from the start, Stresemann's volte-face in 1924 now left the Soviet adventure on an even less firm foundation especially since Trotsky had been forced out of political leadership of the Red Army after Frunze had criticised its readiness for war. Von Seeckt had suffered some weakening of right-wing support after his crushing of Hitler's 'Beer Hall Putsch' and was losing ground to Stresemann in foreign affairs. Germany was now reliant on Western financial help after its catastrophic inflation crisis and looked to Stresemann, with his more Western-oriented policies, rather than von Seeckt to claw its way out of its dilemma. He had not lost sight of the Soviet target, however, and maintained his even-handed approach by saying 'it is necessary to so bind up the Russian economy with the capitalist system of the Western European powers that we thereby pave the way for an evolution in Russia which in my opinion presents the only possibility of creating a state and an economy out of Soviet Russia with which we can live'. Herbert von Dirksen echoed the sentiment when he advocated a policy to 'gradually to moderate the revolutionary and subversive tendencies of the Soviet government and bring it closer to the West'.[25]

At the start of 1924, however, the prospect were far from bright. German exports to the Soviet Union were a only a little over 1 per cent of its total and were destined to fall. When Lenin died on 24 January, Stalin grabbed the Soviet helm and steered the country away from Lenin's New Economic Policy towards a more introverted, radical and brutal doctrine. The Germans saw the 'glimmerings of economic reconstruction' that had promised a new economic and political dawn turn into bitter disappointment but the strategy could not be abandoned and while the Soviet Union remained a vital component of German foreign policy, the country was now viewed with renewed caution and suspicion.

In the Soviet Union, a special high-powered military commission had been set up in January 1924 to look at the personnel and supply issues in the Red Army. Frunze, Ushlinkht and Kliment Voroshilov were amongst the distinguished inquisitors and the target was clearly the person of Trotsky who had been accused of 'de-politicising' the Red Army. It took just two weeks for Andrei Bubnov to report that 'the Red Army [was] unfit for combat'.[26] Shortcomings and deficiencies were found at every level as a result of Trotsky having left administration in the hands of Ephraim Skylansky and Lebedev who 'were not qualified'. Frunze piled in with damning criticism of supply and organisation. Skylansky was summarily removed as Trotsky's deputy and Frunze appointed in his place. Trotsky's political position came under attack which meant he was powerless to oppose Frunze's restructuring of the army and his eventual appointment as People's Commissar for Army and Navy Affairs. With a much more pedantic approach in contrast to Trotsky's fiery enthusiasm, Frunze concentrated on rekindling the spirit of Alexander Suvorov (1730–1800) that had centred around discipline and rigorous training.

This was at a time when Soviet-German cooperation on the ground had seen substantial results but all was not well. Germany's first cooperative efforts in working with Moscow had resulted in the construction of the Junkers factory in Fili near Moscow and other smaller sites at Kharkov, Taganrog and Rostov.[27] The Germans equipped the plant and supplied the skilled labour while the Soviets provided raw materials and unskilled labour. Negotiations had started in October 1921 but were slow and tortuous, eventually resulting in a signed agreement in December 1922. The plan was for 300 metal-skinned aircraft to be built at the plant each year, with 60 of them being bought by the Soviet Union, but disagreements over the manufacture and supply of aero-engines, which the Soviets preferred to buy direct from German factories, dogged the collaboration from the start and because of this, and the financial catastrophe of galloping inflation in Germany in 1923, production never even got close to targets. To compound the tension the Soviets, impatient at having to wait so long for aircraft to come out of Fili, further undermined the viability of the enterprise by purchasing 100 Fokker aircraft from Holland. German capital set aside for investment was wiped out and the financial controller of the operation, General von Borries, proved incapable of finding solutions to keep the plant viable. Junkers were pressured into putting eight million gold marks of capital into the venture, with von Seeckt underwriting the investment with guarantees from the Reichswehr and the German government, emphasising that it was less an economic enterprise than a military-political matter. Elsewhere in the Soviet Union, Krupp had set up an experimental tractor station at Rostov and Factory No. 8 to manufacture 30mm infantry weapons while Soviet plants at Zlatoust in the Urals and Tula in Leningrad were producing large-calibre artillery and grenades with German help.

In early 1926, GEFU would be dissolved having come under suspicion by the French and British of illegal activity (there was also accusations of misusing its funds for financial speculations in Holland) and its activities would be taken over by a new body, *Wirtschaftskontor* (WIKO). All investment to this point had been in industrial concerns with armament application such as aircraft factories but they had not been a great success primarily due to the low skill base from which workers could be drawn. Germany had made a point of hedging its bets in the Soviet Union by encouraging other German aircraft manufacturers to invest in factories in countries such as Sweden where civilian aircraft with potential military uses were being built. After 1924 in the Soviet Union, therefore, emphasis shifted from production of war material to testing of military equipment and the training of personnel. This led to the secret establishment of three experimental and training stations.

The bizarre nature of the collaboration was thrown into focus by the communist Hamburg Uprising of October 1923 in the planning of which Red Army members had been involved. Although swiftly crushed, the incident showed that Soviet-inspired insurrection was still a major threat to the political situation in Germany. Only two weeks later, however, large numbers of Reichswehr officers and business leaders were guests at a glittering reception at the Soviet Embassy in Berlin to celebrate the sixth anniversary of the Russian revolution. In 1924 a number of countries, including Britain and France, officially acknowledged the Soviet Union and established diplomatic relations but Britain would retain its very deep-seated animosity to the communist creed.

The rivalry between the Reichswehr and the German embassy in Moscow was threatening to derail the whole German-Soviet venture in 1924 and emergency talks were held between Brockdorff-Rantzau and Niedermayer to clear the air. This seems to have been successful since a number of practical steps were taken to aid cooperation. All communications between Z. *Mo* and GEFU would now go through the Moscow embassy and Brockdorff-Rantzau was given a greater role in military dealings with the Soviets. It was he who, when Junkers threatened to pull out of Fili in April 1924, urged Berlin to intervene saying that liquidation of the manufacturing base had to be avoided 'at all costs'.[28] He even prevailed upon Trotsky to use his influence to improve relations at the plant which had deteriorated due to German accusations of pilfering by the Soviet workers and a general feeling in the Junkers management that the Soviets were not investing sufficient goodwill and effort into the venture.

Trotsky, however, was feeling a bit unloved in Moscow. Stalin had called into question his performance in a speech of January 1925 but despite attacks against him personally, his policy of cooperation with the Reichswehr did not seem to have been derailed and continued almost seamlessly under Voroshilov. Indeed, the far-reaching commitments made between the militaries, whilst not exactly showing success in encouraging wider economic relations as envisaged by Brockdorff-Rantzau, could not be undermined without significant negative political repercussions. There was, however, a shift away from manufacturing war materials, which had never been successful, to training and testing. This seemed to show more promise as direct contacts between the German and Soviet military continued apace despite grumblings in the commercial sector. A delegation of German officers was assigned to participate in the Red Army's manoeuvres in August 1925 and in return several high-ranking Soviet officers, disguised as Bulgarians, were to visit the Reichswehr's autumn manoeuvres. Brockdorff-Rantzau was uneasy about this, fearing the consequences if the news leaked out which, given the uncharacteristically casual Soviet approach to secrecy in Soviet-German affairs, was a distinct possibility but he understood that the exchange of military personnel might help political relations.

There was a hint that the Soviets played fast and loose with security to keep the Germans a little off balance and also to keep open back-door communications with Western intelligence agencies.

It was a piece in a Soviet military publication written by Voroshilov in early 1926 that had spooked the Germans. The article, backed up by a piece in *Izveztia*, gave details of the strength, organisation and structure of the Reichswehr in what could only be seen as gross negligence or provocation. Berlin began to question whether the risks of collaboration were beginning to dwarf the benefits and once again it was Brockdorff-Rantzau who made the greatest effort to build bridges which saw him rewarded by being given more control over German military budgets in the Soviet Union.

Chapter 5

THE LOCARNO TREATIES

In October 1925 representatives of the principal Western Powers, Germany, France, Belgium, Great Britain and Italy, met at Locarno in Switzerland. German Foreign Minister Stresemann had made his highest priority the restoration of German prestige and privileges as a leading European nation after the 'moral, political and economic death sentence' of Versailles.[1] With the deliberate exclusion of the Soviet Union and Poland from the talks, they discussed ways of securing borders of the nations of Europe after the First World War, achieving the permanent demilitarisation of the Rhineland and ways to allow Germany into the League of Nations and normalise relations. They concluded the Locarno Treaties (seven agreements) between 5 to 16 October and formally signed them in London on 1 December.

The principal treaty concluded at Locarno was the Rhineland Pact between Germany, France, Belgium, Great Britain and Italy. Germany formally recognised its new western borders as set out in the Treaty of Versailles but relations between Germany and France remained frosty. The first three signatories undertook not to attack each other, with the latter two acting as guarantors. In the event of aggression by any of the first three states against another, all other parties were to assist the country under attack. Subsequent to the main treaties, France signed further treaties of mutual assistance with Poland and Czechoslovakia in the event of conflict with Germany. These essentially reaffirmed existing treaties of alliance concluded by France with Poland on 19 February 1921 and with Czechoslovakia on 25 January 1924. While Locarno guaranteed the western borders of Germany, its eastern borders with Poland were left open for revision.

In London *The Times* editorial said:

> The little town of Locarno . . . now has its assured place in history. Last evening the representatives of Powers and peoples who for eleven years had struggled in war, or with the bitter consequences of war, registered their free and deliberate agreement in a pact of genuine peace. . . . Humbled and chastened by an unimaginable calamity, the peoples of Europe . . . have learned to limit their hopes and purposes. Safety for a time that may be foreseen, some real confidence that the work done to-day will not be undone to-morrow, even that would mean a marvellous release of energy in the present state of Europe. This, at the very least, is the result of the work that culminated yesterday in the Treaty of Locarno. It is a genuine Treaty of Peace.

It seems odd that Germany would come to Locarno so full of enthusiasm for the talks when the probable outcome would be a weakening of the cooperative ventures established with Soviet Russia as a result of Rapallo. It was very much the efforts of Stresemann that had brought Germany to the table and it was his strategy of 'balance' between East and West that was on show here. It was a risky move to recognise Alsace-Lorraine as legitimate French territory. Count Kuno von Westarp, leader of the conservatives in the Reichstag, fulminated against the 'renunciation of German land or people' in return for Germany's entry into the League of Nations or the conclusion of a security deal. Stresemann's strategy was based on the relative value to Germany of Alsace-Lorraine and the Danzig Corridor. He reasoned that Germany could not reasonably expect to reclaim both but by placating France with Alsace-Lorraine he hoped for French support over Danzig and it was with anticipation of this and the prospect of resolving the Rhineland issue that he was able to persuade the Reichstag to support him.

In September 1926, the Assembly of the League of Nations had before it the problem of Germany's admission, divisions over which had brought the previous March session to an abrupt end. As a preliminary, a special committee had been sitting since June in an attempt to devise a plan for reorganisation of the League's Council which would permit Germany's admission with a permanent seat on the Council, and at the same time satisfy as nearly as possible the ambitions of other states. The success of the Locarno agreements led to the admission of Germany with a seat on its Council as a permanent member, and the withdrawal of Allied troops occupying the Rhineland. The Treaties marked a dramatic improvement in the political climate of Western Europe promoting expectations for continued peaceful settlements, often referred to as the 'Spirit of Locarno'. The Treaties were seen in Poland as a humiliation, leading to the fall of the Grabski government and contributed to the worsening of relations between Poland and France.

The League of Nations was an international organisation that had been created at the end of the First World War to be an arena for the resolution of international disputes and so avoid another war. Germany was excluded from joining and the USA never joined. The Soviet Union was not one of the founding members and caustically referred to it as the 'League of Imperialist Aggressors'.[2]

In 1919, the German government had taken strong exception to the fact that it had been excluded from the general 'Association of Nations' in the Treaty of Versailles that laid the foundations for the League. When the first Assembly of the League met in November 1920, most of the neutrals and some of the belligerents deplored the omission of Germany but through the influence of the Great Powers the discussion was cut short. From then on, each successive Assembly showed increasing friendliness to the idea of German admission while Germany had shown less and less inclination to join. The League came to be regarded in Germany as an association of states under the control of former enemies rather than an international association for the promotion of universal concord.

In 1924 the political climate altered as the Poincaré government in France fell and Ramsay MacDonald became Prime Minister in Britain. In September 1924 MacDonald expressed his dismay that Germany was still excluded and urged her to apply for admission. This encouraged the German government to re-apply but they required conditions before agreeing to do so. There had to be discussions on questions relating to war guilt, disarmament, sanctions and mandates since the full development of the League could only proceed along lines of absolute equality between the member states.

In the meantime, negotiations had begun for the Locarno conference in which Germany told the French that the adoption of a security pact could only be agreed if Germany herself joined the League of Nations, placing any Locarno agreement above the League in importance. In February 1926, Stresemann requested that the question of German membership be put on the agenda as soon as possible. On 8 September, by unanimous vote of the Assembly, Germany was admitted to the League and given a permanent seat on the Council.

The success of the Locarno negotiations and Germany's accession to a seat on the Council of the League of Nations were a major setback for Soviet diplomacy which saw Germany being drawn back into the fold of Western capitalist nations and lined up in a united front against Bolshevism. Chicherin had failed to prevent Germany's drift towards the West and told von Seeckt that Germany was being lined up as a 'battering ram' against the Soviet Union. Radek labelled Germany's 'subordination' to be a step on the road to 'an alliance of capitalist powers . . . directed against the Soviet Union'.[3] It was essential for the Soviets now to do something to counter Western influence and it was in this context that Chicherin made plans for a Neutrality and Non-Aggression pact with Germany. The moment seemed favourable since Britain was distracted by the 'Mosul' dispute with Turkey. The Soviets had already signed a treaty with Turkey that had begun to undermine the foundations of Locarno and was now used as a template for negotiations with Germany.

There had been three articles in the treaty with Turkey. Article 1 stipulated the neutrality of one if the other was attacked, Article 2 stipulated that neither would attack the other or engage in hostile agreements with an aggressor and Article 3 stated the duration of the agreement (with Turkey that was three years). None of these were incompatible with Locarno or the League of Nations. The Soviets made it clear that they were willing to enter into similar binding agreements with all of its neighbours with which it had normal relations.

Relations between the Soviet Union and Germany had actually been amicable since Locarno and the appointment of Brockdorff-Rantzau to the Moscow embassy. While Locarno had been a blow for Soviet diplomacy it had not been a death-knell and there was optimism that swift action might persuade Germany that it should not put all its eggs in the 'Western' basket, given the hostility it still faced from France and Poland. Chicherin nibbled away at German confidence over Locarno, waiting for a chance to make his case. It soon came when Germany's admittance to the League of Nations was met with deep anger inside the country for its apparent reinforcement of Germany's humiliation at Versailles. At the same time Poland and Romania renewed their alliance which seemed to the Soviets to be outside the 'spirit of Locarno'.

The speed with which Stresemann agreed to Chicherin's overtures was astonishing. On 24 April 1926, Stresemann and the Soviet Ambassador in Berlin, Nikolai Krestinsky, signed the Treaty of Berlin (German-Soviet Neutrality and Non-Aggression Pact). Article 1 affirmed relations based on Rapallo and the other three articles were based on the Turkish treaty. A group of private German banks had granted the Soviet State Bank a short-term financial credit of 100 million marks in October 1925 and the German Cabinet followed this gesture, approving a long-term credit of 300 million marks in February 1926.

Although private German funds accounted for the credit, both the Reich and Länder governments agreed to guarantee 60 per cent of the credit against default. By extending a credit facility, Germany was hoping to bind the Soviet Union into a closer economic and political partnership.

Even though relations between Germany's Moscow embassy and Z. *Mo* had improved, they were still not particularly good and the lack of any real political benefits accruing to German industry from either military or civilian cooperation up to that point was worrying. While Soviet involvement was at the highest political level, Brockdorff-Rantzau wrote in 1926, the German military were conducting negotiations without the involvement of leading political figures and it was that imbalance where hardened Soviet political manipulators were dealing with politically naïve German military officers that was giving the Soviets such control of the whole strategy.

The Soviets had dangled offers of a full-blown military alliance but the German embassy was distinctly opposed to that. Brockdorff-Rantzau's ambitions were inclined much more to achieving a political agreement to serve as a counterweight to diplomatic moves in the West and also to use Soviet influence to keep up the pressure on Poland. He claimed that he had never been reliably informed about the actual status of the negotiations and so had been unable to exercise the sort of control that might have gained more political and economic advantage in return for military concessions. He demanded that the Reichswehr be prevented from maintaining direct relations with Soviet politicians and a single representative of the Reichswehr, Colonel von der Lieth-Thomsen, be appointed in the Soviet Union responsible to him and that he be given exclusive control over German funds to be spent for military purposes in the Soviet Union to ensure that they would be used not merely for the military strengthening of the Red Army but to procure war materials for Germany.

Ongoing negotiations to conclude a neutrality agreement between Germany and the Soviet Union, however, meant that his objections had little effect. A Soviet mission headed by Vice Commissar of War Iosif Stanislavovich Unshlikht (Herr Untermann) visited Berlin in the spring of 1926 and told German Chancellor Luther, Stresemann, Secretary of State von Schubert, von Seeckt and General Wetzell of Soviet plans for the production of heavy artillery, poison gas and precision instruments for which they needed Germany's financial support and guarantees that Germany would buy a certain share of the products. In return Germany could send officers to be trained at these new industrial centres. The offer was met with some surprise and consternation. Luther said that of course Germany was ready to collaborate in projects of peace but he showed little enthusiasm for military cooperation. As von Seeckt sat silently in the background, Unshlikht dropped a bombshell by then telling the meeting that he had already discussed the matter with the Reichswehr and was bringing it up now simply as a formality to get political approval. Von Schubert wrote to Brockdorff-Rantzau showing guarded enthusiasm but warned of huge political repercussions if news of the venture ever got out given the current negotiations for better relations with the West. He was familiar with covert operations, having been involved with Radek in the sealed-train transfer of Lenin to Russia in 1917. Overall, he agreed with Stresemann that 'to pursue this project cannot be reconciled with the general lines of our policy'.[4]

While there was no direct threat to the Soviet Union, a war scare swept the country in 1927 that may or may not have been a ruse by Stalin to hound his internal enemies, such as Trotsky and Zinoviev, by claiming disloyalty at a time of extreme national danger, and the manipulation of the fear of war to increase his control of the Politburo. After Locarno, Moscow had encouraged Franco-German cooperation in an attempt to open a rift between those two and Britain and, at the same time, had tried to come to an agreement with France over Tsarist debt. Britain went out on a limb and proposed a deal with Poland to cede the Danzig Corridor to Germany in return for all or part of Lithuania. This was not a comfortable prospect for the Soviet Union which suspected German connivance in an arrangement that brought both its near neighbours a step closer to its borders.[5]

In late 1926, the Soviet press warned of 'a new danger of war', blaming the British for stirring things up and the French for considering 'the crushing of the Soviets to be the necessary condition for the triumph of European civilisation'.[6] Politburo members Nikolai Bukharin, Alexei Rykov and Kliment Voroshilov all piled in after the New Year with warnings of imperialist aggression that got the Soviet public alarmed almost to the point of panic. Stalin was forced to make public statements to calm things down but further tension was raised by events on the other side of the continent.

In April 1927 the Soviet embassy in Peking was raided and Chiang Kai-Shek began his brutal repression of the Communist Party in China. In May, Britain broke off diplomatic relations with the Soviet Union and raided Soviet offices in Moorgate in London. The assassination of Pyotr Voikov, the Soviet plenipotentiary representative in Poland, by Boris Kowerda on Warsaw railway station on 7 July 1927 rekindled war fever, with Stalin saying 'It can scarcely be doubted that the main issue of the present day is . . . the real and actual threat of a new [imperialist] war'. German officers in the Soviet Union, however, reported no mobilisation measures and the only troop movements were the annual manoeuvres. Finally, in September, Franco-Soviet economic negotiations broke down and France expelled the Soviet ambassador, Christian Rakovsky. This was a serious embarrassment for Stalin that his enemies in the Politburo were not slow to exploit. Stalin was forced to defend himself against attacks by his main critics Trotsky and Zinoviev, who had called for the removal of 'incompetent leaders [who were] ignoramuses and scoundrels [and who had] blundered so badly'.[7]

As the threat of war continued to hang over the country, Stalin chose to announce in September that he had agreed to pay France sixty-one annual payments of 60 million gold francs to French holders of Tsarist bonds. It took some effort to persuade Soviet public opinion that such a high price was worth 'several years of relative calm' but the Soviet press informed them that it had been the 'threat of war hanging over us' that had forced the decision. They further justified the deal by implying that the debt would never be fully paid and simply 'liquidated' when the capitalist economies collapsed. Externally, Moscow saw the deal as mollifying a significant and influential section of French society who would receive the payments and, hopefully, would persuade the French government against joining Britain in an anti-Soviet campaign.

Bukharin, in particular, made a number of speeches blaming Western governments for creating a hostile environment in which war fever was circulating. Many of the Soviet Union's internal difficulties including shortages and price inflation were directly attributable to measures forced upon the government by the need for more investment in the military to meet the threat of war. It was all part of a long process, he said, to wean the Soviet economy off Western capital and introduce 'a whole series of measures which could secure our independence from foreign economic ties'.[8] Stalin was unable to persuade the Politburo to expel Trotsky and Zinoviev from the Party in October and had to settle for a motion of censure but when demonstrators disrupted the anniversary parades in November in support of the two men they were ruthlessly dealt with and used as an excuse to eventually have Trotsky and Zinoviev, along with a number of other prominent critics of the leadership, kicked out of the Party. A badly fractured opposition to Stalin was dealt a further crushing blow when Trotsky was exiled to Alma Ata a few weeks later. The war scare had served its purpose.

Chapter 6

LIPETSK, TOMKA AND KAZAN

As the few tanks the Soviet Union possessed in 1923 rusted away under Kotovsky's impoverished gaze, it fell to the new Red Army commander Frunze to redefine armoured doctrine which he did by depriving tanks of their 'special' status and relegating them to peripheral roles. Few new machines were ordered in view of their diminished importance in Red Army planning. Kotovsky was left to develop doctrine almost from a purely theoretical point of view with little opportunity of putting any of it into practice. The problem for Trotsky had been that he was too much of a realist in a country where dogma predominated. His pragmatic concept of modern military doctrine based on Western concepts made him an easy target for Frunze who embraced the ideological Bolshevik ideas of a proletarian militia that would inevitably prevail over decadent capitalist doctrine.

Like their German counterparts, Soviet military theorists, in their search for an armour doctrine, looked to the writings of the British tank experts J.F.C. Fuller and Basil Liddell Hart and the Frenchman George Soldan. Fuller, in particular, championed the idea of massed formations of tanks in a 'war of machines', almost eliminating the need for infantry, while Liddell Hart emphasised speed of manoeuvre as the key to victory. This may still have been pure fantasy given the current state of tank technology, but it could not be ignored given that there had not yet been observed any discernible slowdown in the pace of technological innovation.

It was becoming accepted by all modern military establishments that aircraft and mobile armour would eventually revolutionise warfare but until new machines had been tested in combat, theory allied with technology would be all that strategists could rely on.

The need for such ideas to be explored was heightened in the Soviet Union after Stalin had stirred up fear of Western nations threatening military action against them. In so doing he had collected to himself the power to further dictate domestic policy especially in the matter of industrialisation and, as a central part of that, the creation of a hugely expanded military-industrial base. At the core of this transformation of the economy was technological change.

In Germany the much-anticipated withdrawal of the Inter-Allied Control Committee that had tried, albeit without much success, to keep a check on any moves to expand the German military beyond the confines of Versailles encouraged a more aggressive attitude to rearmament with less fear of reprisal. General Werner von Blomberg, Chief of the *Truppenamt* (German General Staff), told his staff to beef up its planning for rebuilding the German armed forces. Plans were laid for a much-expanded army with an emphasis on technological developments, much as in the Soviet Union. Trials carried out in Britain had greatly widened the field of planning of tank warfare which was now benefitting from the greater speed and manoeuvrability of the latest experimental models. Exercises had shown that the tank need no longer be restricted to infantry support roles and could be used independently in, for instance, rapid flanking attacks. Some military thinkers even called the tank 'the supreme battle weapon' that would soon dictate the momentum and overall tactical employment of all forces on the battlefield.[1]

While tanks were gaining popularity as the weapon of choice, it was the motorisation of the whole army, giving infantry and artillery the ability to move at speed, upon which future leaders such as Heinz Guderian were concentrating. While Guderian would achieve fame as a Panzer leader during the Second World War, at this stage it was Fritz Heigl and Friedrich von Rabenau who laid the foundations of the tactics that Guderian would employ to such stunning effect in 1940. Fast-moving tanks in cooperation with motorised infantry and artillery were seen as the obvious way forward but the number of obstacles to overcome before this could be realised were great.

- Where was the protection from aircraft for units caught in the open?
- How could tank tracks be made sufficiently robust to withstand continuous wear over hard terrain?
- How could trucks follow the tanks across broken countryside?
- How could communications be maintained between the different components in a volatile environment?

- Who would dictate tactics once the battle commenced?
- How far ahead of field headquarters was it possible for a mobile force to go?
- How would tanks be rearmed with shells and refuelled during a battle?
- How would maintenance crews keep up with the tanks?
- Was the advantage of mobility sufficient compensation for the limited firepower of the tank compared to artillery?
- Were tanks best used *en masse* or in smaller units striking at a number of points simultaneously or in waves?
- Was it wise to mass produce a weapon that could be outmoded by the time it entered the battlefield?
- Where were the analysts that would keep track of technological developments and integrate that with evolving military doctrine?

In 1926, the Soviets had launched plans for large-scale production of tanks far exceeding anything being considered in Germany. Stalin's ambitions, however, seemed to have little influence on Tukhachevsky's mind which seemed to have little space for tanks despite Poland, the Soviet Union's most obvious potential adversary, having a large number in their ranks. Stalin was in charge and Stalin's plans would be followed. Production of the first MS-1 tank started up but was slow, as might be expected. Still, there were a few available for the autumn manoeuvres but not enough to give scope for exploring the theories that tanks were to be used in large numbers.

It was dawning on both the Germans and Soviets that the problems of working towards an effective doctrine for tank warfare might be shared, in a 'two heads are better than one' scenario. After early contacts which had mostly been in the area of armaments manufacturing, the concept of joint military testing and experimentation gained traction. Von Seeckt had become a keen advocate of tank development but realised that, of course, Germany was severely hamstrung by Article 171 of the Treaty of Versailles which had stipulated 'The manufacture and the importation into Germany of armoured cars, tanks and all similar constructions suitable for use in war are also prohibited'. The ambition was that one day Germany would cast off the shackles of containment and expand its military capability with impunity and when that day came, it would be good to have a great deal of experimental design knowledge to inform industry and ensure rapid progress towards the ultimate goal, but to be seen to move too soon towards rearmament while military resources were still constrained would inevitably invite intervention from Poland or France, or probably both together, with consequences that would mean further trauma for Germany.

German arms manufacturers like Krupp and Junkers had established factories in Sweden, Switzerland and the Netherlands after 1919. Krupp had signed an agreement with the Swedish gun manufacturer Bofors whereby Krupp supplied capital and technological information in return for a shareholding in the company and access to a number of patents. While the arrangement seems to have been of small benefit to Krupp it allowed the German government, through Krupp, to keep abreast of developments in artillery manufacture at the highest level. In 1920, the Swedish tractor-maker Landswerk, which produced tracked vehicles for agriculture, had sold shares in its business to the German manufacturer Gutehoffnungshütte (GHH) who developed the technology in relation to tank propulsion. Junkers had moved into Sweden in 1925 and set up what was essentially a German company in Malmo with few Swedish connections, AB Flyingindustri (ABF). It is interesting to note that the British did not object to the establishment of a factory in Sweden and even agreed to provide it with aero engines but insisted that it was sited close to the coast. Obviously suspecting that the factory would be producing aircraft that could easily be converted to military use in time of war, Britain ensured that the manufacturing base would be well with the range of its naval guns. Many of the aircraft coming out of the Malmo plant later went to the Soviet Union either for Soviet use or for the Germans at Lipetsk.

Only two options seemed to be on the table to achieve von Seeckt's ambition of rebuilding the German armed forces. One was continued collaboration with the Swedes, and the other was cooperating with the Soviets. It was clear that the second option, although riddled with political and doctrinal issues, allowed much more scope for experimentation, training and testing in a region that was very much less open to scrutiny by the Western Allies.

In 1921 the Germans had already established aircraft manufacturing capabilities at Fili but in 1924, they also built the Lipetsk training facility. The German military never wore uniforms while in the Soviet Union, only civilian clothing, to maintain their cover as much as possible. The training programme was very flexible and the main concept was one of creative thinking, experimentation and innovation. Initially only existing pilots received refresher courses but this was extended in 1926, when Reichswehr officers would be trained to become pilots and flight leaders and later, in 1928, *Jungmärke* (young pilots) were being accepted into the training programme.

The first suggestions in the Western press that there was some sort of military collaboration between the Weimar Republic and Soviet Russia were in 1922 when *The New York Times*, *The Wall Street Journal* and *The [London] Times* printed a number of articles about it. In June 1922, just two months after Rapallo, a *New York Times* article reported the arrival of the first German army officers sent to Soviet Russia to help train the Red Army. This group of officers included Colonel Max Bauer, Ludendorff's Chief of Staff in the First World War.

In terms of giving the Germans a military aviation base in the Soviet Union, the Soviets offered them the use of the military aerodrome at Odessa whose facilities seemed to meet all requirements, especially for naval aviation, but when the Reichsmarine decided that it didn't want to be part of the arrangements with the Soviets, Lipetsk (north of Voronezh) seemed to be a better alternative.

In late 1923, a Special Moscow Group (*Sondergruppe Moskau*), attached to the German *Sondergruppe R*, had been set up headed by Hermann von der Lieth-Thomsen, former German Air Force Chief of Staff. Ritter von Niedermayer, a former intelligence officer in the Middle East, was his deputy while Captain Ratt, Lieth-Thomsen's adjutant, was responsible for aviation matters. Versailles had banned development of German military aviation meaning that pilots could only be trained in Germany legally at the Civil Aviation Pilot Training Centre (*Deutsche Verkehrsflieger-Schule*) in light training aircraft or Junkers passenger planes and in sports flying clubs.

The first practical steps towards establishing facilities in the Soviet union were taken in 1923, when the Reichswehr, through the mediation of the German industrialist Hugo Stinnes, bought fifty single-seat Fokker D.XIII fighters from Holland and shipped them on the SS *Hugo Stinnes-IV*. The aircraft had originally been produced for the Argentine Air Force. The aircraft and other equipment were shipped as commercial goods through Metachim, a specially-founded joint stock company, and German pilots were sent disguised as tourists or employees of private companies, with passports issued in fictitious names.

The Germans established their flight school at Lipetsk in 1924 and operated it under Soviet cover. In Soviet documents the German aviation unit appeared as the 4th Aviation Detachment of the RKKA (Workers' and Peasants' Red Army) Air Forces 38th (later 40th) Aviation Squadron, while the German personnel were called 'friends'. In German documents the Lipetsk organisation was called the 'scientific aviation testing station' or just 'the station'. The first group of German airmen arrived under the command of Martin Fiebig, K. Lite, G. Johanenson, R. Hasenor and J. Schroeder, ostensibly as consultants with the RKKA Air Forces Directorate and the Air Force Academy in Moscow but then became the central staff members under Major

Walter Schtaar at Lipetsk. Schtaar was at first glance a strange choice but it may well have been selected because of rather than despite his being 'a Nazi of stern temper, demanding, and merciless . . . extremely hostile towards Soviet power and [intolerant of] Russians', to ensure that fraternising was kept to a minimum.

Pilot training began on 15 July 1925 under K. Schoenebock. Experienced instructors led the fighter pilot training course of four weeks of intensive flying with six to seven cadets in each training group. The Soviets took the opportunity of using the sessions to familiarise themselves with modern aircraft through competitive actions against German pilots. Early collaboration proved popular and successful as shown by the comments of Lieutenant Wilberg, Chief of the Reichswehr Aviation Department, who announced plans to expand the fighter school to include the training of reconnaissance aircraft crews and to conduct experiments in aerial photography. Eight Heinkel HD 17 reconnaissance aircraft were especially commissioned from Germany and although the company agreed to accept the government contract, it had grave misgivings about breaching Versailles. The Soviet Military Commissar, Romuald Adamovitch Muklevich, concurred and declared that Germany could 'count on total assistance and support on our part'. The first Fokker D.XIII aircraft were supplemented by more modern aircraft over the years. There was some friction over the issue of aircraft when the Soviets complained that the Germans were not making available to them their most modern aircraft although the Junkers Ju 87 dive bomber saw its first test flights there.

Numerous technical innovations in military aviation were also tested and evaluated while battle strategies and tactics evolved. During the summer of 1931, experiments and training extended to German and Soviet squadrons participated in mock attacks against daylight bombers devising the most optimal attack and defence techniques. By 1933, when Lipetsk was close down, over 1,200 Luftwaffe pilots had been trained there.

The German-Soviet project for chemical warfare development in the Soviet Union was code-named 'Tomka' (*Gas-Testgelände Tomka*) and based at Ivshchenkovo in the Samara Region of the Volga near Podosinky and operated by a fictitious joint German-Soviet company Bersol but which in reality was a branch of I.G. Farben. It was co-directed by Yakov Fishman and Dr Hugo Stolzenberg and managed by German chemists Alexander von Grundherr and Ludwig von Sicherer. It was officially described as an agricultural plant producing superphosphate fertiliser but its function was to manufacture mustard gas and phosgene. Its location allowed for German-speaking personnel living in German colonies in the Soviet Union to provide many support functions but everywhere on the site each German technician was always accompanied by two Soviets. Construction began in 1924 but 12 months later production had hardly started and the quality of the first batch of mustard gas produced which was tested in large-scale trials near Luga was far below standard. The plant failed to survive Soviet criticism of Stolzenberg's 'personal corruption and inefficiency' and it was closed down in 1927, not least because the Soviets had built their own mustard-gas manufacturing plant under the management of Evgeny Ivanovich Shpitalsky.[2]

Elsewhere another joint-venture experimental station was operated at Orenburg on the Ural river testing the dispersal of the gas from aircraft-mounted spray tanks. The relative success of this then led to another site at Shikhany (Saratov Oblast), again led by Fishman, on the Volga where the focus was on the toxicology and field behaviour of the gas. This site was expanded in 1928 with some German staff still working there as late as 1933. At first, the Soviet staff were 'very backward in the technique and evaluation of experiments' but eventually proved to be 'good, teachable pupils'. Cooperation had been reasonably good for the first couple of years but soon the Soviets clamoured for more control of the experimentation and persisted to the point where termination of the German contribution became a 'foregone conclusion'.[3] The Soviets, however, continued to use the sites to further their own research right up until the German invasion in 1941. Documents retrieved by the Germans from the French military archives in Paris in 1940 indicate that the French were well aware of the Tomka project and may actually have had a spy on site during the period of German collaboration.

In 1926, von der Lieth-Thomsen signed a three-year agreement with the Chief of Soviet Army Intelligence, Yan Berzin, to establish a *Panzerschule* (tank school) named Kama in Kazan. Berzin was wholly supportive of any military cooperation with Germany. He wrote:

> The most appreciable results are yielded by our officers' manoeuvres observation and field trips as well as by their attending academic courses in Germany. By studying the organisation of individual branches of the service, the arrangement of staff work, methods of instruction and training as well as the development of military thought, our officers not only acquire a good amount of useful knowledge and broaden their outlook, but also get some stimulus to examining certain problems and trying to solve them independently as applied to our conditions.

> In short, our officers, enriching their knowledge, acquire so called 'military culture'.[4]

The Germans would come up with the finance and the Soviets would attend to construction and maintenance of premises. The Reichswehr internal budget for the purchase and manufacture of permitted weapons set their value at inflated prices which allowed for a margin of creative accounting, making money available for transfer to a 'black' fund to finance Kazan. The main purposes of the establishment would be to train officers in the handling of tanks and to test new German models alongside foreign designs for comparison. The Reichswehr sent Lieutenant-Colonel A.D. Malbrandt to liaise with the Soviets and together they chose the city of Kazan, some 500 miles east of Moscow. The name Kama was derived from Kazan and Malbrandt but it was quickly renamed TEKO (Technical Courses of the Society for Defence, Aviation and Construction of Chemical Weapons). The Soviets chose as its representative at Kazan the old Bolshevik Józef Unshlikht, a close ally of Lenin whom Trotsky called 'an ambitious but talentless intriguer' and who was paired with the German appointee, General Oswald Lutz. TEKO's teaching covered both practical and theoretical studies. Construction of the site was slow which prompted von der Lieth-Thomsen to make official his complaint to von Blomberg that the Soviets were preoccupied with putting their main effort into building their own new aerodrome at Bryansk.

Already there was a feeling amongst Soviet political leaders that they were not getting equal benefit out of the cooperative projects already in train and, as a result, were giving them lower priority than purely Soviet developments. Commercial ventures such as the Fili plant had failed and the danger was that the experimental military schemes could follow suit but there was still sufficient enthusiasm in the military of both sides to continue even if the politicians were daily finding new reasons to scale them back. Soviet prevarication can also be seen in the light of their ambition to acquire as much technical and engineering experience with modern German machine tools while sending the minimum number of tanks to fit out Reichswehr armoured units. The Germans held the purse-strings to a very great extent but the Soviets were on home turf and it was a long way to Berlin.

At first the engineers had to improvise by modifying a pair of agricultural tractors (*Hanomags*) into primitive self-propelled guns for testing and practice but by 1929, the basic infrastructure was in place with garages, workshops and 400 workers on site as the first Panzers started arriving for training exercises. These were six 23-ton tanks with BMW engines and 75mm main guns and three 12-ton tanks armed with 37mm guns. Along with the armour, the Germans assembled a substantial engineering and mechanical team at Kazan including representatives of Rheinmetall-Borsig and Daimler-Benz. The Soviet Army provided a number of British Carden-Loyd tankettes that went on to play a role in the development of the German Panzer I. As part of the deal, Germany provided the Soviet Union with a number of industrial and manufacturing tools which the Soviets did not yet have the capacity to make for themselves. Tukhachevsky, who was intimately involved with Kazan, had visited German facilities in the Soviet Union and had even gone to Germany himself to see German tank designs and training methodology. He became one of the Soviet Union's top experts on Soviet-German co-operation and developed good relations with a number of German staff officers.

Deprived of any type of armour under Versailles, von Seeckt had created a Motor Troops Inspectorate, which was headed by young officers with considerable experience with armoured vehicles from the First World War. Using 'paper Panzers' (cars with wood and sacking added to give the rough appearance of a tank), these officers began experimenting with ideas of armoured warfare.[5] In the Soviet Union, Frunze had died whilst undergoing surgery for an ulcer on 31 October 1925 and Voroshilov had taken his place. Voroshilov had never distinguished himself as a military innovator or inspirational leader. His traditionalist military philosophy may well have been why Stalin chose him but Trotsky was scathing about the abilities of a man who was 'capable [only] of handling a regiment'.[6] The biggest influence on the Red Army going forward, however, would prove to be Tukhachevsky, who became the Soviet military's 'most influential thinker and strategist'.[7]

Tukhachevsky had served as one of the senior Red Army officers in the Russian Civil War, as an adviser to Trotsky. As early as 1920 he had gone on to write extensively on mobile armoured warfare and was appointed Director for the Study of Strategy at the Red Army War College. His philosophy was underpinned by Clausewitz's thinking and was based on his theory of 'Deep Battle', a concept that involved the concentration of armoured vehicles. Politically, like Clausewitz he held that 'warfare itself is only a means to a political end'. This meant that strategic considerations must inform tactical decisions and he was sufficiently emboldened to assert that political leaders should not interfere in the execution of tactics; a viewpoint that would later get him into serious trouble under Stalin. He concluded that Germany had lost the First World War because of economic collapse that left the army without the means to continue fighting. Technology and mass production were his watchwords.

His concept of 'Deep Battle' was formulated in Field Manual PU-36 and argued for the concentration of force using 'shock troops' of armoured vehicles at a narrow point to achieve penetration of enemy lines after which it would use speed of advance to bring about destruction of enemy logistics and communications. Encirclement and annihilation of enemy units would follow. This required the separation of tanks and mechanised units from infantry units and was deeply unpopular with influential and traditional Red Army commanders such as Voroshilov. Furthermore, he believed that modern warfare depended upon the successful relationship between all military branches, particularly emphasising the need for close air support and communication between shock troops, armour and infantry. Successful application of 'Deep Battle' tactics required the concentration of a vastly superior force at the point of attack but perhaps the most revolutionary of his ideas was in the use of aircraft acting independently of ground forces to focus on strategic objectives. The similarities of 'Deep Battle' tactics to those of the German 'Blitzkrieg' employed during the Second World War are inescapable.

From the very first German-Soviet contact, the Kriegsmarine had been little interested in working with the Soviets. A couple of naval missions had gone to Moscow in the early 1920s but neither side showed much enthusiasm given that naval operations were much more difficult to disguise. In 1926, a Soviet naval delegation visited Berlin and offered to build German-designed submarines and torpedoes in the Soviet Union in return for German assistance in a number of associated fields. There were two areas of possible collusion. In the event of a joint Soviet-German offensive against Poland, the Soviet Navy would blockade Danzig and if the French intervened to support Poland it would be essential for the Soviet Black Sea Fleet to interfere with French Mediterranean traffic but the Soviet navy would be quite unable to carry out any of these manoeuvres without a significant elevation of their combat efficiency which could only come from German input.

Muklevich and von der Lieth-Thomsen discussed the possibility of opening a submarine training station on the Black Sea coast on similar lines to the stations at Lipetsk and Kazan at the end of 1926 but the German navy reviewed the proposal and declined to accept it, no doubt because they already had a Dutch firm Ingenieurskantoor voor Scheepshouw (I. v. S.) in The Hague constructing submarines in a covert operation. They also did not wish to upset the Royal Navy who the Germans knew were monitoring them very closely. Only in 1938 and 1939 did the Kriegsmarine take a more serious interest in Soviet naval matters, but by then it was already too late to establish reliable contacts.

The way in which these new military developments affected the *Auswärtiges Amt* can be seen by the way they impacted on negotiations, in the summer of 1926, for an exchange of political prisoners between Germany and the Soviet Union. One of the Soviets in German jails, Skoblevsky, had been convicted of planning the assassination of no less a figure than von Seeckt but the Soviets were anxious to have him repatriated. When Germany refused to release him, Brockdorff-Rantzau felt compelled to urge Stresemann to comply with the request fearing that the Soviets would act with 'ruthless brutality' and expose the cooperative military ventures to the world. Stresemann conceded that they were 'in the hands of political blackmailers' and persuaded the German Cabinet, despite a number of threats to resign in protest, to agree to Skoblevsky's release.

The *Auswärtiges Amt* decided that they had to get to grips with the problem and took steps to clarify the situation. First of all, they observed that German financial and logistical support for parts of the USSR's armament industry and the firm of Junkers in Moscow violated Article 170 of the Treaty. Secondly, the Bersol partnership at the poison gas factory at Ivshchenkovo, which produced gas for import into Germany, was in violation of Article 171. Furthermore, Germany's decision to send repeated military, naval and air missions to the Soviet Union under Hasse, Mentzel, Fischer, Wilberg, Vogt and Spindler violated Article 179. It was also noted that other German activities in the Soviet Union, such as participation in Soviet military industries and the training of German personnel at Lipetsk and Kazan which might not have actually constituted a direct violation of Versailles were clearly against the spirit of the Treaty, and would, if they became known, compromise the German government.

Again the Western press came up with reports describing clandestine operations between Germany and the Soviet Union but no politician in the West seemed remotely interested in pursuing the matter. On 23 January 1927 *The Observer* reported that

> two German workmen who were employed up to May last year, in the poison gas factory which the Reichswehr, with the help of the Soviet authorities, set up at Trotzk, near Samara, on the Volga, have given names and have cited facts which involve the Reichswehr, and, therefore, the German Government in the person of the Reichswehr Minister very

deeply. The preliminary effect of this intrigue seems to have been to provide the Reichswehr with a secret store of 1,000,000 poison gas shells; and though the factory was washed out by the Volga floods last May, there is no certainty that it has not since been re-started.[8]

Germany's concern over possible Soviet blackmail, however, was really unnecessary. The Western Powers had known for some time about the illicit operations through French and Polish Intelligence. They had become aware that, during the summer of 1926, the Reichswehr was getting ready to move to Germany large quantities of shells that had been produced in the Soviet Union. Both Brockdorff-Rantzau and von Dirksen, one of Stresemann's team, had warned the Reichswehr against so dangerous an operation at a time when Germany was about to enter the League of Nations, but they were told that all necessary precautions would be taken. The false optimism of this assertion was exposed when, on 3 and 6 December, the *Manchester Guardian*, in two articles considered to be amongst the most important yet most ignored stories of the Weimar era, reported not only details about the transport of ammunition from Leningrad to Stettin but also revealed many other aspects of Russo-German military collaboration.

The Berlin correspondent Frederick Augustus Voigt had acquired a copy of a memorandum sent by a furious Junkers company to selected members of the Reichstag after the company had been denied state funds to keep its Fili plant going. This formed the basis of his article but he had also discovered that a Soviet cargo vessel that had sunk in the Baltic en route to Germany was discovered to have a cargo consisting of weapons and ammunition for the Reichswehr, and implied that most of the cargo the Germans received from Russia was of a military nature. He wrote:

> an aeroplane factory has been built by the Junkers' Works in Russia for the purpose of manufacturing military aeroplanes for German as well as Russian use. Arrangements for erecting chemical works in Russia to manufacture poison-gas for both countries were also made by German and Russian military experts. These activities began at least five years ago but have been going on ever since. To make the necessary arrangements officers of the *Reichswehr* have travelled to and from Russia with false papers, visaed by the Russian authorities. General von Seeckt, until recently Commander-in-Chief of the *Reichswehr*, was on the best of terms with the Russians, particularly with officers of high rank in the Soviet Army. It seems that he was not unaware of the facts mentioned above.[9]

Three days later he followed up with a second article.

> The Junker Works in Moscow were as a preliminary to further production to manufacture a hundred aeroplanes. Almost the entire expense of fitting out works, dispatching and maintaining experts, as well as of providing material and constructing aeroplanes, was borne by the Germans. The construction programme was to reach 300 aeroplanes yearly, of which the majority were to be for German use.

This was compounded by a sensational speech on the subject delivered by Socialist deputy Philip Scheidemann before the Reichstag on 6 December in which he demanded the resignation of Defence Minister Otto Gessler, the ending of all illegal military collaborative efforts with the Soviet Union, and parliamentary oversight of the actions of senior military officials and the funding of Reichswehr operations. The *New York Times* reported that Scheidemann's speech was greeted with cries of 'Traitor! Blackguard! That's treason!'. German Chancellor Wilhelm Marx called the claims untrue and denied that funds were being diverted illegally for military purposes. The Reichswehr and von Seeckt were held in such awe by German politicians at the time that Scheidemann's attack was easily parried but it had been a severe embarrassment and a warning for Germany. Brockdorff-Rantzau's worst fears were materialising. Tschunke tried to calm things down by saying that German military activities in the Soviet Union underwent 'a number of important changes' as a result of Scheidemann's speech but in reality little changed.

Brockdorff-Rantzau again claimed that he had never been properly informed by the Reichswehr of what was going on and worried that further exposure would show him up as *'als Esel oder als Schweinhundt* [an ass or a scoundrel]'.[10] He didn't have long to wait. Reports came in indicating that ammunition was being unloaded at Stettin on ships coming from the Soviet Union. This forced the closure of some small factories in the Soviet Union but a number had never been successful anyway, and another consequence was the resignation of Gessler for 'health reasons'. Brockdorff-Rantzau tried to divert attention by proposing that certain factories producing non-military material should be converted to civilian use but only on condition that, in an emergency, they could be used for war production. There was, however, the question of how they would explain this to the Soviets without alerting them to the fact that German policy was changing dramatically. It was agreed to tell Chicherin of the changes but to emphasise that they would take effect only slowly and would not have any immediate impact. There would be no urgency to make the changes that would have a deleterious effect on the political climate, neither would there be a need to curtail production of items not proscribed by Versailles and anyway doubtless the military would try their best to ignore any political directive and carry on as normal. The Reichstag chose to ignore Scheidemann and concentrate on maintaining the balance between East and West they had fought so hard to achieve with Rapallo, Locarno and Berlin. The Reichswehr responded by tightening security and, after a short hiatus, resumed operations on a more intense level.

The Soviet Central Committee, meanwhile, approved calls for greater investment in indigenous military industrial projects, especially aviation. There were a number of experienced aircraft designers coming through such as Nikolai Polikarpov and Andrei Tupolev who had worked with Junkers at Fili. By early 1927, most of these proposals were already being carried out. Germany had almost entirely withdrawn from the Junkers works and the poison gas works in the Soviet Union and Lipetsk and Kazan had been transformed into private enterprises supported by German government funds and in which there were no active Reichswehr members employed, while WIKO had disappeared altogether. Indigenous Soviet aircraft manufacture, prioritised in the First Soviet Five-Year Plan, had increased but manufacturing standards were pitiful and the quality of aircraft coming out of the factories made the flying of them something of a gamble. Debate was fierce as the military and diplomats engaged. It was absolutely necessary, Wetzell argued, to gain some experience in aerial and tank warfare, since those two weapons would play a decisive role in any future war. Von Schubert told a meeting that 'it was no longer possible for the *Auswärtiges Amt* to follow its past practice of wanting to know as little as possible about these things, so as to be able to say that these matters were unknown to them'. He doubted that 'the military advantages were so decisive as to make up for the political risks which the continued operation of Lipetsk and Kazan incurred'.[11] Wetzell assured him that the Soviets were still sufficiently motivated in the operations to keep them secret but if Germany was to withdraw precipitously the Soviets might approach France or some other power and Germany would lose all the political and military advantages she had accrued to date. 'All current operations' he stated, were 'vital for our army', and he urgently requested continuing them. Von Schubert felt unable to argue further without consulting Stresemann.

General August Wilhelm Heye replaced von Seeckt on 9 October 1926 when the latter had been forced to resign after having become embroiled in a scandal involving the appointment of one of the Kaiser's sons to a prominent military position. It was President Hindenburg himself, however, who became the German Army Commander-in-Chief with Heye, although titular head of the Reichswehr, very much in a subordinate role. Stresemann went to Heye and came back with an agreement to continue operation in Kazan and Lipetsk but specified that no currently serving German officers should be sent to these schools during 1927. The military were disdainful of what they saw as *Auswärtiges Amt* capitulation to international disquiet but were minded to exercise the greatest caution. The Finance Ministry took a hand in facilitating the transport of war materials to the Soviet Union and even Stresemann agreed to Germany's continued participation in experiments with poison gas.[12] In reality Germany's enthusiasm for military collaboration with the Soviet Union had actually appeared to intensify after 1926 but, especially at Kazan, the Germans had been embarrassed at not being able to manufacture the agreed number of tanks to be sent out from Germany. The Soviets suspected that this was a deliberate plot but in fact it had come about as the result of manufacturers such as Henschel failing to meet specifications.

Nothing daunted, Soviet and German theorists set about discussing battlefield doctrine, especially in relation to how tanks were expected to work with infantry. While the infantry slowed down the rate of advance of the tanks, they were left without any heavy armour if they failed to keep up with them. Any loss of contact was seen as a recipe for disaster. Since there were no tanks to use, when exercises were conducted, they were represented by bicycles with wooden mock-ups build around them. However risible this might seem at first, the results of exercises carried out in 1928 with slightly better mock-ups allowed General von Alfred Vollard-Bockelberg, head of the *Heereswaffenamt*, to put his theories into practice.

Results of exercises came under scrutiny when reports of new French high-speed Renault-built 'chars' dropped on his desk. There was no way that these would be held back by slow-moving infantry. This meant that rather than moving together in carefully choreographed ways, the tanks would forge ahead to make the initial breakthrough using speed as a decisive factor and the infantry would then be activated to drive into the breach and consolidate the salient. This was all well and good but in reality the Kiev exercises in 1928 brutally exposed the shortcomings of Soviet capabilities. Commanders showed no understanding of how to employ tanks. One tank unit was even attached to an artillery unit, presumably on the basis that they both fired shells. Tukhachevsky must have had his head in his hands when it was clear that infantry had been given no instructions how or when to follow tanks.

All this was in sharp contrast to German exercises where Soviet observers were impressed by the way that German tactics were evolving at such a pace and reported to Voroshilov how tanks and motorised infantry were becoming increasingly effective in combination. While von Vollard-Bockelberg forged ahead with more elaborate tactics, there was a growing body of opinion in the German General Staff that improved anti-tank weapons would quickly nullify the effectiveness of tanks and that the sums currently being lavished on tank development might be better spent elsewhere. The Soviet view was that first must come the tanks in huge numbers as the result of Stalin's drive for industrialisation of production and then would come the doctrine according to how many there were.

This was especially important to Tukhachevsky who was working on revolutionary ideas and had already gone to print with his papers on artillery and aviation but now turned to tanks. Modern war looked quite different to Tukhachevsky than it had done to either Trotsky or Frunze. New technologies required new doctrines. His drive on Warsaw in 1920, even though it ended in ultimate failure to take the city itself, had opened his eyes to how war could be conducted beyond the confines of static positional trench warfare. Not for him the single decisive battle to determine the outcome but a continuous series of operations that succeeded each other seamlessly so that pressure was applied to wear down the enemy and gave them no respite or chance to regroup or reinforce. This required constant resupply throughout the campaign and continuous management of the changing circumstances. The key to developing the doctrine of 'Deep Battle' was motorised infantry, tanks and aircraft but theory was all well and good if there was the necessary equipment to hand which, in the case of the Soviet Union, was still a long way off. At this stage the theory, however, only went as far as stipulating the need for large numbers of vehicles and aircraft: it had nothing to say about exactly how all the different elements would work together.

Unfortunately for Tukhachevsky, at this point he came off second best in a dispute with Voroshilov over army command structure as well as getting Stalin's attention for all the wrong reasons. Both his adversaries saw Tukhachevsky as a threat to their own positions and together these two powerful enemies forced his resignation as Chief of Staff. While this relegation removed him from the centre of power, it had the effect of allowing him to develop his theories relatively free from interference and opposition. The scale and composition of Soviet forces, he decided, was to be determined by those of its potential enemies, Poland and Germany. In this he had the support of many of his fellow commanders who peppered Voroshilov with reports outlining the inferiority of Soviet arms in this respect. While Poland was modernising its tank force, the Soviets still relied on the relics of the Civil War, some of which did not even have working guns fitted.

The message got through. General Staff officer Pavel Dybenko argued for more tanks at a Defence Cabinet meeting of April 1927. Together with Lukin, head of Financial Planning, he called for as many as 900 MS-1s as well as 180 heavy tanks and a large number of light reconnaissance vehicles. There was huge support for Dybenko but, of course, the problem was that Soviet industry was far from capable of manufacturing this number of machines. The growing awareness of the need for rapid mechanisation of the army had the effect of bringing Tukhachevsky back into the limelight as the one who had championed the cause in the first place. It was he, supported by Unshlikht, who presented the military five-year plan in 1928 in which he bemoaned the lack of manufacturing facilities but insisted that this had to be addressed with the utmost urgency with a programme to equip the armed forces with high-speed tanks and long-range aircraft.

Political opposition to Stalin's industrialisation programme foundered and plans were approved for industry to meet the requirements of the military but it was soon made clear that the myriad formidable obstacles in the way meant that, in the short term at least, they would need outside help. Voroshilov was urged to seek German assistance, especially in dual-drive technology, invented by Oswald Lutz, to provide blueprints and specifications for the next generation of tanks. This revolutionary propulsion method involved both tyres and tracks to be used according to the terrain. The German designer Josef Vollmer eventually signed an agreement but the tank school and workshops at Kazan were behind schedule meaning that no exercises could begin before spring 1929.

Z. Mo, re-named *Heim Deutscher Angestellter Moskau,* under the direction of Niedermayer, continued its activities in close collaboration with the Moscow embassy. The *Auswärtiges Amt* was kept informed about the number of Reichswehr members assigned each year to serve in the Soviet Union and other officers continued to go on temporary missions. An example of the continuing close cooperation was the visit of von Blomberg together with several other officers to observe Red Army manoeuvres in the autumn of 1928. The visit was carefully managed so as the German delegation avoided meeting the military attachés of other powers.

Von Blomberg reported that they had been shown everything they asked for and the reception they received everywhere was friendly, often cordial, and very hospitable. He visited Lipetsk, Kazan and Tomka and found all of them in the best condition, expecting to reach their full capacity by 1929. 'The great value of these institutions for our military preparations,' he said, 'is beyond a doubt [and even though] the Russian interest in them is considerable, the advantages from these installations predominantly favour the German side.'[13] When Voroshilov tried to engage von Blomberg in the wider issue of mutual military aid in the event of a Polish attack against either country which was a fundamental issue for the Soviets, von Blomberg demurred and somewhat disingenuously pleaded military separation from such 'high policy' decisions. Despite this prevarication, Voroshilov seems to assume that he had got a 'nod and a wink' to indicate that the Soviets could count on Wehrmacht support in any action against Poland.

What has rarely been addressed in the whole collaborative venture is the German objective of gaining access to the inner circle of Soviet command to acquire some understanding of military capabilities and long-term strategy. Colonel Hillmar Mittelberger's report of spring 1928 shows that the Soviet military high command under Tukhachevsky was trying to distance itself from communist control but the question of Red Army efficiency remained difficult to answer. At most it was thought to have the means of repulsing an attack from Poland, which was what motivated most of its strategy, but it had little offensive capability. Von Blomberg had also made his assessment of the Soviet leaders. Tukhachevsky had been removed from the Red Army Staff and made commander of the Leningrad Military District for his belligerent advocacy of an aggressive war capability against Poland but von Blomberg found him to be 'a lively and shrewd questioner' and 'a personality very worthy of notice'.[14] His demotion was taken as an indication that the Soviets harboured no immediate plans to attack Poland.

Von Blomberg had only praise for his reception in the Soviet Union and heard only enthusiastic approval of the links now established between the Reichswehr and the Red Army. Niedermayer's Moscow headquarters was shown to have excellent rapport with Voroshilov, Kazan was almost running at full capacity and the Tomka poison gas project was being expanded but Lipetsk was the jewel in the crown. Von Blomberg considered the value of all ventures to be 'beyond any doubt'.[15] Voroshilov, like Tukhachevsky, was eager to disengage the army from politics and he saw collaboration with the Reichswehr as a vital part of that strategy.

Conditions at Tomka were very favourable for the German workers. An interview with German operatives at the plant revealed that the wages were 700–900 marks per month which included 'danger money' and a family allowance paid to families back in Germany. However, letters home were censored and only right-wing German newspapers were allowed. German officers visiting the factory were treated with 'great politeness'. German workers had to sign a contract which stated:

> You undertake expressly the duty to keep the strictest secrecy about all occurrences in Russia which should come to your knowledge directly, as well as about your own work, and all business affairs which should come to your knowledge, both within and outside the factory. You are strictly forbidden to publish any thing or to deliver a lecture on any subject whatsoever. Any offence under this clause will lead to immediate dismissal, and, in case of need, to claims for damages, as also ruthless prosecution by the competent Courts.[16]

Chapter 7

THE MIDDLE YEARS

Von Blomberg made a return visit to the USSR in 1929 along with General Kurt von Hammerstein-Equord and Colonel Kühlenthal to observe the Kiev manoeuvres. His compendious report of the visit contained a section on the Red Army command structure which was split between political 'non-soldiers', who held many of the highest posts, older ex-Imperial officers and younger trainees. German influence through military literature was deep and assignment to Reichswehr units was considered to be a major boost for any Soviet military career. In conclusion, he stressed that the Red Army should not be viewed as the bodyguard of a hated regime but as a military force which could not be ignored. All military joint ventures were on firm foundations, the Red Army was most important as a restraining influence on Poland and collaboration, which must continue, was vital to German interests.

Once again Brockdorff-Rantzau felt aggrieved to be sidelined and complained to Stresemann in April 1928. It was he, he wrote, who had played a leading role in Russo-German relations for the past five years and had always seen them as one of the most important bonds of common policy but now, without his knowledge, an agreement was being concluded between Stresemann and the Reichswehr minister according to which the secret deals between Germany and the Soviet Union were not only being continued but extended. And all this at a time when Russo-German political relations were at a particularly low ebb, due to a number of incidents, especially the notorious Shakhty trial.

Early in 1928, five German technicians who had been installing equipment in the North Caucasus town of Shakhty for AEG and another German firm, Knapp, were arrested together with forty-eight Soviet specialists and charged with espionage and sabotage. Chicherin, powerless to influence his own political masters, told Brockdorff-Rantzau he feared that a public trial would follow and urged the ambassador to use whatever influence he had to intervene and prevent a breakdown of Soviet-German relations. AEG threatened to discontinue all its operations in the Soviet Union. Two of the Germans, Goldstein and Wagner, were released ten days later. Three others, Maier, Otto and Badstieber, however, remained in prison. After his release, Franz Goldstein reported to the *Auswärtiges Amt* that he believed the real reason for the arrests was to cover up a catastrophic decline in Soviet industrial production. It was clear that the German and Soviet specialists were to be used as scapegoats for Bolshevik failures. 'Let this be a warning to every German engineer not to make his ability available to the Soviet government', he said.[1]

The *Auswärtiges Amt* was aghast at the development and could not understand why Moscow had chosen to attack German industry just when relations were strained. All and sundry were desperately trying to find some way out of the predicament. The management of AEG informed the *Auswärtiges Amt* that the arrests were not the private concern of the firm, as the state had insisted, but an issue for the government. Stresemann issued a resolution objecting to the Soviet action, threatening to withdraw all AEG employees from the Soviet Union, but a special committee of the Reich Association of German Industry (*Reichsoerband*) declared that such a move would constitute a breach of contract. AEG responded by recalling all employees who were not bound by any contract and refused to send any more but was anxious not to go too far and prejudice its already substantial investment in the Soviet Union.

Germany was determined to do nothing that could be interpreted as a breach of Rapallo and hoped against hope that the Soviets would see sense and let the remaining three Germans return home but the Soviets would not agree and the men remained in prison. Brockdorff-Rantzau lodged an emphatic protest against the unhygienic and despicable conditions in the jail, as described by Goldstein, and demanded that the German prisoners receive humane treatment according to the 'procedures established among civilised peoples'.[2]

On 29 March, the *Narkomindel* (Soviet Foreign Commissariat) granted the German Consul in Kharkov permission to visit the three technicians. Brockdorff-Rantzau bluntly declined the offer on the Consul's behalf and insisted that the more senior figure of the Secretary of Legation, Schliep, must be allowed to see them; if not he would cause a diplomatic incident by going himself. As a result, Schliep was granted access to each of the men, who had been given single-occupancy cells, for ten minutes but overall the Soviets paid little heed to German protests. Maier appeared to be in good health,

Otto seemed 'in good spirits also but Badstieber appeared depressed and feeble.'[3] Brockdorff-Rantzau was sure that it was a proxy war and all had something to do with issues between the Reichswehr and the Red Army.

On 17 April, Politburo member Nikolai Bukharin intervened and in an undisguised threat, claimed that Soviet Intelligence had uncovered a plot by foreign capitalists to sabotage Soviet industry. Foreign engineers, he said, were members of the German fascist organisation *Stahlhelm*. There was even the possibility that the defence and chemical industries had also been affected. Stresemann and von Schubert continued to protest but the Soviets insisted that it was an internal matter. The Germans objected to the unseemly haste with which the arrests had been carried out and called the whole thing an example of 'lamentable foolishness'. In reply, the Soviets made a telling reference to the haste with which current economic negotiations had been curtailed by the Germans, indicating that they may have had an underlying agenda. Stresemann promised to press for a resumption of talks as soon as the men were freed but pointed out that it was hardly an encouragement for other German firms to invest in the Soviet Union.

The three men had been transferred to Moscow on 7 April and kept in the Butyrka prison to await the trial and eventually, on 8 May, Brockdorff-Rantzau was able to visit them. He discovered that the men were not entirely innocent of illegal activity, having been instrumental in offering bribes to Soviet officials to increase state orders from their factories but the charges were excessive and based on hearsay. AEG refused to get involved in the bribes scandal saying that no charges had been brought against the company but Polish intelligence had documentary proof to the contrary and showed it to the *Auswärtiges Amt*. Furthermore, the Poles said that there was not a shred of evidence to indicate a counter-revolutionary cell in the Donbas. Just to complicate the matter further, the Lithuanian ambassador told Brockdorff-Rantzau that sabotage in the area had been the work of the Poles.

The trial, the first of the great Stalin show trials, opened on 18 May. Brockdorff-Rantzau, with 'a tired, unfathomable expression', was there to observe.[4] Proceedings were clouded in political interference and characterised by particularly Soviet forms of justice. Charges were not read out, apparently on the basis that they involved the French and Polish governments and could not be made public. The German defence lawyer, Gustav Hilger, was refused permission to act for the men and German witnesses were not called because it was claimed they were also complicit in the crime. It became perfectly obvious to Brockdorff-Rantzau that the trial had been well prepared down to the last detail and that the verdict was a foregone conclusion, and he wondered why Germany should be treated differently to Poland and France who were handled with greater consideration. He concluded that it was because the Soviets thought they had Germany 'in their pocket' with the hidden threat of exposing the military cooperation to keep them in check. He furthermore surmised that the Soviets had concluded that they could proceed with impunity and deal with him as they saw fit and were determined to prove it as a show of strength. However, despite the ever-present danger that the Soviets would leak information about the secret collaboration, neither Stresemann nor the Reichswehr were willing to cause a fuss and risk disrupting what they saw as a profitable relationship. The access to training facilities for tank crews and combat pilots as well as to the Soviet defence and chemical industries were much too important. German military experts had made it repeatedly clear that even the threat of dire political consequences was not sufficient to discontinue the training of experts in the arms which would be decisive in any future conflict.

Quite soon, however, the Soviets changed tack and appeared to moderate their position. The Soviet newspaper *Izvestia* reported 'The German Reich does not sit in the dock, neither does German industry nor German firms as such, but individual German citizens who are accused of a number of unlawful acts'. Mikhail Kalinin said in a speech, 'Maybe our Government was a bit incautious . . . considering that Germany is a friendly state . . . with whom we have good-neighbourly relations, we should have been more careful with the arrests . . . the leaders of the USSR had the highest regard for German industry'.[5]

As for the trial, one of the defendants had put the cat among the pigeons by implicated not only AEG and Knapp, but also two other German firms, Eickhoif and Siemens, in the financing of the alleged sabotage. Otto and Maier defended themselves with great spirit. The latter did especially well. He told the prosecutor Krylenko that the examining judge had put statements into the record which he, Maier, had never made. He had signed the protocol because in his nervous state he had felt that it was better to do so.

On 29 June, Krylenko summed up. He said that AEG as such was not accused but pointed out that there was evidence that meetings of foreign members of the counter-revolutionary organisation had taken place in AEG's Russian Department. He asked that the charges against Maier be dropped. Otto, he said, belonged not only to the *Stahlhelm* but also to the *Freunde des Neuen Russlands* (Friends of the New Russia) indicating that he was politically active. He called for Otto to be given a six-month sentence. Babsteiber had admitted the charge of bribery but had also maintained that Knapp machinery delivered to the Soviet factories was of poor quality. Krylenko called for a suspended sentence. It was clear that the Soviets regretted ever involving the German technicians in the trial and were trying to get out of the mess as quickly as possible.

Brockdorff-Rantzau's threat to disrupt diplomatic relations resulted in Soviet Ambassador Krestinsky's hint to von Schubert in Berlin that the Germans could expect a light sentence. Von Schubert informed Brockdorff-Rantzau and told him that every effort would be made to renew negotiations on the extension of the Commercial Treaty but insisted on definite assurances that the talks, once resumed, would be concluded successfully.

On 7 July the verdict was delivered. Eleven Soviet defendants were condemned to death. Otto and Maier were acquitted and Babsteiber was given a suspended sentence. The trial had seriously undermined Brockdorff-Rantzau's belief that Germany and the Soviet Union were tied together by a community of fate (*Schicksalsgemeinschaft*). His close personal relationship with Chicherin had, in some measure, compensated for the disappointments with the other Soviets but Chicherin was a very sick man and his star was on the wane. Brockdorff-Rantzau's own health, which had been poor at the start of the trial, had been worn down by the end of it also.

He left Moscow on 18 July, arriving in Berlin on the 24th, and took part in a conference during which the entire relationship between Germany and the Soviet Union was thoroughly discussed. Besides the Ambassador, von Schubert and von Dirksen were on the German side while, for the Soviet Union, the People's Commissar for Foreign Affairs, Maxim Litvinov, an associate of Lenin during the revolution and a man who was probably the most pro-Western of all Soviet statesmen of the time, and Ambassador Krestinsky attended. The talks were based on a memorandum which Moritz Schlesinger had drafted. Litvinov, a Pickwickian figure in gold-rimmed pince-nez spectacles, was reminded that recent developments showed the Soviet government to be exhibiting a tendency to undermine friendly relations.[6] German firms were attacked and Germany's leaders were constantly subjected to the worst vilifications. The Shakhty trial had proved that all of the recent actions of the Soviet government were part of a well-conceived plan to blame German firms for the actions of international capitalism against the Soviet Union. If this was a shift in the policy of the Soviet Union towards the German government, then this would indeed bode ill for future cooperation.

After the conference Brockdorff-Rantzau left for his estate in Schleswig. He returned to Berlin on 28 August suffering from cancer of the throat. He died on 8 September 1928. He had been quite right to call the bond between the Reichswehr and the Red Army one of the most important and steadying factors in Russo-German relations. Despite all the problems, changes of personnel do not seem to have made any difference to a policy that was evidently so advantageous to both partners. In the Soviet Union, Trotsky and Chicherin were replaced and for the Germans von Seeckt, Gessler, Brockdorff-Rantzau and Stresemann were all replaced over time but the fact is that the Reichswehr's operations in the Soviet Union were continued, regardless of who was in charge of German military or foreign policy.

By 1929 the number of aircraft at Lipetsk had grown to forty-three Fokker D.XIIIs, two Fokker D.VIIs, six Heinkel HD 17s, six Albatros L 76s, six Albatros L 78s, and one each of the Heinkel HD 21, Junkers A 20 and Junkers F 13. However, according to a report by senior Soviet pilot S.G. Korof, only a fraction of the aircraft were ever employed in training. The others were dismantled and kept in hangars. Accidents also restricted the number of aircraft available at any one time. More than 10 per cent of aircraft were lost to accidents, especially landing accidents which, fortunately were low-speed incidents and rarely resulted in fatalities.

There were deaths, however. In 1930, two German aircraft, a single-seat fighter and two-man reconnaissance aircraft, collided at an altitude of 3,000m. The observer-gunner, Amlinger, in the reconnaissance aircraft was unable to get out and was killed. Later the same year, two Fokker D.XIII fighters flown by German pilots collided at a height of 700m. One pilot, Paul, baled out too late and was killed. To avoid bad publicity the dead bodies were shipped to Germany in wooden boxes marked 'Machinery Parts'. And, if word got out, the dead were to be described as having died in an incident involving a sports aircraft.

The training programme now included blind flying, firing practice at towed targets and simulated dogfights. Bombing (including dive-bombing) was practised at a range to the north-west of Lipetsk, and new types of bombsights were tested. The pilots practised air reconnaissance and aerial photography too. High-altitude flights were planned, but, due to a shortage of liquid oxygen, it was decided not to go beyond exercising at altitudes of 5,000–6,000m where it was possible to do without oxygen masks. For the first time the Germans used gun cameras, the films being processed at a special laboratory set up in Lipetsk.

One more area of collaboration was working with the Tomka organisation to investigate the potential of aircraft to deliver toxic agents. This was of particular interest to the Soviet Union where, in 1925 two public organisations, the Society of Friends of the Air Fleet and Dobrochim, merged into one organisation called Aviachim. For the chemical warfare experiments the Lipetsk workshop fitted Albatros L 76s, capable of carrying relatively large payloads, with so-called aviation spray tanks (VAP). In 1926, Unshlikht reported directly to Stalin;

> The entire first part of the programme is complete where experiments were conducted spraying the liquid from different altitudes. A liquid similar to mustard gas was used in the experiments and confirmed the full capability for aviation to employ toxic agents. Our specialists believe that, based on these experiments, it can be presumed that employment of mustard gas by aviation against enemy personnel and to contaminate the terrain and populated areas is entirely feasible from a technical point of view and is of great value.

German personnel lived in clean and comfortable barracks built specially for them with officers and their families renting accommodation in the town. It is surprising to note that Soviet authorities essentially did not restrict the flight routes of the German aircraft that flew, often with Soviet markings, over the region and took pictures of Voronezh, Yelets and other inhabited localities and railway stations. A Junkers aircraft with a German crew of four flew to a German colony in the Volga region landing in Kuibyshev, Saratov and Kazan. Berzin, however, seemed unconcerned even though he accepted that espionage to some extent had to be expected and did 'some harm' but was 'less dangerous than covert spying'. His sanguinity was balanced, to some extent, by the arrest of nineteen Soviet citizens in the town in 1929 who were charged with espionage and whose fate remains undocumented.

Reichswehr Minister Wilhelm Groener said on 20 February 1930, 'Only relations with Russia give the army the opportunity to familiarise itself with the most modern weapons and to keep abreast of manufacturing processes'.[7] The Soviets too were enthusiastic. Unshlikht was clearly pleased with the result of the collaboration when he reported that the benefits included the fundamental reconstruction of the Soviet air base. The opportunity to work jointly with German operational units, a cadre of good specialists, mechanics and blue-collar workers was welcomed, as was gaining experience of the latest tactical procedures of the different aviation types, participation in the testing of armaments, photography, radio and other auxiliary services employing the latest innovations. By 1930, not only pilot training but the testing of new aircraft types became part of the daily routine. This resulted from Soviet pressure since they had no real interest in training German pilots and saw the real value of Lipetsk as a research establishment using the latest materiel and equipment. The station then became known as WIVUPAL (*Wissenschaftliche Versuchs und Preussanstalt fuer Luftfahrzeuge* – Scientific Experimental and Test Establishment for New Aircraft) under a new leader, Major M. Mohr, who replaced Schtaar. The Germans had agreed to this since it fitted into their own broad strategy and in 1931 completely new types of aircraft, including prototype four-engined bombers, were ordered from German factories. As compensation, the Soviets agreed to pay an extra share of the costs of running the station.

New aircraft types tested were the Arado SDH, SDIII, SSDI (floatplane), Ar 64 and Ar 65 fighters, two-seater Junkers K 47 fighter, two-seater Dornier Do 10, single-seat Heinkel HD 38, and Heinkel HD 45 and HD 46 and Focke-Wulf S 39 and A 40 reconnaissance aircraft. The promised four-engined bomber, however, was abandoned by the German Air Force as too expensive and failed to materialise. Work began instead on converting Junkers G 24 and Rorbach Ro VIII passenger aircraft into bombers by the addition of bomb racks, bombsights and machine guns. German personnel in Lipetsk were shown a few examples of Soviet equipment such as the Degtyarev DA aircraft machine gun, only recently adopted by the RKKA Air Forces. Officers Schoenebock and Reidenbach were allowed to visit an experimental TsAGI factory and the Ikar Engine Production Plant in Moscow. They were also shown a Tupolev ANT-14 heavy aircraft and R-5 reconnaissance aircraft.

While von Mittelberger and von Blomberg confessed themselves well satisfied with the 'splendid' facilities, Voroshilov was less enthusiastic and told them when they visited that although Lipetsk had yielded good results for the Reichswehr, the Soviets had got very little out of it. The Reichswehr, having handed over their side of the operation to private German or joint-stock companies, said it was sorry but there was little they could do about it since, although they continued to benefit from the results of work at Lipetsk, they no longer had much say in the matter of policy. Voroshilov saw this as the Germans merely hiding behind words while they 'dig their paws even deeper into our aviation'. Expecting the Soviets, who were more used to political than commercial wrangling, to negotiate successfully with the private capitalist reactionary German firms was very optimistic to say the least. It was now not only a matter of military conservatism to restrict Soviet access but also a commercial issue since private manufacturers were less inclined to show off their latest innovations to potential competitors.

Berzin reported to Voroshilov that the Germans seemed 'less eager' to bring in the newest technical devices for testing and did not always share with the Soviets the full results of research and experimental testing work. When in March 1932, during talks with von Mittelberger in Moscow, aviation commander Yakov Ivanovich Alksnis asked to see the latest high-altitude aircraft and new diesel engines developed by Junkers demonstrated in Moscow along with new Focke-Wulf helicopters, the Germans made it abundantly clear that they had no intention of bringing any of them to Lipetsk, not least because there were now greater opportunities to advance their latest designs in Germany itself. Some 2,000 future Luftwaffe pilots had already received training at illegal military flying schools within Germany at Braunschweig and Rechlin air bases. The Soviets reacted by insisting that under the terms of the agreement they were entitled to visit factories in Germany and this they did by going to the Junkers works at Dessau but agreement to develop the new experimental high-altitude Junkers aircraft with its supercharged 720hp Jumo engine came to nothing as Junkers hit an economic barrier and faced bankruptcy. A visit to the Siemens factory to see the new air-cooled Siemens engine resulted in orders but Siemens demurred, saying that they could not guarantee a delivery date due to the complexities of the revolutionary design.

Among the German firms most heavily involved in the Soviet collaboration had been Krupp who supplied such items as tank tracks, gun barrels etc. which had been manufactured by a consortium *Konstruktionsbüro* in neutral countries such as Sweden. The *Auswärtiges Amt* was becoming increasingly uneasy about arming the Soviets with modern weapons but the Reichswehr assured them that the Soviet Union had no offensive military capability. They were also quick to point out that intelligence had confirmed that exploratory talks had begun between the Soviets and the Glen Martin aircraft manufacturing company in the US.

In the short time between 1930 and 1933, Kazan had expanded massively with large numbers of new students arriving accompanied by new machines and prototypes. In 1928, von Blomberg had already been impressed by the Soviet BA-27 armoured car and the T-24 tank but there were no large-scale facilities to manufacture them before 1932. As a result of von Blomberg's visit, Malbrandt was recalled to Germany in 1930 and replaced by Ludwig Ritter von Radlmaier. He, in turn, was replaced by Josef Harpe in 1931. Both von Radlmaier and Harpe would become Panzer commanders during the Second World War.

The training staff during this period expanded considerably. By late 1930, there were nine academic instructors at Kazan. The *Lehrgangsleiter* taught classes on tactics, supervised war games and oversaw the curriculum and there was a team of radio technicians, who worked on engineering radios that could function in the difficult conditions of a moving tank.

Captain Ernst Volckheim, viewed by some historians as the real genius behind German Panzer development, joined the staff at this time. A total of eight different German and British tank models were tested at Kazan between 1931 and 1933. Rheinmetall-Borsig, MAN, Krupp and Daimler-Benz had all supplied eight prototypes that served as the models for almost all future German tank development, as well as having a huge impact on Soviet tank designs.

The first step in tank development at Kazan had come in 1927 when Reichswehr engineers began experimenting with turning Hanomag Corporation commercial tractors into self-propelled armoured guns. The first modification was the addition of a 37mm anti-tank gun mounted on a pedestal and then a machine gun was mounted on the rear. The next prototype used a 50hp tractor with a 75mm gun which was to become standard fitting on many German vehicles including the Sturmgeschütz and Panzer IV.

The first German experimental tanks due to arrive at Kazan in spring 1929 were delayed due to what the Germans called 'transportation difficulties' in the port of Leningrad but which had more to do with the German insistence that the tanks should be documented as private purchases from Rheinmetall which Stalin refused to go along with. Eventually, six 18-ton, six-man crewed Grosstraktor I tanks and other equipment reached Kazan but these were still inferior to the French 26-ton Char B-1 heavy tank. Because of the requirement for secrecy in Germany these vehicles had been shipped straight from the factory and had not been tested. When they arrived at Kazan, the Daimler-built machines were found to be defective and remained in the workshops for a whole year. The first ten German tank officers came with the first shipment and reported that, with the few tanks that could be operated, satisfactory results were achieved. It is hard not to conclude that whilst giving the impression that they were cooperating fully, the Germans were now employing delaying and spoiling tactics to minimise the benefits that the Soviets were getting out of the relationship.

When Voroshilov met Kurt von Hammerstein-Equord, who succeeded Heye as Chief of the German General Staff, the talks centred around ambitious Soviet plans for Kazan which meant much more in the way of German technical know-how. The Soviets wanted joint design teams and resulting blueprints to be available to both sides and, crucially, wanted German tanks to be built in Soviet factories under German supervision and shipped back to Germany. It doesn't take much imagination to see how easily that could become Soviet tanks (built to German specifications) being built in Soviet factories. Von Hammerstein-Equord said that German technicians in Kazan were not qualified to design tanks, only repair them, and secondly, no agreement could be made about the production issue until extensive testing showed which designs were the best ones to use. The talks probably signalled the first appearance of negative exchanges over Kazan. Stalin assumed that the Germans were being evasive and obstructive. For their part, the Germans had no interest in building a tank-manufacturing capability in the Soviet Union. Their only objective was to test and analyse prototypes as a basis for indigenous manufacture once Versailles had been consigned to history.

Soviet tank design was severely hindered by a lack of their own manufacturing capabilities which was only overcome in 1932 as the first of their prototypes were rolled out for evaluation. The results were not good. Transmission units were unreliable, tracks were poorly designed and prone to breakage, and all this was compounded by poor training of crews and inadequate maintenance which left many vehicles unusable. General Ludwig reported that 'the thirty tanks that the Soviets possessed simply did not work' but the German models were not much better.[8] Theory, however, advanced with exercises in tank support for infantry, high-speed tank engagements and anti-tank defences as Soviet-German cooperation in the military sphere reached its peak while the political landscape continued to be strewn with difficulties.

The first prototype 21-ton Grosstraktor II had been introduced in 1928 to compete with the British Medium Tank Mk III. It too had a 75mm gun, but mounted three machine guns rather than one. Two Grosstraktor III prototypes arrived in 1933 along with three new Daimler-Benz, C.D. Magirus and Büssing Corporation experimental armoured cars. Another tank under scrutiny at Kazan was the German-Swedish designed Rader-Raupen Kampfwagen M-28 whose treads could be removed for fast road travel but the Germans did not like it and it was abandoned like most of the designs tested at Kazan. All did, however, serve as models for a new generation of mechanised vehicles which would become the basis of Germany's Panzer formations in the Second World War. The VK-31 would see mass production, eventually morphing into the Panzer I that would see action in the

Spanish Civil War. The influence on Soviet design was significant with the T-28 using a Krupp running suspension and a welded chassis of German design, optical monitoring devices, gun sights, and the idea of combining electronic components with the machine gun. The testing and development that went on at Kazan validated Tukhachevsky's concept of 'Deep Battle' with his first armoured corps being created according to German doctrine.

One of the most observed comments from available sources concerned the Soviet tendency to denigrate its own army and praise the Reichswehr organisation which, to them, exuded professionalism and efficiency but because only fragments of the German military were ever in contact with the Soviets at any one time, its internal structure and administration remained a mystery. In particular the independence of decision-making and decisiveness of the Germans during field exercises in the Soviet Union impressed their contemporaries but higher up the chain of command, such characteristics were not encouraged and were 'no example for the Soviet Union to follow'.[9] Such attitudes may have been politically motivated but Soviets working with Germans during the exercises were more than willing to emulate them and build on that to developing a doctrine that suited their circumstances, but it was still mostly theoretical. It was not only the lack of machines to work with; it was the whole tank construction programme that was faltering and opening ever further the divide between ambition and achievement. It was all very well for the Five-Year Plan to call for thousands of tanks to be built and decrying as defeatist any questioning of its capacity to produce them but Voroshilov still did not know what sort of tanks the army needed, let alone how many of each type to make. The heavier the tank, the more expensive it was to make and therefore the fewer would be made.

Strong support grew in the Soviet Union for buying foreign tanks until domestic production could be expanded. The obvious source was Germany but production there was limited while it was still required to operate secret factories. However General of Armour Innokenty Khalepsky went to Berlin to meet representatives of Krupp and Daimler to discuss technical help setting up the Soviet production lines and an agreement to train Soviet engineers in German factories. A Soviet delegation visited the Vickers-Armstrong Company in Britain where they were impressed by the 6-ton Mark E and obtained a licence to make it even though the British Army had rejected it due to its unreliable suspension. The problem was that it was not possible to specify what sort of tanks were needed until actual field trials had been carried out and that could not be done on any scale with the few machines available. The Soviets had little choice but to place orders for a few Carden-Loyd and Vickers tanks from Britain as well as some T1E1s from James Cunningham and Son in Rochester, New York. The American tanks were a disappointment and never actually went into mass production even in the US.

By the end of the decade, the Soviets had at least defined their ambitions, begun to create a tank warfare doctrine and incorporated armament manufacture as a huge part of their Five-Year Plan of industrialisation even if they were still a long way from realising its fruition. The Reichswehr, for their part, had developed their own strategies and were committed to making the most of facilities at Kazan for training and experimentation but actual manufacture of tanks was now in the hands of private German companies working with the Soviet government.

In 1930 both Germany and the Soviet Union were undergoing major upheavals. The Soviets were in the throes of transforming their economy, collectivising farms and progressively destroying the kulak class as they drew labour in from the countryside to man their burgeoning manufacturing industries. Germany, on the other hand, was staggering under the weight of worldwide economic depression and political upheavals as the Nazis started to make their presence felt using violence and propaganda to punch far above the weight of their limited public support.

Tukhachevsky became more and more ambitious for his 'Deep Battle' concept, calling for ever greater numbers of tanks and aircraft to be produced. Stalin and Voroshilov thought this 'fantastic' and 'science-fiction' but it did not deter Tukhachevsky from dreaming his dreams despite Soviet industry's conspicuous failure to come anywhere near to fulfilling its tank production quotas for any year up to 1931.[10] Industry was plagued by shortages of skilled labour and raw materials. Khalepsky had talked to Rheinmetall, Krupp, Mafei, Daimler-Benz and Linke Hoffmann about help to jump-start tank manufacture in the Soviet Union with new specifications the Soviets had now decided upon. He also travelled to Britain, France and the US where he placed orders for twenty Carden-Loyd tankettes, fifteen 6 ton and fifteen 12-ton Vickers-Armstrong tanks and two Christie tankettes to study their design and construction and test their capabilities. Voroshilov, parroting Stalin's line, was not overly supportive of Khalepsky's shopping trip, fearing that reliance on foreign experts would deny the Soviets the chance to develop their own special tank doctrine and self-reliant military-industrial infrastructure but he had to concede the urgent requirement for foreign technological expertise.

Vickers had accepted the orders but had difficulty in adapting their tanks to Soviet specifications which demanded solid, heavy construction along with speed. Neither could the heavy-gun specification be accommodated within existing body types. Khalepsky suspected political interference from the British government to scupper the deal but German deals had been equally dogged by disputes. Vollmer took two years to come up with a design which, with all its compromises and limitations, proved to be no better than machines already under construction in the Soviet Union. Only the Carden-Loyd and Christie tankettes made it to the Soviet Union and it was these which informed Soviet tank production in the early 1930s.[11] This was only part of the problem, however. Military spending was not the only demand on the Soviet economy and fierce debates continued over allocation of funds. While politicians looked for ways to cut back on the excessive funding for motorisation and mechanisation of the army, Tukhachevsky and his acolytes, with unrealistic demands, wanted more and more without making any allowances for budgetary constraints.

Although tank production was way below target, by 1932 it had been possible to form an experimental mechanised brigade with some sixty tanks. When these were tested in exercises it was soon clear that crews were poorly trained, machines broke down continually and lack of support units for them often left them being stranded without fuel. Commanders showed almost total lack of any understanding of how to employ either tanks or motorised infantry, often holding back tanks to move at the pace of infantry, a tactic that had last seen the light of day in 1918. To address this issue, more tank officers were sent to Kazan to study under the Reichswehr.

German officers at Kazan, including Stülpnagel and Guderian, reported that the installation was 'the only place where really positive work on the area of tanks can be achieved . . . the effect of its weapons, the possibilities for its employment, the tactics to follow . . . can only be acquired there'.[12] It was their opinion that Kazan was of the utmost importance and the Reichswehr should exploit it to its full potential even to the extent of expanding the facilities. Technical deficiencies in the machines were glossed over to encourage greater investment both in Germany and the Soviet Union but while both sides wanted to proceed with urgency there was no consensus about how to do so. The argument was quality against quantity where the Reichswehr, given the limitations of the personnel pool from which they could draw, wanted to concentrate on long training programmes with detailed instruction for each trainee but the Soviets preferred to train larger numbers to a lesser degree of proficiency. The German selection process had the advantage of a small professional core of men from which to choose, which ironically was a consequence of Versailles, whereas the Soviets needed to start with a larger number of less well-prepared trainees in order to apply the selection process as training progressed in order to end up with the same number of qualified tank crews and commanders.

Urgency for Germany was now a crucial factor. Its breaching of Versailles was becoming daily more apparent to the international community and risked a pre-emptive strike by the French and Czechs, both of whom had mechanised brigades far in advance of the meagre resources the Germans had in that area. It would be a fine line to walk between boosting the very capabilities that would be required to meet that threat while pretending that it was complying with the restrictions imposed upon it.

The Germans were far from happy with the Soviet attitude to cooperation and were frank with their Soviet counterparts in discussions, but they knew how important Kazan was to their programme of rearmament and, for the moment at least, it was the only viable option available to them. While the large number of poorly prepared trainees was a problem for the Soviets, their facilities for mass production of tanks were growing at a tremendous pace. The Germans, by comparison, might have had the better personnel but for the moment they lacked the means of creating the armoured brigades they needed. Both, however, could only develop doctrine from a theoretical angle given the very low numbers of tanks available at Kazan for field exercises to put theory into practice.

By 1932, collaboration at Lipetsk, Kazan and Tomka seemed to be going well. Exchange of personnel increased a little and generally cooperation was good both in the factory and in the field. These facilities, however, were becoming more and more pools and eddies of tranquillity in a political stream that was becoming increasingly turbulent. Soviet manufacturing facilities were now turning out significant numbers of tanks which entered service alongside machines bought from Britain and France, making its reliance on German cooperation less important by the day. This was against a background of growing Nazi influence in German domestic politics and an understanding by the Red Army, derived from their visits to German factories, of the increasing contempt shown by the Reichswehr for Versailles as they started investing heavily in home industries that were either producing armaments or could be converted to military production at the drop of a hat. Both sides knew that the days of cooperation were coming to an end but neither wanted to see that happen overnight.

Now that the Reichswehr could see the day coming when German industry might, in all its unconstrained efficiency and expertise, manufacture all the tanks they called for, in 1932 it was still not clear to them what they wanted. They were realistic enough to know that they would have to compromise on numbers and size but striking the balance between the light and heavy machines fuelled intense debate. The light tank, the 5-ton Krupp-designed *Landwirtschaftlicher Schlepper* (La S, agricultural hauler) was based on the Carden-Loyd chassis but was beset by what Krupp called unspecified 'technical problems' and was very slow to emerge despite Lutz threatening to buy complete machines direct from England.[13] Guderian was firmly of the opinion that the heavy tank was the answer to the Reichswehr's needs but development of that was still some way off and it was the 5.4-ton Panzer I that became the stopgap main battle tank. Also based on the Carden-Loyd tankette, it had a 3.5-litre 60hp petrol engine, 13mm of armour and was armed with two 7.92mm machine guns. Whilst not a particularly good battle tank, the Panzer I was an excellent training vehicle.

Both German and Soviet designers were adapting Carden-Loyd designs which they tested in exercises at the German Grafenwöhr and Jüterbog testing facilities where it became clear that poor command and control of fast-moving mechanised units soon led to chaos. Fortunately, radio communications, which had advanced significantly in recent years, came to the rescue. Germany recognised its military importance rather earlier than anyone else and repeated the exercises in a *Funkübung* (radio exercise) in 1932. These showed how important it was for each radioman in his tank to have a clear understanding of his mission and a broad grasp of the way the battle was progressing so that his messages were meaningful to his command base and messages received from there and from other units could be interpreted in accordance with his overall assessment of what was happening before his eyes. From the moment that these exercises were analysed it was clear that radio was absolutely indispensable for the new mobile units.

By the end of the year Lutz was confident enough to assert that armour was now a 'main branch' of the army on a par with artillery and infantry and that a whole new doctrine was required to address the anomalies thrown up by this new addition to the concept of combined arms. The question of how armour that, by its very nature, could be used both independently and in concert with much less mobile units was to exercise the minds of military theorists for many years. The character of the argument was brought into focus by Tukhachevsky who, after attending the combined autumn manoeuvres, claimed that 'conservative' German generals were mostly 'against mechanisation' and lagged far behind their British and French counterparts.[14] There was no attempt here to sugar the pill of criticism and may well have been an indication of the fracturing relationships between German and Soviet military leaders that were beginning to reflect those of their political masters.

In the Soviet Union it was now becoming a distinctly uncomfortable position to be seen as too close to the Germans. Kazan, however, continued to be important for both sides. The Soviets expressed satisfaction in the sixty-five of their officers that had graduated from the tank school to achieve command rank and were not ungrateful for the tactical and technical skills acquired in the workshops and there was still more to be had in terms of supply and maintenance of active units. Many of their tanks were fitted with Krupp-designed suspensions and German-designed periscope viewing devices. At the end of 1932, despite rumblings of discord from above, Soviet personnel active at Kazan were still clearly enthusiastic. It was the case, however, that tank manufacture in the Soviet Union was growing at a rapid rate and Soviet doctrine was now seen as becoming less compatible with German ideas of tank deployment. It was becoming a matter of pride that the Soviets could start looking to their own resources much more and showing less reliance on the Reichswehr.

The Lipetsk venture began to collapse in 1933. Pilot training continued but relations between the Soviet Union and Germany got progressively worse as plans to close the training school down became known. During March the heads of the RKKA decided to severely constrain the movement of German pilots throughout Soviet territory and cut the school's Soviet staff to the minimum. According to one cadet, Harro Harder, 'the situation was very tense'. In August 1933, Lipetsk was handed back to the RKKA Air Forces and forty-eight aircraft with most valuable equipment on board flew to Moscow and then on to Germany, via the Deruluft Company route. They left behind fifteen obsolete Fokker D.XIII aircraft and a few vehicles.

It is undoubtedly true to say that the Lipetsk venture was of much greater benefit to Germany than ever it was to the Soviet Union. Brockdorff-Rantzau's early assertions that 'the Soviets needed the German more than the Germans needed them' became an 'idée fixe' and dominated Germany attitudes throughout the period of collaboration. The Soviets were slow to appreciate that they had been outmanoeuvred and, when the Germans began to withdraw, became anxious to prolong the venture in order to improve their technological and matériel yield.

As well as testing new aircraft and weaponry at a time when development of military aviation was prohibited, Germany had been able to train some 200 military pilots, many of whom later held command positions in the Luftwaffe. The Soviets had fared less well and were only privy to some innovations of the German aircraft industry and the number of Soviet specialists trained in Lipetsk with German assistance was very small. Much of what the Soviets learned from the whole collaborative venture was derived from visits by high-ranking RKKA officers to facilities inside Germany. Over the years Soviet Air Forces leaders such as Alksnis, Sergei A. Mezheninov, and B. M. Feldman, Revolutionary Military Council Deputy Chairman Unshlikht, RKKA Chief of Staff Tukhachevsky and others visited Germany where they were shown many aircraft companies and factories including Junkers, Heinkel, Siemens, Hirt and BMW, flying schools and scientific institutions. Innovations such as wings with leading-edge and trailing-edge flaps to increase the range of speeds, as developed by Arado and Heinkel. New ideas of diesel engines design and superchargers were absorbed as well as innovation in development of radio navigational equipment.

The downside for many Soviet air force leaders in the years to follow was that their contact with German businessmen and military leaders made them prime targets for Stalin's paranoia during the purges. Tukhachevsky, Unshlikht, Alksnis, Mezheninov, Rosengoltz and Feldman would all be executed for their 'friendship' with the Reichswehr. During the years after the death of Lenin, Soviet politics had been rife with factionalism that left its mark on the military. Frunze had been able to protect the Red Army to some extent, bringing a level of stability, but more and more the military had been drawn into supporting one individual or another that had played into Stalin's hands in his drive for total power. Voroshilov had been far from universally liked or trusted and Tukhachevsky had been banished to Leningrad. Shaposhnikov, made Chief of Staff in 1928, brought conservatism back into fashion with ex-Imperial officers still an invaluable core of the command structure but would soon suffer disgrace for aligning too closely with Trotsky. The inexorable concentration of power into a smaller and smaller base dominated by Stalin, however, was the overriding trend. In terms of military policy, it was clear also that doctrine was being formulated not only by Marxist dogma but by the very existence of new weapons such as tanks, which heralded mobile aggressive war potential, and modern theory evolved through collaboration with the Reichswehr. These new concepts of warfare with emphasis on mechanisation, specialised equipment and training were to have huge internal political consequences.

Military power, the lack of which had restricted Soviet foreign policy options and dictated diplomacy since 1920, was now starting to change Soviet perceptions of its place in European affairs. The armed forces were becoming embroiled in a permanent technological revolution as a result of the preceding ten years of German collaboration. Voroshilov, who had been a keen advocate of that venture, praised the 'sound work which had been accomplished [in becoming] a modern military instrument'.[15] As a result, German officers serving in the Soviet Union commented on the optimism within the Red Army but cautioned that they found it a little unwarranted. Even though Tukhachevsky had been virtually banished from Moscow, his influence and enthusiasm for continued cooperation with Germany was still considerable and he made it his business to keep abreast of all developments. Younger officers, especially, showed eagerness to absorb his theories of mobility and technical excellence. He first experimented with paratroops in 1929 as part of a strategy employing combined mechanised ground forces with aviation which had the backing of commanders Alksnis (aviation), Sedyakin (artillery) and Khalepsky (armour), all of whom had benefitted from extensive contact with the Reichswehr.

By 1930, the Soviets had, to some extent, become the victims of their own success in their dealings with the Reichswehr. Rapallo had opened the door for Germany to start breaking the chains of Versailles by building a military capability which was now allowing them to flex its muscles to demand better terms with the West and this in turn made her less reliant on the Soviets.

Chapter 8

THE RISE OF NAZISM

The years 1930–3 were confused ones of constant change with countries and their relations in flux. Talks between Poland and the Soviet Union which had been going on since 1926 to prepare the ground for a non-aggression pact that recognised the terms of the 1921 Treaty of Riga were stalled. Similar talks between Poland and Germany were planned at the same time but never got off the ground. The Soviets had been minded to discuss terms with Poland primarily because they had been unnerved by French moves in the Far East to reach an understanding with Japan, who were looking to the West for capital to invest in Manchuria which they had occupied. The Soviets feared that any Sino-French agreement might include Poland, France's great ally in Eastern Europe, but the terms the Poles demanded included a requirement for the Soviets to conclude a similar pact with Romania and Romania refused to sign anything until the Soviet Union renounced its claims to Bessarabia. This proved to be an insurmountable stumbling block, which illustrated just how complex negotiations were in that part of the world. Meanwhile, the German government refused to renew the 1926 Treaty of Berlin with the Soviet Union for an extra five years, stipulating instead that only a two-year deal was acceptable after which it should be allowed to lapse. This left the door open for a closer understanding between Germany and Poland, but Piłsudski was not in favour of a short term fix and was adamant that any agreement between the two countries should stand for a ten-year period.

Stalin cannot have been pleased to agree to renewal of the Treaty of Berlin. Neither was he thrilled to have to repay $500 million to Germany which had been advanced in medium-term credits for goods delivered to the Soviet Union by German industrialists, under a guarantee by the German government. Timely repayment of these credits was essential, however, to maintain the services of German industry for repairs and replacements in many industries contributing to armaments production. Even in subsequent years he supplied Germany with oil, minerals and other raw materials in order to guarantee supply of the machinery and instruments necessary to maintain his own armaments production in accordance with the third Five-Year Plan.

While Stalin and Hitler were openly scrapping with each other using propaganda in all parts of the world, each using the other as a bogeyman with which to win over or consolidate public opinion, their armies continued to maintain the friendly relations that had been established in 1924. Stalin had his own policy of making treaties with countries and observing them fairly correctly while simultaneously trying to stir up civil war in them. Nazis strategy followed a similar trajectory and between them the Bolsheviks and the Nazis succeeded in bringing just about every country near them into active or latent civil war. Hitler and Stalin, while careful not to appear to collaborate, even operated a common front from time to time in certain circumstances for purely tactical reasons. For instance, in 1931 Stalin, in a 'miserably inadequate and hopelessly distorted view of priorities',[1] had ordered the German KPD to cooperate closely with the Nazis to prevent the Reichstag from functioning normally, which contributed significantly to Hitler's rise to power. The following year, Stalin again exerted his control over German communists by calling irresponsible strikes, in conjunction with the Nazis, to destroy the authority of the German trade unions.

With Germany in the throes of revisionist dynamism, it was no longer possible for the Soviets to simply think in terms of defence. In order to have a say at the international table, especially in relation to its dispute over the Polish borders, its military also needed an offensive capability. Litvinov had to lie to the Germans when he went to Berlin in August 1931 and told them that there had been no approach to the Poles but diplomatic contact had certainly taken place to try and discomfit Germany as Stalin continued to nibble away at Rapallo but it was a fine line with continuing cooperation with the Reichswehr still a vital part of Soviet strategy.[2] It was certainly the case that the tank training centre at Kazan was still producing results that were appreciated by both sides, with exchanges of personnel as extensive as ever.

In October 1931, Litvinov proposed to the Poles that they finalise the non-aggression agreement that had been on the table since 1926. Meanwhile German experts in the fields of military transportation, aviation and chemical warfare continued to travel to the Soviet Union and significant contracts were signed with Junkers and Bayerische Flugzeuwerke for aeroengines and spares. These moves disturbed the balance of power since the mutual threat between the Soviet Union and Poland was being reduced to the detriment of Germany who had hitherto been confident that Poland would be pacified by the threat from both east and west if it started trouble.

When Fischer went to Moscow in April 1932, his intention had been to persuade the Soviets to maintain their forces on their western borders rather than see a large-scale transfer to the Far East where Japan was flexing its muscles in Manchuria. When Tukhachevsky, the hammer of the Poles in 1920 and now chief-designate of the Red Army High Command, had been invited to Berlin to shore up German-Soviet relations a number of important contracts were signed with German factories and licences granted for the manufacture of military equipment inside the Soviet Union. French Intelligence had long suspected exchanges of intelligence between Germany and the Soviet Union but could not, or chose not to, go public. This did not, however, prevent the signing of the Franco-Soviet Non-Aggression Pact on 29 November 1932 just as the Reichswehr had been unable to prevent the signing of a similar deal between the Soviets and Poles four months earlier.

Soviet attitudes were changing towards France whose relationship with Poland had long influenced both German and Soviet thinking. The Soviets had become anxious during the Lausanne Conference in the summer of 1932. It had been a meeting of representatives from Britain, Germany and France held to discuss the suspension of First World War reparations imposed on Germany at Versailles. During the conference rumours circulated suggesting that the German Chancellor Franz von Papen had offered the French Premier, Edouard Herriot, a military alliance against the Soviet Union. Whether or not there was any truth in this, it was taken seriously by the Soviets who feared that the German government was distancing itself from Rapallo and seeking a rapprochement with the Western Powers. In response, they quickly negotiated the Russo-French Non-Aggression Pact along with a similar agreement with Poland, talks about which had been stumbling along for a number of years.

There was further encouragement for Moscow as, politically, the mood in Germany had temporarily changed in favour of the KPD which increased its vote in elections at the end of 1932 when it seemed as if there was a groundswell of opinion opposing Hitler. Any hopes that the Nazis could be stopped, however, were quickly shredded when Hitler came to power only weeks later. Stalin was stunned into inaction as he waited to see what the reaction was in the West. As for Hitler, he moved cautiously, having grasped power and not being inclined to see it slip. He told Soviet Commissar of Trade Lev Khinchuck that he would endeavour to maintain German-Soviet relations 'on a permanently friendly basis'. It was still a guiding principle that Germany needed the Soviets as 'cover for [its] rear with respect to Poland'.[3]

Neither was Hitler blind to what he saw as the strengths of Soviet communism. In the early days before his grab for power, he had even spoken of having 'learned a great deal from Marxism' and had adapted their methods for his own purposes. He rationalised this by drawing a distinction between reactionaries who were 'only interested in the advancement of their own children' and 'communists and fascists who are interested in the whole nation'. As far back as 1925, Hitler's henchman Goebbels had said that he would 'rather perish with Bolshevism than live [under] the slavery of capitalism'. It is ironic that while street battles between the KPD and the Nazis were fought with great ferocity there seemed to be nothing in Nazi ideology in the 1920s and early 1930s that erected barriers to friendly relations with Soviet Russia. The Foreign Office diplomat Erich Kordt even said that he would have been a 'fantastic communist' if he hadn't encountered Hitler.[4]

Despite electoral defeats in 1921 and 1923 the KPD had remained pledged to lead the proletariat to victory in the class struggle in Germany and establish a soviet dictatorship but in practice it laboured under too many doctrinal constraints and concentrated on expanding membership and campaigning in parliamentary elections while its main challenge for recruitment of members, a mass political movement, the *Nationalsozialistische Deutsche Arbeiterpartei* (NSDAP), was winning the hearts and minds of the proletariat. On most issues and foreign policy, the KPD's approach was dictated by Moscow which allowed little leeway. Ernst Thalmann, the KPD's chairman, had dismissed the NSDAP as little more than a nuisance whose propaganda and rousing street parades could not be allowed to detract from the real battle against the SPD, the largest party in the Reichstag at that time. In the second half of 1929, however, the NSDAP's fortunes began to improve, as the party scored gains in Landtag elections in several German states.

During the latter part of 1929 both the KPD and NSDAP campaigned aggressively against the Young Plan, a new arrangement that was designed to lighten Germany's reparations burden under the Versailles Treaty. Although advantageous for Germany, the new deal was rejected by these two rival parties who used it instead to rouse voter anger against the injustices and humiliations of Versailles that had laid the country low and continued to oppress it. Already the Nazis were winning the propaganda war and showing themselves to be more imaginative and radical by introducing new slogans with mass appeal claiming that the Young Plan was 'sucking Germany dry'.[5] It was clear that the NSDAP's campaign had been much more successful than that of the KPD in the Landtag elections where it had trebled its number of seats in the Reichstag but the KPD remained fixated on targeting the SPD. Eventually the KPD was persuaded by Thalmann to do more to counter NSDAP propaganda and step up its campaign to recruit members that resulted in even more bitter confrontations at street and shop-floor level as both sides copied each other's propaganda slogans, and even wore each other's insignia.

Long before the Nazis got their hands anywhere near the levers of power, during the Weimar years the KPD and NSDAP had worked, if not harmoniously at least with common purpose, to subvert the democratically-elected government of Germany. Their common enemies within Germany were free-market capitalists and democratic socialists and they both used Germany's meek acceptance of the choke-hold of Versailles and the onerous reparations payments as examples of how the government was failing the people. For a time, it looked as if it was the KPD that was winning the votes of the German working class since the number of NSDAP members in the Reichstag had fallen from 32 in 1924 to 12 in 1928 but they were still able to retain a high profile and make their voices heard in the domestic political debate by standing alongside the 50–60 KPD members to vote against import tariffs, to vote for progressive taxation and increased state expenditure on social welfare and for the restoration of the eight-hour working day. Both stood to applaud when unemployed workers stormed the Reichstag to stage a protest in January 1929.

Throughout the 1920s, KPD policies had been directed by Moscow with the overall strategy of waiting for capitalist states to succumb to ever worse economic and social crises, many of which it helped to inflame, and exploit the situations to bring about world communism. The most powerful support for capitalism and anti-Bolshevism even to the point of war against the Soviet Union was seen to be Social Democracy. It therefore followed that the main attentions of Communist parties everywhere had to be directed at the 'French and Polish imperialist' puppets in the SPD.[6]

Up until about 1929, the KPD had been confident that it could manage any threat posed by the NSDAP as a mass movement, but elections started to indicate a rise in its popularity, in some cases talking support from the KPD. Their confidence seemed to have been justified when the NSDAP movement stalled in 1928 with no growth in membership but it was the NSDAP that proved more adept at exploiting the worsening economic conditions in the country after that time and when the speaking ban on Hitler was lifted it made a modest recovery. The KPD had also increased membership as a result of the economic downturn which blinded it somewhat to the growing popularity and increasing threat of the NSDAP.

When competition for recruitment at the street level intensified in 1930, both propaganda machines found themselves battling for the same ground which meant not only recruiting from the previously uncommitted but also drawing in supporters from the opposing camp. The KPD based its campaign on its perception of the typical NSDAP voter as a radical and an anti-capitalist, who had not yet found his way into the communist camp. This was not supported by the evidence, however, as Nazi–communist street violence increased and election results in Saxony showed votes migrating from the KPD to the NSDAP whose slogans and arguments were new and fresh compared to the same tired old communist line that everyone had heard so many times before. When the Reichstag was dissolved in July 1930, the real battle for hearts and minds of the working classes began with rallies for autumn elections. Both parties gained extra seats, but the Nazis were by far the greater beneficiaries. The communist factions responded badly to this setback by turning inward and blaming each other and offering conflicting strategies which prevented the KPD from putting up a united front. While some wanted to calm things down and launch a concerted campaign to persuade NSDAP members to defect, others urged their followers to take control of the factory floor by driving them out of workplaces and meetings with fist and club.

Moscow persisted with its line to the German communists that it was still the Social Democrats who were the main enemy and all attacks should be aimed at them rather than the Nazis. Stalin's man in Germany and the KPD number two, the Berlin-born Heinz Neumann, disagreed. Neumann was the son of a Berlin grain wholesaler and had joined the KPD in 1920. After his arrest in 1923, he had fled to Moscow where he acquired a reputation as something of a 'desperado', both resented and feared by his contemporaries and considered intellectually superior, arrogant and ambitious.[7] He was a popular rabble-rousing speaker whose cry of 'Smash the fascists [*Schlagt die Fascisten*] wherever you may find them!' found very receptive audiences and became a battle-cry for street fighters. His sights were firmly on the Nazis whose novel appeal and dynamic movement contrasted so effectively with the tired communist propaganda.

The Moscow directive blinkered the KPD which lacked the resources to launch an effective campaign against the much better organised and financed SPD. It was soon obvious that, in order to progress the Moscow-dictated agenda, they were going to have to seek an accommodation with other parties and it was becoming increasingly obvious that the main candidate was the NSDAP.[8] They had flirted with the fascist movement ever since 1923 and believed that they could once again combine their efforts in a 'community of interests' with the new, more strident Nazis while maintaining their independence and control of the relationship in an 'objective collaboration' as together they heaped scorn on the ruling Social Democrats and undermined their authority at every turn. One KPD memorandum called for 'united action of the Communist party and the Hitler movement to accelerate the disintegration of the crumbling democratic bloc which governs Germany'. The Hannover branch of the Nazi movement referred to 'casual understandings' with the communists.[9] In practice, this saw communists and Nazis working together to organise and lead strike actions. Violence was a common result of picketing and strike-breaking and it was here that the KPD should have seen the danger as it was the Nazis who provided the bulk of the manpower to intimidate and cause damage to facilities even to the point of using explosives.

Moscow looked at how German foreign policy might evolve if the increasing popularity of the Nazis was reflected in a growing representation in the Reichstag. The fierce opposition the NSDAP had shown against the Young Plan gave hope that the anti-Western wing of the party would dominate policy and thus prove less antagonistic towards the Soviet Union. Radek anticipated that this Nazi anti-Western stance would be strengthened if, as seemed likely, the French would encourage internal opposition to any increase in Nazi power by withdrawing its short-term loans and sending further shockwaves through the German economy. There was, however, an element of wishful thinking in this analysis. If increasing mass hysteria as a means of sparking revolution was the KPD's ultimate aim, it was unfortunate for them that Moscow still saw the rise of militant nationalism in Germany as an essential requirement of Soviet foreign policy whilst failing to recognise that the aroused populace was responding more to the Nazi message than the communist one.

The KPD seemed to have won a major propaganda coup when, in September 1930, three German army lieutenants, Hans Friedrich Wendt, Hanns Ludin and Richard Scheringer, a former *Freikorps* fighter, were put on trial in Leipzig for high treason having tried to form an illegal Nazi cell in their garrison at Ulm as a cornerstone of the 'people's army of [anti-Versailles] national liberation'. No less a person than Hitler appeared as a defence witness and he got huge publicity given the high-profile nature of the trial which was covered by all the German press. He won a major propaganda victory by 'underlining his party's commitment to legality' and won a standing ovation in the courtroom by saying that 'heads would roll after the NSDAP came to power'.[10] It was a surprise, therefore, when Scheringer then bizarrely denounced Hitler and the Nazis a few months later and declared his conversion to communism. The seemingly casual ease with which Scheringer had leapt from fascism to communism underlined what was a significant similarity between the KPD and the NSDAP, both of which were wedded to political violence and had an ethos of tough proletarian masculinity, militarism and the idea of war which found its expression in symbol, dress and prejudice. This threatened to be a body blow to the NSDAP. For maximum publicity, a KPD deputy, Hans Kippenberger, interrupted a debate in the Reichstag on the military budget to read out a letter sent by Scheringer in which he calls the KPD the 'most war-like of parties'. Scheringer's conversion, however, was less to do with communist idealism than his own sense of the 'adventure and romance' of being a warrior in the 'defence of the Fatherland' and the problem of choosing 'which army to fight for' against the Western Powers.[11] Neumann chose to interpret the Scheringer trial as exposing the internal arguments between the socialist and nationalist elements within the NSDAP and meant that it was time to act and expose those divisions but Moscow urged caution.

Outside parliament the rival parties combined to undermine public support for the government by backing strike actions, marches and protests, most notably during the five-day Berlin transport strike of November 1932 on the eve of the Reichstag elections. KPD chief Ernst Thälmann said in 1932 that 'it is absolutely essential and desirable that Nazis are invited to take part in the strike committees'.[12] It is clear from the evidence that Stalin eagerly supported the Nazis at the turn of the decade. Hitler's trajectory to power was becoming apparent. Whether or not Stalin thought that the KPD could rise and govern with the Nazis in some sort of bizarre coalition or whether his long-term plan was to foment a confrontation between Germany and the Western Allies that would ultimately weaken both and leave the Soviets to take control of Eastern Europe is a matter of conjecture but on a number of occasions his comments suggested that the latter was his preferred option. He is reported to have said to Neumann in 1931, 'Can you not see Neumann that if the National Socialists come to power in Germany, they will be so completely occupied with the West that we will be able to get on with building Socialism in peace.'[13] Radek was a huge fan of the Nazi paramilitary *Schutzstaffel* (SS) and *Sturmabteilung* (SA) who, he believed, would lead Germany through civil war to a communist future but as Hitler drew more and more support and raised his profile more and more KPD activists went over to the NSDAP where they were welcomed with open arms. The flow of recruits was so great that whole SA units were made up of ex-KPD men. The numbers joining up were both a consequence of and, in a positive feedback loop, the result of burgeoning support for the Nazis and certainly helped later to sweep Hitler to power in January 1933.

The mass of ex-*Freikorps* men in the NSDAP, inflamed by campaign propaganda and by the election triumph, had expected power to fall into their hands within weeks of election victories but when it did not they thought Hitler had betrayed their sacrifices and that he was as much a 'system-politician' as any of the others. It looked as Neumann had been right in his view that Nazi support had peaked and was on the wane. The Berlin SA, under Walther Stennes, revolted and public squabbles broke out within the NSDAP leadership. The KPD believed that the NSDAP was not a truly revolutionary party and would fragment as internal divisions widened so it increased its propaganda drive with pamphlets and more meetings, but the movement showed itself weak, tired and lacking the motivation to rise to the challenge. Such effort as there was proved to be disjointed and lukewarm and what had seemed to be a great opportunity for the KPD to build momentum was frittered away.

While Neumann demanded that 'blood must flow' as street battles intensified,[14] others in his movement were fearful of Nazi mob violence and urged him to scale back his rhetoric. Moscow also warned against targeting the Nazis with violence and terror as Stalin reiterated his message that the Social Democrats were still the main enemy. By lowering the temperature, Moscow hoped to allow infiltration of KPD members into the NSDAP to act as spies and informers at the same time as taking all possible steps to attract defectors to go the other way and also stem the flow of recruits, especially younger ones, into the Nazi ranks. KPD propaganda was stepped up in the armed services but it did not have the same appeal as the Nazi message. KPD membership rose to of a quarter of a million but competition for new members both in industry and within the ranks of the unemployed remained fierce.

Violence on the streets between the KPD and the NSDAP escalated but on the political front, the KPD were instructed to support the Nazis during a drive to force new elections in Prussia to topple the Social Democrat government there. There was a limit to what control Moscow could exert, however, and when two Berlin police captains were ambushed and murdered by communists the KPD headquarters were occupied and several top-ranking members were arrested. Despite his closeness to Stalin, Neumann suffered a major defeat when the Central Committee condemned 'individual terror' and once again pointed the KPD away from confrontation with the Nazis. Neumann's days were numbered and he would soon be ousted from all offices within the party as the gulf between the Moscow line and the mood on the street widened. It is likely that he, like Radek, was scapegoated, 'in a well-tried method that had claimed many victims before',[15] when it was clear that Moscow was becoming embarrassed by its underestimation of the Nazis and searched for a rationale to change its approach.

On 30 January 1933, the German President Paul von Hindenburg appointed Adolf Hitler Chancellor of Germany at a time when unemployment was at critical levels and communism and socialism constant threats to his leadership. Initially, Moscow welcomed this change in the German leadership saying 'Hitler's rise to power hastens the revolutionary crisis' and anticipated that extreme fascist terror on the streets of Berlin would merely serve to sharpen the class struggle and the growth of the KPD. Radek predicted that Hitler's election represented the first step toward the proletarian revolution in Germany

When the Weimar Republic fell in January 1933, a fundamental shift occurred in German-Soviet relations. Up until the moment of Hitler's accession to power it could be said that the Rapallo Treaty was still largely intact but that was soon to change. The period of military and economic cooperation would come to an abrupt end. Stalin may well have been discomfited by the rise of Nazism but it would hardly have surprised him and it was not opposition to fascism per se that informed his strategy over the next few years but the desire to join with a grand alliance of states to oppose the Nazi expansionist doctrine. It was Litvinov who asserted that Soviet relations with Germany would be determined by Germany's external and not its internal policy and Krestinsky hoped that Hitler's policy would be dictated by 'the necessity of not breaking with [the Soviet Union]'.[16] He was in no doubt, however, that Germany would seek its new territories at the expense of the Soviet Union and warned that the German government could not be relied upon to remain friendly. It was of particular and continuing concern that a Franco-German rapprochement be averted at all costs.

With the Nazis very much in the ascendant, it was now too late to recover lost ground and the German communists were starting to suffer the consequences of their miscalculations. Armed Nazi thugs

Signing the truce between the Central Powers and Soviet Russia on 15 December 1917 in Brest-Litovsk.

Kapp Putsch conspirators under arrest 1921.

Enver Pasha.

Karl Radek.

Carden-Loyd tankette of the type used at the secret Russian Kama facility where the German Panzer I was developed

Soldiers training at the Soviet-German Tomka chemical weapons facility.

Junkers aircraft manufacturing plant at Fili 1923.

German communist anti-Fascist demonstrators

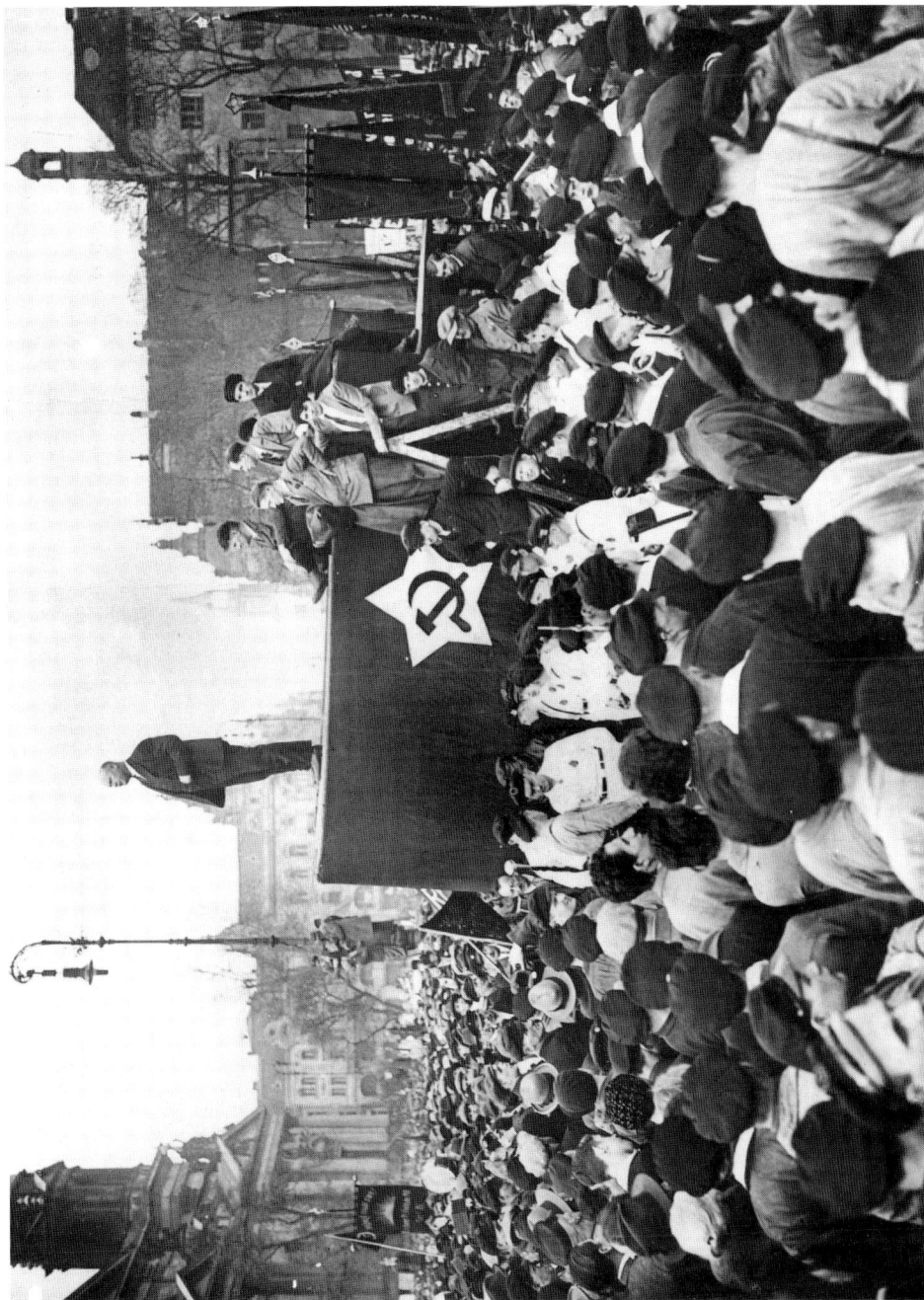

Ernst Thalman addressing a communist rally in the Berlin Lustgarten 1931.

Hans von Seeckt and Adolf Hitler.

Soviet Foreign Minister Molotov and German Foreign Minister von Ribbentrop after signing the Molotov-Ribbentrop Pact on 26 August 1939.

Moskau, den 23. August 1939.

Für die
Deutsche Reichsregierung:

[signature: Ribbentrop]

In Vollmacht
der Regierung der
UdSSR:

[signature: Molotov]

Molotov and Ribbentrop's signatures.

German and Soviet commanders meet in Poland, September 1939.

German troops burn a Russian village during Operation Barbarossa.

German troops hang Russian civilians during Operation Barbarossa.

Soviet prisoners of war captured by German forces during Operation Barbarossa.

stormed and closed the KPD headquarters, Karl Liebknecht House, on 23 February 1933 and banned its newspaper, *Die Rote Fahne*, a few days later and then the Reichstag fire on 27 February was used to justify concerted action against them. The Reichstag Fire Decree that Hitler pushed through on 28 February destroyed most civil liberties including free speech and freedom of assembly and was followed by the declaration of a state of emergency which enabled mass arrests of political enemies. Over 1,500 KPD members were arrested that night in Berlin alone. Unable to fit so many political prisoners into the existing prison system, the Nazis erected the first concentration camps during this wave of terror.

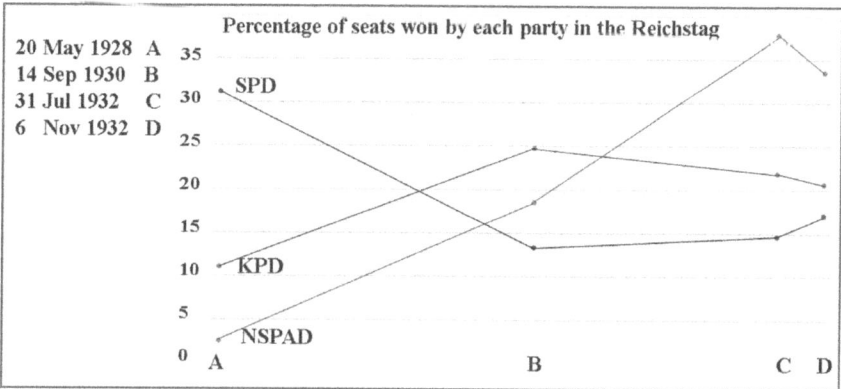

The last federal elections were held on 6 March in which, despite the Nazi repression, the KPD still received 12.3 per cent (4.8 million votes) and the SPD 18.3 per cent. The Nazis had enough seats to form a government in coalition with a right-wing party, however, and this allowed Hitler, who had banned the KPD from attending the Reichstag vote, to force through his 'Enabling Act' against SPD opposition giving his government the right to pass laws contrary to the constitution. Most communists deputies by this time had either gone underground or had been arrested.

Hitler was quite open about his ambitions to revise the terms of Versailles and was clearly willing to show contempt for international opprobrium by blatantly flouting many of them. This made secrecy much less important and in fact counter-productive since it became a tenet of Nazi policy to openly boast of its military prowess as a means of backing up its aggressive diplomatic initiatives. This was against a background of growing Nazi domination of the German political agenda with anti-communism now one of its guiding doctrinal concepts, which inevitably made the continuation of cooperation with the Soviet Union problematic to say the least. Of course, the German government had never been anything other than hostile to communism but now there was no longer any need to swallow pride and feign friendship with the Soviets to advance its military agenda. The severance of cooperation needed to be carefully managed though given the German resources still deep inside Soviet borders that needed to be repatriated.

Niedermayer was now military attaché in Moscow and still fervently in favour of retaining amicable relations with the Soviets and likewise General Putna, the Soviet ambassador to Berlin, kept up pressure to continue with cooperation which, by now, was almost entirely to the benefit of the Soviets. Putna continued to pursue this line even when re-assigned to the London embassy, until he fell foul of Stalin and perished in the purges of 1937 following a trial for high treason that also took, amongst many other high-ranking military personnel, the Chief of the Red Army, Tukhachevsky. While Hitler's public castigation of communism never wavered, and his political ambitions had clearly been stated in *Mein Kampf* to encompass expansion in the East, his first adventures were likely to stir up France in particular and he was anxious to avoid unnecessary tensions with the Soviets while these first acts of his drama played out. Poland was a major component of his strategy viz-a-viz the Soviet Union. He was at pains to instil in Poland a false confidence, telling Piłsudski and the Polish ambassador to Berlin, Józef Lipski, that he was ready to protect Poland against Soviet aggression in the hope of diverting Poland's gaze east to contemplate danger from that source and distract it from the machinations of its western neighbour. German ambitions, he said, were confined to annexing the Baltic States and establishing German dominance of the Baltic Sea.

The Soviet leadership was not blind to Hitler's wider ambitions. Indeed it is fair to say that Stalin was, at this stage, much more aware of the threat posed by Nazism than many Western leaders seemed to be, with the notable exception of Winston Churchill, who was outside government and whose influence at that time was restricted to rhetoric. The only advantage that the Soviets saw in the growth of the Nazi threat was the distant prospect that, as the menace grew and the Western Powers started to get nervous, they would look more favourably on cooperation with the Soviets and be more willing to allow them to take a place at the table in the European family of nations.

When Hitler came to power in early 1933, Russo-German relations became inherently unstable. This was greeted with dismay by the Soviet Union which had no desire to see a deterioration of its relations with Germany beyond what was obviously unavoidable given the Nazis' strongly anti-communist stance. Not only that, but the Nazis took repressive measures against Soviet trade missions and Soviet companies operating in Germany while Soviet citizens came under political surveillance and interference. Hitler tried to calm things by drawing a sharp distinction between the internal treatment of communism and international relations with the Soviet Union. There was every reason for him to resist any real change in the political, economic or military policy with the Soviets but with anti-communism as one of the populist campaigns that had propelled him to power there was a very fine line to follow.

The ex-German ambassador in Moscow, von Dirksen, summed up by saying that the Soviet Government did not wish 'to reorient its policy or to permit a cooling of its relations with Germany', but, at the same time, was minded to view any deterioration of Soviet-German relations as an invitation to 'develop its relations with France in a positive direction'.[17] Inevitably, however, relations with the Soviets did get worse. In late March the Soviet newspaper *Izveztia* launched a vitriolic attack on the German government in retaliation for the ban imposed on *Pravda* and *Izveztia* journalists who had been denied access to the grand opening of the Reichstag on the 21st. German-language broadcasts sharply critical of the Nazis also began from Moscow. Hitler had embarrassed the new Soviet ambassador by delaying an interview until 28 April and had ignored Soviet requests to renew the Treaty of Berlin for a further two years. There was a clear impression that an organised anti-Soviet campaign was being conducted at the highest levels of the German government which indicated to Moscow that opposition to the Nazis was crumbling inside Germany. Von Dirksen saw the inevitable conclusion as the eventual severance of mutual relations and required a reversal of German economic and military policies but for the moment, Hitler took note of diplomatic and military advice which assured him that Germany was not yet strong enough to make a complete break with the Soviet Union either militarily or economically.

At a conference of ministers in the Reich Chancellery on 7 April, the Foreign Minister, von Neurath, pointed out that Germany's major foreign policy objective was still revision of the Versailles Treaty and nothing should interfere with the achievement of that goal. Until that could be done, Germany would continue to be militarily at the mercy of a French-Polish alignment and needed to tread carefully and in this context, an alliance of sorts with the Soviet Union was vital to maintain the balance of power. 'At the present moment,' cautioned von Neurath, 'it is uncertain whether this can be counted on . . . we cannot do without Russia's cover for our rear with respect to Poland.'[18] Besides, the Soviet Union was still Germany's biggest market for industrial products and owed Germany 'about a billion Reichsmarks'. News that the Soviets apparently now wanted to break off cooperation at Tomka was filtering through to further cloud the issue although it was not clear if it was a political or economic decision.

Chapter 9

THE END OF COLLABORATION

The apparent meandering of Soviet foreign policy during the 1930s may be explained by the fear of a resurgence of imperialist aggression of the sort experienced right after the revolution in 1917. The establishment of diplomatic relations and the signing of the Rapallo Treaty had edged the country further away from that scenario, but it never really fell off the agenda.[1] Lenin had pursued the strategy of exploiting rivalry between the Great Powers in order to prevent a concerted effort against the Bolsheviks but he was careful to avoid sparking a major conflict between them. If it came to war between Germany and the Western Powers, neither an Anglo-French victory nor the spread of German power was in the strategic interest of the Soviet Union. The Soviet approach was the cautious traditional balance of power strategy, not one of reckless gambling. Stalin was also seen to be one of the most cautious of the Bolsheviks in assessing foreign policy and revolutionary initiatives, as his opposition to the adventurist course in Poland during 1920 and in Germany during both 1921 and 1923 demonstrates.

Neither Stalin nor the KPD had been overly apprehensive about the rise of Nazism in the 1920s, which was not seen as an impediment to an eventual communist victory in Germany. Even when Hitler seized power, it had remained Stalin's belief that the German capitalists, aristocrats and military would continue to hold onto the reins of power behind the scenes. This view lost validity over time as Hitler repeatedly made it abundantly clear that the focus of his expansionist ambitions lay in the East at the expense of Poland and the Soviet Union. While Stresemann's strategy had been for the slow and steady reacceptance of Germany as an equal in the community of Great Powers, Nazi Germany made repeated grabs for unlimited power and, most importantly, presented a fundamental threat to the very existence of the Soviet state. In the face of this, Soviet foreign policy had changed to unequivocally espouse the concept of collective security against the Nazis.

The public record shows that, aside from a few tentative advances toward Berlin, Litvinov and his colleagues at the *Narkomindel* devoted themselves tirelessly throughout the 1930s to the struggle to secure collective guarantees against Fascist aggression. The suggestion of the American political scientist and historian Professor Robert Tucker that Stalin had deliberately fostered the Nazi menace, which was a danger to the Soviet Union above all, must be questioned. It seems more likely that Stalin had, unwisely as it happens, used it as a makeweight ally against the SPD to be crushed at the appropriate time. The Nazi-Soviet Pact of 1939 represented not, as Tucker would have it, the fruition of Stalin's decade-long diplomatic policy, but was forced upon him by the failure of his collective security strategy.

To test the mood of cooperation, the Reichswehr told the Soviets that Alfred von Vollard-Bockelberg, the ex-head of the Reichswehr Weapons Office and now involved with synthetic fuel production, would be pleased to accept Tukhachevsky's invitation to visit the Soviet Union. The German Military Attaché in the Soviet Union, Otto Hartmann, prepared the ground for the visit by meeting Tukhachevsky to try and clear up a number of matters that von Vollard-Bockelberg would address if progress stalled. The first item on the agenda was Tomka but Tukhachevsky would not commit to an extension claiming, without foundation, that during his visit to Germany in the previous autumn, it had been made clear to him that financial constraints had caused the Germans to scale down their activities. Tukhachevsky did not feel that even if Tomka was closed it necessarily meant any fundamental change in military cooperation and if the Germans wanted to put Tomka back into full production, he would not object. In reality the Soviets had not got much out of the plant and didn't really care what happened to it as long as it didn't impact on Soviet finances. After some difficulty, agreement was reached with Yakov Fishman, the Red Army Chief of Chemical Warfare, on a compromise proposal for renewed operations at Tomka. The final details were worked out when von Vollard-Bockelberg visited the site and saw demonstrations of equipment but he was dogged by persistent Soviet complaints that they were being prevented from getting access to the latest developments, especially those emanating from experiments in Germany. Von Vollard-Bockelberg promised Fishman full access on his next visit to Germany.

Before that could happen, however, when a 'new chemical warfare agent' failed to arrive at the station, Fishman took it as an affront even though the Germans claimed that no such 'new material' existed. Soviet obstructions to continuation of the German presence were explained when one Soviet official let slip that 'perhaps' the German contribution was now rather less important since Soviet chemical warfare research at the purely Soviet-operated site of Bobriki was more advanced than at Tomka. Von Vollard-Bockelberg petitioned Tukhachevsky again to calm things down and promised the fullest cooperation. Hartmann was realistic enough to see that military cooperation was no longer able to bridge the gaping political divide. On 26 July, Hartmann told the Soviets that, in response to the cancellation of a visit by Red Army officers to Berlin, the proposed visit of German officers to Red Army exercises and manoeuvres was cancelled also.

While von Vollard-Bockelberg's visit was a success and his reception by the Red Army was noticeably friendly, it was clear that there had been a shift in policy when it was emphasised to him on more than one occasion that, although the Red Army leaders placed the greatest value on close cooperation with the Reichswehr and German industry, armies were only servants of their governments and a close cooperation was only possible if governments led the way. Rather than a criticism of their own government, von Vollard-Bockelberg understood this to be a commentary on the anti-Soviet rhetoric in Berlin. It seemed, however, that military collaboration was set to continue for at least another year but soon after von Vollard-Bockelberg's return to Berlin, suddenly and without warning, the Soviets demanded an immediate termination of the Reichswehr bases in the Soviet Union. Soviet officers who had been scheduled to attend courses in Germany were peremptorily reassigned elsewhere. An embarrassed Tukhachevsky had, apparently, been unaware of the terseness of the note which was sent to cancel the visits. He apologised for the manner in which the notice was given and repeatedly expressed the hope that the traditional friendship between the two armies would continue. It was clearly a political decision coming, probably, from Stalin himself.

The Reichswehr leaders sympathised with Tukhachevsky and responded with personal messages expressing disappointment at the abrupt actions of the Soviet government but made it clear that they did not consider them to reflect the feelings of the Red Army Command. Von Hammerstein was clear that, in carrying out orders to liquidate the stations, great care was to be taken to avoid attitudes or actions that would prejudice further friendly relations with the Red Army. Soviet officials, however, irked by virulent anti-Soviet speeches in Germany, had no such qualms about ruffling feathers. Reichswehr personnel sent to decommission the stations were refused visas and German personnel at Lipetsk were forbidden to leave the site. All aircraft there were grounded, which immediately sparked fears that the Soviets would impound the latest experimental models under evaluation. Rising tensions were eventually relaxed a little when the Soviet military, after heated arguments in Moscow, were able to regain some control by allowing the Germans to begin repatriation of all movable equipment. All transportable equipment was crated and sent by rail to Leningrad and then by ship to Germany. The experimental aircraft were flown out along with some of the personnel, the rest going by train. At the same time General Lutz arrived to supervise the closing down of Kazan.

Germany, for its part, responded with what was to become typical pugnacity by publicly repudiating the military clauses of Versailles on 16 March 1933. Britain and France recoiled in some disarray as the spectre of German resurgence began to seep into their consciousness. Both were anxious to avoid seeming intimidated, but neither were they going to make any rash moves. This left the Soviets without willing allies in any anti-Nazi coalition especially after Italy refused to contemplate sanctions and Britain went on to sign the Anglo-German Naval Agreement allowing for a significant increase in German naval tonnage. Any lingering hope that the French might want to come on board peremptorily vanished later when the French Foreign Minister Louis Barthou was assassinated in October 1934 and French foreign policy came under the control of Pierre Laval who was by no means pro-German but neither would he prove to be particularly anti when he later joined the Vichy government in occupied France in 1940.

By 12 September all Germans had left Lipetsk and a farewell dinner was held for Z. Mo staff on the 26th as the Moscow office was closed also. Several top Red Army leaders who had been invited, including Alksnis and Fishman, in a show of contempt, sent representatives but others who did turn up spoke of their fond memories of collaboration and expressed the hope that the foundations that had been laid for friendly relations at Rapallo would not be disturbed.[2] By the end of September all German military personnel had left and with that had ended any hope for renewed contact with both militaries now coming firmly under the control of governments that were moving further and further apart. Hartmann wrote that '[no] very strong gestures for rapprochement can be expected from the Russian side in the very near future'.[3]

It was noticeable that gaps left in the Soviet side of their administration section which had been devoted to Reichswehr relations were now being filled with Polish-speaking and French-speaking officers and Tukhachevsky had made a not very subtle gesture by giving part of his farewell speech on 26 September in French, a language in which he was fluent, and in which he, perhaps ironically, referred to *'nos sentiments les plus amicaux pour le Reichswehr'*.[4] The Russophile French Air Minister, Pierre Cot, visited the Soviet Union in September but the Red Army staff officer M.M. Smagin assured Hartmann that there was no ongoing military discussions with France. Notwithstanding Smagin's denial, which may well have been his true opinion since he had spoken in a personal capacity, France had a clear interest in weakening what was becoming an already fragile relationship between Germany and the USSR, not least because it eased some pressure on Poland and might even prise Turkey away from the German camp.

On 21 September 1933, a secret dispatch arrived at the Reichswehr Ministry in Berlin from Colonel Hartmann in Moscow. It read; 'The stations were discontinued on September 15. Therewith the period of many years of German-Russian military cooperation has been terminated in its previous form.'[5] The stations referred to, of course, were the three main Reichswehr military bases in the Soviet Union. After nearly a decade of collaboration the Reichswehr and the Red Army looked upon the results of cooperation with mixed feelings but from a military perspective, the partnership, despite some statements to the contrary, seems to have been mutually beneficial; indeed, had it not been, there were certainly many occasions when it could have been terminated.

In a speech to the Central Committee of the Soviet Communist Party on 29 December 1933, Litvinov said that the world was 'standing at the junction of two eras [one of] bourgeois pacifism [and] a new era of wars of imperialist redivision'. 'Peace', he continued, 'requires the collaboration and cooperation of other states.' In what effectively sounded the death knell of Rapallo, that period of extensive economic, political and military cooperation, he blamed the new German government for 'preaching the most extreme anti-Soviet ideas' and whose leader openly aspired to 'enslave the Soviet peoples' but was careful not to close the door completely on future cooperation.[6]

France was the first to reach out to the Soviets and seek rapprochement, having seen its long-time ally in the East, Poland, being wooed by Germany, a move which bore fruit in January 1934 when Lipski and von Neurath signed a German-Polish declaration of non-aggression. Barthou tentatively suggested that an 'Eastern

Locarno' pact be negotiated to bring the Soviet Union, the Baltic States and Finland into the general agreement drawn up with Germany, Poland and Czechoslovakia but Germany and Poland threw the idea out. Slightly panicked somewhat, the Soviets reacted by agreeing immediately to inclusion in the League of Nations, an organisation they had previously derided and shunned, where they were given a permanent seat on the Council. Straightaway, they began energetic, and for them revolutionary, efforts to build a coalition opposing Nazism and secretly plotted the 'encirclement' of Germany.[7]

The German government was now much more reliant on domestic manufacture for its armaments but, unlike the Soviet Union, the state did not own industry in Germany but that did not mean that it did not hold sway over it. In order to give the maximum attention to its rearmament plans the government needed to have a legal framework for its cooperation with industry. They signed long-term contracts with industry groups to buy their output at fixed prices but while these were nominally contracts expressing agreement by both parties, the two parties were decidedly unequal. The Nazis viewed private property as conditional on its use and not as a fundamental right. If the property was not being used to further Nazi goals, it could be nationalised. Professor Junkers of the Junkers aircraft plant refused to do the government's bidding in 1934. The Nazis thereupon took over the plant, compensating Junkers for his loss.[8] This was the context in which other contracts were negotiated.

Hope that the 'spirit of Rapallo' might linger a little longer were dashed when a number of Reichswehr officers who had been amongst those most friendly to the Soviet Union were cut down in Hitler's 'Night of the Long Knives' on 30 June 1934 when around eighty of his political opponents within Germany were murdered. It was a turning point for German-Soviet relations in as much as it was a clear indication to Stalin that Hitler was every bit as ruthless as he was and would, in future, need to be handled with a little more circumspection.

The Soviet Airforce (VVS), having benefitted greatly from the Lipetsk venture, was now beginning to re-equip with Soviet-designed and built aircraft but crucially was now reliant much more on French support, especially in the development of the Soviet aluminium industry. In a move towards closer cooperation, aviation specialists Alksnis and Tupolev had visited French factories to see what new ideas the French were working on. At the same time they discussed doctrine with French air force officers and returned home to work with aviation theorist A.N. Lapchinsky to develop Soviet doctrine.

This turned out to favour aviation over armour, although combined operations were still of paramount importance. The crucial difference in Soviet aviation which separated it from other mainstream doctrines was the strategic concept of 'independent air operations' carried out by long-range bombers that would put the industrial centres of both Germany and Japan within range.[9] It was clear that the role of aviation was becoming every bit as important to battlefield doctrine as mobile armour.

The growing strength of the Luftwaffe, in particular, was ringing alarm bells in Moscow. Both Radek and Tukhachevsky had parroted the Stalinist line of German threats to the Soviet Union's western borders but it was mere rhetoric since it was clear that the Reichswehr was in no position yet to move in the East. It was the Soviet view that Hitler would have to move first in the West to subdue the French before contemplating any move against either Poland or the Soviet Union. The French were not averse to talking to the Soviets but had, as their primary motivation, a desire to merely prise them away from German influence. There was a clear division within the Red Army between those like Voroshilov who, somewhat nostalgically, wanted to recharge the spirit of cooperation with Germany and those who now saw Germany only as a threat and one that was growing by the day. In this regard, the French connection was important enough for a Soviet military attaché, S.S. Venstov, to be sent to Paris and once there he wasted no time in opening up dialogue with General Maxime Weygand's staff.

After 1934, in practical terms, the 'spirit of Rapallo' dissipated as cooperation between the Red Army and the Reichswehr dwindled but the Soviets still hoped to retain good relations and proposed a joint Soviet-German guarantee of the territorial integrity of the Baltic States. This was mere window-dressing given the simmering animosity between Poland and Czechoslovakia, as only one instance of lingering discord, and Poland's reluctance to believe any friendly overtures emanating from Moscow. It was probably never meant to be taken seriously but the 'Eastern Pact' had been mooted alongside a number of other initiatives doing the rounds of European capitals. Britain, France and Germany had, rather optimistically, discussed an 'air pact' which never got off the ground. At the same time, Göring was in Warsaw making vague references to a possible anti-Soviet agreement in alliance with the Poles. Some forty French officers and the same number of Soviet officers had been involved in an exchange whereby the French were asked to look at Soviet tactics with a view to loosening them from the rigidity imposed by socialist dogma while the Soviet officers would try, unsuccessfully, to make close acquaintance with French armoured units and, while the visits were a disappointment, it was this initial exchange that was the catalyst for a Soviet-French agreement.

While the Soviets were winding down their commitments to Germany, they had become embroiled in disputes on the other side of their massive continent thousands of miles from Moscow. Following the Japanese invasion of Manchuria in 1931, Japanese expansion had led to disputes with the Soviet Union, each accusing the other of border violations. The first armed clashes occurred in 1935 when the Soviets and Japanese, through their proxies Mongolia and Manchukuo, fought a series of escalating border skirmishes. The whole confrontation never escalated beyond a bad-tempered dispute and there were few casualties but it did have the effect of distracting the Red Army from giving its full attention to the European theatre since the region of Outer Mongolia that was under threat was central to Soviet Far East defences. It was also of some concern that the Germans were making diplomatic advances towards the Japanese, prompting further expansion of the Red Army and re-evaluation of its relationship with the Reichswehr.

Although collaboration had been rapidly dismantled at the end of 1933, the Red Army, with Stalin's full approval, was still anxious to retain a level of contact with the Reichswehr. While Litvinov was edging towards the French, leading members of the Red Army were 'singing the praises of the Reichswehr' and affirming that 'no injurious intent' had been intended by Soviet withdrawal from collaborative ventures.[10] The Non-Aggression Pact agreed between France and the Soviet Union on 29 November 1932 was updated in the form of the Pact of Mutual Assistance signed by Pierre Laval for the French and Vladimir Potemkin for the Soviet Union on 2 May 1935.

Both sides agonised over the wording of the agreement which was, after all, a dramatic shift in allegiances and would inevitably be seen as a provocation by Germany. Progress was halted halfway through negotiations when its main protagonist Barthou was assassinated and his successor, Laval, showed himself to be sceptical of any advantage that might accrue to France but after the declaration of German rearmament in March 1935 he lost no time in putting his signature to a Franco-Soviet Treaty of Mutual Assistance alongside that of Litvinov on 2 May. Fearing that it would be rejected by the French Parliament which contained a strong peace lobby, he had hoped that Germany might be persuaded to become a co-signatory but nothing came of that. It was a weak agreement in reality, as can be seen in article 1:

In the event that France or the USSR. are subjected to the threat or the danger of aggression on the part of a European state, the USSR and France engage themselves reciprocally to proceed to an immediate mutual consultation on measures to take in order to observe the provisions of Article 10 of the League of Nations Pact.

It required the agreement of other members of the League of Nations before any of its terms could be enacted but, at least, it was a statement of intent and a recognition of how the diplomatic sands were shifting as the winds of change blew all across Europe with war being the sub-agenda of all major deliberations.

The French government, however, was not at all enthusiastic about cooperation with the Soviets. The very weakness of the treaty indicated that it was 'devoid of military interest' and Paris showed only lukewarm enthusiasm in the process.[11] For the Soviets, the treaty was little more than a public declaration of its loosening ties to Germany and a prompt in the direction of Berlin that economic ties with them could go the way of the military ones if the Nazis continued with their obstructionist attitude and vitriolic damning of communism. After all, the Soviets still owed vast amounts of money to Germany. Radek noted that 'German business circles . . . were the pillars of German-Soviet relations'[12] and, with his customary cynicism, made clear his view that for purely financial reasons as much as anything else 'nothing will happen that will permanently block our way to a common policy with Germany'.[13] A complete rupture with the Soviets could prove to be a very expensive mistake for German industry.

Two weeks later the Soviets managed to sign another treaty of mutual assistance, similar to the one it had with France, with President Edvard Beneš of Czechoslovakia who was already experiencing internal disturbances caused by the country's pro-German minorities. Again, this treaty was little more than a cosmetic chimera lacking any credibility since the two countries were separated by Poland and Romania, neither of which would, under any circumstances, consent to Soviet troops crossing their borders. The Soviet treaties with both France and Czechoslovakia were treated with contempt and ignored by Hitler who declared Germany to be 'the deadliest and most fanatical enemy' of Bolshevism.[14] On the other hand, he was pleased to note that the signing of the Anglo-German Naval Agreement had visibly annoyed the French whose anti-German position had been weakened. Hitler wasted no time in going onto the diplomatic offensive against the French, now unbalanced by the British move, by condemning the

Soviet-French treaty as a violation of Locarno and using it as an excuse to reoccupy the de-militarised Rhineland with German troops.

The Soviet Union, however, was not willing to allow the Czech treaty to be so easily dismissed and opened talks with Romania, represented by the grand old man of Romanian foreign policy Nicolae Titulescu, in 1934. Titulescu had voiced support for collective security as the only alternative to what he saw as the inevitable carving up of Poland by Germany and the Soviet Union and the occupation of Romania which would swiftly follow that. The Soviet agreements with both France and Czechoslovakia had put significant pressure on Romania given that Voroshilov had assured Beneš that the Red Army would come to aid the Czechs in the event of war 'with or without' the consent of Romania.[15] Surprisingly, the Romanian army High Command was in favour of talks with the Soviets but that can be seen in the context of their only other meaningful international security treaty being with the French, who were a very long way away indeed and their agreement with them was merely a treaty of friendship. They had few suitors and beggars could not be choosers. The Poles were not impressed with the way things were going in Bucharest but King Carol assured them that any treaty would preserve the Polish alliance and would not be explicitly directed against Germany.

When both Germany and Poland strenuously objected to any Soviet-Romanian deal, pressure mounted on Titulescu, whose power base inside Romania was weak at the best of times, and so to appease international criticism he was dismissed from the Cabinet. The Romanian Foreign Minister in 1938, Nicolae Petrescu-Comnen, did not deviate from the official line but saw major obstacles in dealing with the Soviets. Romania, a monarchy, was fiercely anti-communist and had annexed the territory of Bessarabia while the Soviets had been distracted by civil war and which the Soviets would now like to have back please despite Titulescu and Litvinov having reached a 'gentleman's agreement' never to let the issue interfere with relations. In June 1936, the Romanians made it clear to the world that 'IF Russia remains allied with France and agrees to assist Czechoslovakia, we WILL permit Russian forces to traverse Romania in order to assist the Czechs'[16] but the pact that Titulescu and Litvinov had proposed quietly slipped off the agenda.

Hitler threw down the gauntlet to France on 7 March 1936 when 20,000 German troops marched into what had been the demilitarised zone of the Rhineland. Although this land, lying between the French, Belgian and Dutch borders and the river Rhine, was a part of the

German Reich, under the terms of Versailles the country had been barred from stationing troops there. It had been a constant source of embarrassment to the Reichswehr and the German people as a whole, making it an easy target for Nazi propaganda which had been building up a groundswell of resentment since 1933. It was a bold gamble by Hitler to predict that France was too weak politically to react and that Britain, having repeatedly criticised the French for holding Germany too strictly to the more egregious terms of Versailles, would turn a blind eye.

The Soviet Union noted how the supine response to the Rhineland adventure, especially by the French who were the country most affected, made a mockery of any idea that the Western Powers were ready to stand up to Hitler. Litvinov railed against the occupation at the League of Nations on 17 March but overall, Moscow was not overly concerned with events on the Franco-German border. The Soviet First Minister Vyacheslav Molotov went so far as to say that, despite the Rhineland adventure, 'an improvement in Soviet-German relations [is] possible'.[17] Economically, the Soviet Union and Germany remained tied with huge benefits accruing to both sides, with the Soviet Union, rich in raw materials such as chrome and manganese but industrially backward as a perfect trading partner for the industrial powerhouse of Germany that imported more than three-quarters of all its raw materials.

Throughout the early years of Nazi rule in Germany, they made numerous offers of expanded trade deals with Moscow, all backed up with muted promises of better political relations. The Soviet desire for collective security meant that they could not ignore these advances, especially given their suspicions of Anglo-French motives and a genuine desire for a normalisation of relations with Germany. Through trade might come if not quite friendship, then understanding and acceptance but it was hard for Moscow to gauge the strength of support for a deal within what was, after all, a rabidly anti-communist regime. Their own willingness to continue trading with capitalist governments made them think that in Germany pragmatism too might hold sway over dogma.

The internal conflict between the pragmatic head of the Soviet Trade Mission to Germany, David Kandelaki, and the hard-line Litvinov was at the heart of the Soviet dilemma over relations with Germany. Kandelaki was tentatively supported by the Politburo but such support was only commensurate with results and when he faltered they did not hesitate to applaud Litvinov's vitriol. Kandelaki's initial mission in 1935 was to successfully negotiate new credit arrangements to finance

200 million Reichsmarks worth of Soviet imports from Germany repayable over five years. He held meetings with Schacht who assured him that the German trade strategy had the full approval of Hitler and that as far as Schacht was concerned such cooperation was 'a guarantee of prosperity for both countries'.[18] Further talks planned to propose for an extension of the agreement fivefold were too much for Litvinov and he leaked the information to the French. He could not countenance pursuing economic relations with a regime whose whole foreign policy was so overtly anti-Soviet and he was able to block any new deal by marshalling his supporters in the Politburo to soften the German political stance but that did not quell enthusiasm there for whatever benefits might accrue from the current level of trade.

Kandelaki also found an ally in Karl Schnurre, head of the Eastern European Economic Section of the *Auswärtiges Amt*, and it was through this contact that, over some months, meetings were held to give both sides a chance to ascertain the other side's true intentions but try as they might to use economic ties to normalise wider relations, Litvinov continued to put obstacles in their way. Kandelaki came away after meetings with leading industrialists, diplomats and military convinced that there was a mood in Germany for better relations with Moscow to strengthen their hand in an internal struggle for an economic alternative to the 'unproductiveness and erroneousness of National Socialism's anti-Soviet course' but Litvinov was sceptical and Krestinsky said there were '[no] indications of any changes in [German foreign policy]'.[19] Despite this strong opposition, the Politburo now sanctioned further talks over the extended deal which almost came to an agreement when the economic momentum was stalled by politics as German troops marched into the Rhineland. It was a huge relief to Litvinov whose ambition was and continued to be the containment of Germany until it could be trusted to enter into binding multi-national treaties. Despite having Stalin's tacit approval for his missions (he may even have been acting as his personal agent to look for internal German political divisions), Kandelaki would later be rewarded for his enthusiasm for closer Soviet-German relations with the firing squad in July 1938. Given that he, and other like-minded victims of Stalin's purges, would have played a significant part in German-Soviet negotiations in the lead up to the Molotov-Ribbentrop Pact in 1939, this suggests that there existed no plan in 1938 to create the Soviet-German alliance that preceded the German attack on Poland.

The multifaceted aspect of Soviet strategy at this time was illustrated by Moscow, seeming to lose faith in any Western alliance standing up to Hitler, deciding not to close the door entirely to some sort of relationship with a resurgent Germany but they did feel the need to make some sort of public gesture in protest to the Rhineland occupation and took the precaution of lowering the age of conscription in the Red Army to which Germany, in a tit-for-tat move, increased the period of service in the Reichswehr from one to two years and, in a major speech at Nuremberg in September 1936, Hitler railed against Bolshevism although the Soviet ambassador Jacob Suritz interpreted this as a warning to frighten off any potential suitors for Moscow and was as much a cry of weakness as of strength. Weeks later, Hitler taunted the Soviets, in what might have been no more than misdirection for the benefit of Britain and France, by imagining what Germany could become if it had access to the incalculable wealth of raw materials in the Urals, the rich forests of Siberia and the unending cornfields of the Ukraine. In October of that year, sending shockwaves through the Kremlin, Hitler's secret diplomatic negotiations came to fruition in the forging of the Rome-Berlin Axis between the two Fascist powers of Italy and Germany and a month later by a German agreement with Japan. For their part, the Soviets maintained their diplomatic initiative by opening talks with Lithuania and Czechoslovakia, both of which were being subjected to internal Nazi-led upheavals.

Despite this German provocation, from his perspective at some distance from the centres of disturbance in Europe, Stalin could see that Hitler was in no position to make any move against the Soviet Union and was going to have to find some 'wriggle room' in states immediately bordering Germany before he could flex his muscles further afield and this would embroil him in complicated diplomatic and political manoeuvring which could not, for ever, avoid military conflict. He seemed content to sit back and watch Hitler make his moves and do no more than make vague promises of help to those threatened; help which, in reality, Stalin was neither able nor willing to give. Indeed, it was of immeasurable benefit to Stalin to foment discord and even war between Germany and its neighbours which would keep Hitler occupied and, in this regard, any help he could give to speed up German rearmament would encourage Hitler to make a rash move that might even result in his defeat or, even better, a prolonged military stalemate.

In 1936, despite Hitler's hard-line policies against the Soviet Union, a two-year credit agreement was concluded, which allowed further improvement of trade relations. Germany was accorded increased access to Russian markets and raw materials, especially metals and oil to feed into its rearmament programme. The Credit Agreement of 1936 extended their economic relationship until 1938 during which time Hitler's anti-communist rhetoric did not abate. The conclusion of the credit agreement showed the general inconsistency and inherent contradictions of Hitler's foreign policy that continuously threatened future negotiations between Germany and the Soviet Union, especially in the creation of a new economic agreement over which talks had started even before Munich.

Chapter 10

THE SPANISH CIVIL WAR

Gustav Hilger was a Soviet expert in the *Auswärtiges Amt* and would later be Foreign Minister Joachim von Ribbentrop's translator during German-Soviet negotiations in 1939. In 1953 he wrote; 'There is not the slightest doubt that a deep fear of Hitler's Germany was the essential guide to all Soviet foreign policy in the mid-1930s.'[1] Hitler's renunciation of Rapallo threatened the Soviet Union with diplomatic isolation and resulted in a dramatic change of Soviet foreign policy which saw treaties concluded with both Czechoslovakia and France. This reversal, which took the Soviets away from collaboration with Germany, was intended to impress the Western Powers that they were now intent on pursuing a new doctrine of collective security in Europe based on peaceful opposition to fascism. Stalin hoped to signal to Britain and France that there would be Soviet help in containing the Nazi menace. When war broke out in Spain in June 1936 between the democratically-elected left-wing government and the fascist Nationalist forces under General Francisco Franco Bahamonde, Stalin saw it as a unique opportunity to prove his good intentions.

When Britain and France were getting intelligence in late 1936 that the Soviet Union was sending military aid direct to the Spanish government they warned that any significant escalation would be seen as a violation of international law. Estranged from its First World War allies and having seen its overtures to the West for collective action against the Nazis rejected, the Soviet Union believed it had little more to lose by piling in on the side of the Republicans and much to gain if it could stabilise the socialist government in Spain and establish strong links with it. With Italian boots already on the ground in southern Spain and German aircraft flying Franco's troops across the Straits of Gibraltar, Stalin covertly sent military intelligence (NKVD) officers to evaluate the situation and see how it might be exploited to his advantage without risking becoming directly embroiled in a war with either Italy or Germany.

It was the Italians who had, right from the start, openly and without subterfuge, supplied both equipment and large numbers of troops to the rebel Nationalists in an attempt to extend their influence into the western Mediterranean while Hitler had authorised only transport aircraft in his first response to Franco's desperate calls for assistance. The Soviets had been even more guarded than the Germans when called upon for help from the Spanish Republican government and had initially given only political support and encouragement with the formation of International Brigades of volunteer fighters but, fearing a backlash from the Western Powers, had baulked at any public show of matériel aid. Just like the Germans, however, that did not prevented them from initiating a programme of covert military aid once it was clear that all sides were doing the same thing.

After years of cooperation between the Wehrmacht and the Red Army, the political ambitions of their respective governments had, in 1936, put them firmly on opposite sides of a conflict that had started off as a failed military coup d'état but was now burgeoning into a full-scale civil war. Neither side was particularly pleased about being drawn into the fray but both became victim of 'mission creep' where small deployments of forces begat increasing numbers of support personnel who required extra military protection and so on until pride entered the equation with neither wanting to be seen to back down. Unable now to extricate themselves, both sides saw some benefits by putting years of theory into practice, testing new equipment in battle conditions and seeing how the other side held up in actual combat. The Germans organised their forces under the Condor Legion and opted to make the bulk of their contribution to Franco in air power with only a limited number of ground units but the Soviets had done both and sent not only aircraft but a significant number of tanks, albeit ones that were expected to be manned by Spanish personnel. In fact both sides had planned to provide only equipment to be used by the Spanish fighters, even though Soviet tanks always came with full crews for training purposes, but it was immediately clear that very few of the Spanish forces were sufficiently qualified to operate the modern machines and so, at first, both German and Soviet personnel became directly involved in the fighting until local personnel could be trained. Only rarely did significant numbers of Soviet and German forces come into direct conflict in air battles and never in ground offensives but it is reasonable to think that on more than one occasion air crews that had trained together at Lipetsk would find themselves, unknowingly, up against each other in combat.

Whilst limiting the role of men in combat, the Soviets did send a number of high-ranking tank experts to both train Spanish crews and evaluate the performance of tanks and artillery in combat. Many of these such as Rodion Malinovsky (codenamed Manolito), Nikolay Voronov (Voltaire) and Dmitri Pavlov (Pablo) would survive the Stalinist purges and become four-star tank commanders in the Second World War. On the German side, with its heavy bias towards air support, it was the Luftwaffe that benefitted most from the war. For them it would be fighter pilots, such as Johannes Trautloft, Herwig Knüppel, Kraft Eberhardt, Harro Harder and Rolf Pingel who gained the most and built on their experience of Spain to enter the Second World War as battle-hardened leaders.

It was in many ways an unsatisfactory laboratory for testing machines and methods but throughout the months of war some meaningful results emerged even though many encounters both in the air and on the ground were characterised by poor Spanish leadership at the top of both commands and by inexperience of Spanish crews on the front line. Advantage was often won in the air by the Soviet I-15 and I-16 fighters due to their technical superiority over Nationalist aircraft in the early stages while on the ground the Soviet T-26 tanks were far superior to all other armour and dominated battles in which they fought.

When Soviet arms for Spain started to flow they came thick and fast. The first shipment of 'old and nearly worn out' Soviet machine guns with ammunition and grenades arrived on the SS *Campeche* which sailed from Feodosia in the Crimea and arrived on 4 October 1936 at Cartagena.[2] The SS *Komsomol* arrived at the same port on 12 October with fifty T-26 tanks complete with spares, fuel and ammunition, and fifty-one 'volunteer' crews. Thirty Tupolev SB bombers had been delivered on three different ships within another nine days after that, all with spares, fuel and ammunition and by the end of the month twenty-five Polikarpov I-15 fighter aircraft and thirty armoured cars had followed. Germany immediately responded by sending forty-one Panzer Is to Spain a few days later. These were put under the command of Lieutenant Colonel Wilhelm Ritter von Thoma in Gruppe Thoma (also referred to as Panzergruppe Drohne). This first shipment was followed by four more shipments of Panzer I Ausf Bs, with 122 vehicles shipped in total.

The Soviet military attaché at the Madrid embassy, Kombrig Vladimir Gorev, had arranged for the Spanish to set up a tank training centre near the town of Archene, about 90km from Cartagena. The plan was to train Spanish personnel to operate the tanks and Archene became the main training and technical centre for the Republican tank force for much of the war. Although the original plan was to confine the use of Soviet personnel to training, by the end of October the situation for the Republican forces around Madrid was becoming so desperate that the Soviet attaché V. Gorev was authorised to send Soviet crews to reinforce the Madrid front on the night of 27 October 1936. Soviet armour was also deployed south of Madrid under Colonel Krivoshein before the end of October. Several T-26 tanks under Captain Paul Arman were thrown into a Republican counter-attack directed towards the town of Torrejon de Velasco in an attempt to cut off the Nationalist advance north in the first recorded tank battle in the Spanish Civil War. Despite initial success, poor communication between the Soviet armour and Spanish Republican infantry caused Arman's force to become isolated leading to the destruction of a number of tanks. This battle also marked the first use of Molotov Cocktails (bottle-based improvised incendiary weapons) against tanks. Von Thoma's Panzer Is on the Nationalist side went into action on 30 October and immediately experienced problems when they came up against the Commune de Paris battalion, equipped with Soviet BA-10 armoured cars whose 45mm gun was able to knock out the poorly armoured Panzer I at ranges up to 500m.

Although the Panzer I would take part in in almost every major Nationalist offensive of the war, the Nationalist army began to use more and more captured T-26 tanks. At one point, von Thoma offered up to 500 pesetas for each T-26 captured which hugely incentivised Franco's fierce Moroccan troops. The Panzer I was upgraded to incorporate a 20mm Breda gun capable of piercing 40mm of armour at 250m range. Prototypes were ready by September 1937 and an order was placed after successful results but further orders were cancelled after it was decided that enough Republican T-26 tanks had been captured. Very early on, General Warlimont, the German commander in Spain, had called for Rheinmetall 37mm Pak 35/36 anti-tank guns, twenty-four of which arrived in October 1936 and eighteen more a month later. In all 352 of these weapons would be sent. It is interesting to note that the Soviets also employed anti-tank weapons in the shape of the high-velocity L/46 Model, which had been developed from the Pak 35/36 that they had manufactured under licence from Rheinmetall and the first fifteen of which arrived on 29 April 1937, followed by 100 a week later. It was soon apparent, however, that the Pak 35/36 had a maximum range well short of that of the main gun of the T-26 and was useless as a tank-buster. The British tank expert Liddell Hart, when analysing the Spanish Civil War, seemed unimpressed by the limitations of the 35/36 and took the not altogether valid view that defence against tanks had been developed and perfected more quickly and more effectively than the tank itself.

The German Condor Legion also employed the excellent 88mm/56 Flak 18 anti-aircraft gun, four of which had arrived with the SS *Usaramo* on 6 August. These were later augmented and became the air defence artillery unit of the Condor Legion named Flak Abteilung 88 commanded by Lieutenant Colonel Hermann Lichtenberger, with Lieutenant Colonel Georg Neuffer as second-in-command and chief of staff. Altogether seventy-one Flak 18 guns would be sent to Spain where their versatility was shown both in anti-tank and air defence roles. The '88' literally obliterated T-26 tanks in Spain at the first hit. The initial scarcity of Spanish Nationalist artillery and the general low proficiency of its crews soon forced the use of the Flak 18 gun as a direct-fire infantry support weapon in which capacity they were used at Jamara in February 1937. The Flak 88 group again fought in all the battles along the northern front, where their tasks were divided between anti-aircraft duties and field artillery employment. They took part in the assault against Bilbao's 'Iron Belt', and following the Battle of Brunete, went north again to contribute to the Santander and Asturias campaign. Later they would be used in the Aragon offensive and at the Battle of the Ebro in 1938. The 88mm guns, however, were vulnerable in close engagements and casualties among the Legion's 88mm gun batteries in the Spanish Civil War were second only to those of bomber pilots and crews. These weapons were always manned by German crews and the French War Department verified that 'great secrecy surrounded the operation of these weapons'.

For both sides, but especially the Red Army, the Spanish Civil War had a number of important consequences in tank technology, but on the tactical side, many lessons were ignored or misunderstood. The T-26 was a licence-built copy of the British Vickers 6-ton light tank, but with a Soviet-designed turret and gun. The Red Army had several different types of tanks for specific roles. While the slow T-26 tank gave support to Red Army infantry, the BT-5 'fast' tank, which was employed later in the war, was intended for a deep exploitation role, similar to the British cruiser tanks. The T-26 was the main type of tank sent to Spain during the war, accounting for 281 of the 331 tanks sent, but it was not ideal for infantry support having only thin armour making it vulnerable to anti-tank guns. It was, however, armed with a dual-purpose 45mm gun that was more versatile than the armament on British or French infantry tanks of the period.

Right from the start the Soviet tanks ran into serious problems. The T-26 required an overhaul after 150 engine hours and a factory overhaul after 600 hours but the fighting around Madrid had seen tanks accumulate over 800 operating hours by mid-December, far beyond the regulations, leaving many of them out of service. Not only that but the poor-quality fuel caused engine carbonisation, fouled spark-plugs and other problems which could easily immobilise the tank. Tracks and track pins began to wear out after 500 miles of travel; side clutches became worn out, and the powertrain was gradually knocked out of alignment from hard cross-country travel. Inexperienced Spanish crews were unable to do field repairs, and their unfamiliarity with tank driving led to high rates of clutch and powertrain failures. To extend the combat life of the tanks, the Soviets adopted the French practice of using trains or heavy trucks to transport the tanks whenever units had to move more than a few miles. Co-operation between the tanks and the infantry they were supporting was abysmal. There had been no training by the tanks and infantry in cooperative tactics before missions, and the tank companies seldom worked with the same infantry unit for more than a few days, so no experience was accumulated and the Republicans could not afford to pull the tank companies out of the line for such training, and neither were the Soviets willing to use up precious engine hours drilling with the Spanish infantry. Soviet tank commanders were ordered back to Moscow to brief senior Red Army leaders in January 1937.

Again at Jamara in February 1937, the experience of Soviet tanks with International Brigades infantry was better but still unsatisfactory. Nationalist 37mm anti-tank guns were taking a heavy toll of the T-26s in terrain that was difficult for the tanks to manoeuvre. Soviet armour was called up again at Guadalajara against Italian L3/35 tankettes but despite much success against them, only nine out of the sixty to start the battle were capable of pursuing the enemy as they retreated at the end of the day. The inability of the tanks to advance in the face of enemy anti-tank guns was cited by many as evidence of the failure of the tank to restore mobility to warfare. Even Liddell Hart began to have his doubts in view of the Spanish experience but attributed the tanks' poor performance to a failure of leadership. A hundred new T-26s arrived in March but Spanish crews were not responding well to the training routines and tank commanders looked to the infantry for more suitable men to train. These were sent back to the Soviet Union on a crash training course at Gorkiy.

The last major shipment of fifty tanks were BT-5 fast tanks. They were a licence-built copy of the American Christie tank, but with a Soviet-designed turret and gun, identical to that on the T-26. These were allotted the best of the Spanish trainees and the personnel from the International Brigades who had been set to train at Gorkiy. For many of the Soviet advisors in Spain, the International Tank Regiment was the last, best hope to display the power of tanks on the modern battlefield. These hopes would be crushed in the autumn of 1937 during the Saragossa campaign.

The attack against Fuentes de Ebro on the road to Saragossa began shortly after noon. The forty-eight tanks of the International Tank Regiment started the attack with a salvo of their guns, and then set off at high speed 'like an express train', with Spanish infantry clinging to their sides. In the din and dust of the attack, many of the infantry fell off the tanks, some to be run over and crushed by other tanks. The terrain in front of the enemy positions was of irrigated sugar-cane fields, criss-crossed with irrigation ditches. The tanks soon became bogged down and began to take fire from Nationalist field guns and anti-tank guns. After exhausting their ammunition, the tanks slowly began to make their way back to the start point with little direction or control, leaving behind several tanks stuck in the mud. In total, the International Tank Regiment lost nineteen of its forty-eight tanks in the attack and several more damaged, and a third of its tank crews were killed or wounded. While Soviet tankers would continue to act as advisers, the number of Soviet tank crews continued to diminish and the personnel became mostly Spanish by the end of 1937.

The last major campaign in which Soviet tank crews participated was the bitter fighting for Teruel from 15 December 1937 to 22 February 1938. A total of 104 tanks took part in the operations. Component battalions were assigned to support various attacks. The fighting took place under difficult circumstances – extremely cold weather, heavy snow, poor roads and in mountainous country. What was striking about the campaign was that the tank force was able to function at all. By the end of 1937, the tanks had exceeded their expected mechanical lifespan, yet the tank units were able to maintain a respectable fraction of their tanks in combat on a daily basis and overall tank losses were modest under the circumstances. A total of sixty-three tanks, more than half the force, required intermediate or capital overhaul, which was managed by the units in the field. It was a remarkable accomplishment and reflected the growing skill of the Spanish tank crews, the maintenance units and the tank support infrastructure created by Spanish industry. This legacy helps account for the ability of the Republican tank force to maintain its size and fighting potential for most of the remainder of 1938, in spite of the cut-off in Soviet technical aid.

After the withdrawal of the German Condor Legion from Spain, the Wehrmacht continued to include the aggressive use of tanks in their battlefield doctrine in spite of the poor performance of their own tanks in Spain. They had actually sent few tanks to the war and were not convinced that the experience of small-scale deployment of tanks manned by poorly-trained foreign tankers supporting poorly-trained militia units and all under less than competent Spanish leadership was a legitimate way of assessing the operational potential of large armoured formations and could be disregarded when creating a doctrine for a much larger war under their own total control.

In Moscow, Tukhachevsky, who had been the Red Army's primary architect of its large armoured force and its primary proponent of offensive 'Deep Battle' doctrine, was tried and executed in one of Stalin's purges, giving free rein to Voroshilov to take the Red Army several steps back in its development. Other advocates of armoured warfare in the Red Army suffered similar fates along with many in the tank design sections where the T-26 light tank and BT tanks had been conceived.

The most difficult issue to address in Spain was cooperation between tanks and infantry. In most cases, it had been difficult if not impossible to accomplish and, to a very great extent, was laid at the door of badly trained and poorly motivated Spanish infantry, believing that the situation would be better when operating with Red Army infantry. Many of the Republican infantry units had little practical training and would often refuse to follow tanks into action. Only very rarely had there been time or opportunity for training or instructions in such tactics for either the tank crews or the infantry formations. There was no established procedure for communications between the tanks and the infantry since neither had effective tactical radios. The slow walking speed of the infantry and the much higher speed of the tanks in cross-country travel was also a problem, since once battle was joined, the tankers tried to use the speed of their vehicles to avoid being hit by Nationalist anti-tank guns and field guns. As a result, infantry units and their supporting tanks usually became separated.

Spain had brought into focus the lack of durability of tank designs of the 1930s and the need for expanded Soviet technical support within the Republican armoured units but this was not acted upon, due to the paralyzing effect of the purges as well as army inaction and complacency. The availability of spare parts remained chronically low, and the level of technical competence of the burgeoning officer cadres was inadequate. Calls for better training of tank crews also went largely unheeded.

The issue of command and control likewise went unaddressed. This was in part due to the backward state of Soviet radio technology compared to the Germans' at the time. Although steps were taken to develop a new generation of tactical radios durable enough for armoured vehicle use the importance of radios in particular, and command and control in, was still neglected. The Germans, on the other hand, whilst not heavily engaged in armoured combat during the war, had developed efficient procedures, organisation and learned much about combined-arms tactics, especially with air power.

There was general satisfaction with the performance of the T-26 which had proved to be robust and capable and was viewed favourably in comparison with the Italian L3/35 tankette and the German Panzer I. Both of the Nationalist tank types were armed only with machine guns, and so could not defeat the T-26 in battle, and both were too thinly armoured to resist the T-26's 45mm gun. The T-26's design had taken place before the Red Army had developed any experience in tank combat and the fighting in Spain revealed some significant shortcomings that had not been foreseen by its designers. Its main failing was its poor armour which was immediately improved by adding sloped armour on the T-26S model. Its vision in combat was limited to armoured glass viewing slits and a periscopic sight with a very restricted viewing angle so the crews tended to operate with the driver's hatch and the turret hatch open simply to see where they were going with the result that three-quarters of tank casualties were inflicted on crews through the open hatches.

The designers of the next generation of tanks, basing their views on experiences from Spain, took the view that the new fast tank should have thicker armour to protect it from anti-tank guns and should have a better gun than the old 45mm 'sparrow-shooter' of the T-26 and BT. The new design would emerge in 1940 as the T-34, a revolutionary design which would be the benchmark for world tank design through the first part of the Second World War.

The tank, that was supposed to return manocuvre and offense to the battlefield, had been to a very large extent neutralised as a weapon when anti-tank weapons gave the advantage back to the defence. Military attachés and other observers stressed that to overcome the threat of anti-tank weapons there was a requirement for tanks to be deployed en masse, and not in small groups. They also recommended that tanks be combined with infantry, which could hold the ground gained, and with artillery and aviation, that could protect the tanks by destroying or suppressing enemy anti-tank fire. There followed an escalation in design and technology with an arms race between tank armour and anti-tank firepower. Both proponents and opponents of tank warfare could pick and choose from the evidence of Spain to build their own case. Perhaps the only European military command that drew the correct lessons from the war was the Germans who concluded that Spain had been a special kind of battleground, from which few meaningful conclusions could be drawn. The circumstances imposed in a civil war meant that it had been necessary to take ground and hold it rather than employ fast-moving armour to bypass it. There was little opportunity to test Blitzkrieg-type mobile warfare.

One of the most striking aspects of the Soviet-German confrontations in the Spanish Civil War was the disparity, for the most part, between the effectiveness of Soviet aircraft and those of the Luftwaffe. It is also noticeable that while the Germans employed a total of twenty-six different aircraft types the Soviets sent only three, which suggests that the Germans placed a greater emphasis on using the war to test a range of aircraft whereas the Soviets only sent aircraft that had been proven. Of the German main types deployed, some 90 were trainers, 311 bomber-reconnaissance, 24 dive-bombers and 277 fighters (133 of which were Messerschmitt Bf 109s). The Soviets sent 155 SB bombers, 163 Polikarpov I-15 fighters and 346 Polikarpov I-16 fighters. For the first couple of years, the Soviet fighters far out-performed and out-fought the German equivalent but often came off second-best against the Italian CR.32s. It was only when the Bf 109-Es came on the scene in 1938 that the Luftwaffe swiftly won dominance of the skies but also by then they were almost exclusively up against the less-well trained Spanish pilots in the Soviet aircraft.

Chapter 11

THE
MOLOTOV-RIBBENTROP PACT

Eastern Europe in 1938.

On the other side of the European continent, Litvinov was unnerved by the growing influence of Germany and Poland over Romania and once again the idea of a Soviet-Romanian pact was brought up but the question of Romania allowing the transit of Soviet troops in the event of a German attack on Czechoslovakia was still the stumbling block to Soviet ambitions. The exile of Titulescu in late 1937 had changed the Romanian position somewhat but still they refused to accept Soviet promises that they would retire beyond the Dniestr at the cessation of any hostilities. The formation of an ultra-right government in Romania at the end of December 1937 seemed to once again put an end to talks but the urgency of the need for Soviet transit forced it to remain on the table. Already Soviet aircraft were overflying Romanian airspace, much to the annoyance of the Poles. These aircraft were Soviet SB 2 bombers, sixty-one of which had been bought by the Czechs and almost three times more contracted to be built under licence in Czechoslovakia. These aircraft had been purchased long before tensions had escalated in the Sudetenland and were straight commercial purchases which theoretically did not constitute military aid.

During the 1920s, the question of the *Anschluss* (political union of Austria with Germany) had never been of much concern to Moscow, having been perceived as a 'German question'. As late as 1931, *Izvestia* had published an article welcoming *Anschluss* but as Hitler rose to power it dawned on them that Austria held the key to German domination of Europe. Annexation of that country by Germany would provide a springboard that might launch them into *Drang nach dem Osten* and put them right on the Soviet Union's border. It now became of paramount importance that Moscow oppose *Anschluss*.

At this time, the Soviet Union, Italy and Germany were active participants in the Spanish Civil War. Litvinov denounced fascist aggression and castigated the Western Powers for their failure to support the democratically-elected government of Spain against Franco's insurrection. The ideological war between Berlin and Moscow was now coming to the fore as a dominant factor, having been conveniently relegated to a side issue for almost two decades. And then on 11 March 1938 German troops crossed the Austrian frontier and the *Anschluss* of Austria was declared. Three days later the Soviet Ministry of Foreign Affairs called upon Britain, France and the United States to join them in a conference to discuss international action to prevent further German aggression. The collective show of disdain for such a move was evident and ably articulated by the British Prime Minister Chamberlain when he accused the Soviets of crying wolf by calling for 'a concerting of action against an eventuality which has not yet arisen'.[1] It was, however, a signal to other Eastern European states that the wolf was indeed on the prowl and the shepherds were abandoning the flock.

It became increasingly clear that Czechoslovakia would become the next victim on Hitler's list but Britain and France feverishly distanced themselves from any suggestion of intervention. The Czech Foreign Minister, Kamil Krofta, reported to the Soviet ambassador Sergei Aleksandrovsky that the Poles were massing troops along the Czech border intent on exploiting the fragile situation and asked Moscow to warn them off, which it did by declaring its willingness to abandon its non-aggression treaty with Poland if that state joined in an attack on Czechoslovakia. There was also the small matter of the 1935 Soviet-Czech treaty in which the Soviets had pledged to give aid to Czechoslovakia but that was conditional on France fulfilling its obligations to that country also.

Despite having been snubbed by the Munich negotiators, the Soviets had prepared for action to support the Czechs by calling up reserves and putting their forces on alert as well as urging France to declare support for the Czechs also. Polish sources in the Soviet Union had noted 'feverish' activity' as Soviet forces moved up to the frontier and in Prague the Polish embassy reported 'intensive activity on all Soviet radio stations' transmitting inside Czechoslovakia.[2] On 21 September, Defence Commissar Voroshilov sent orders to mobilise the Kiev Military District. Soviet forces moved up to the Dniestr around Rezina and Rybnica and further south Romanian authorities began evacuating their border areas with the Soviet Union. Polish Intelligence reported on the movement of '600 freight cars passing through Kishinev [at night]' loaded with military equipment and ammunition.[3] The next day the Czech government resigned and was replaced by a Government of National Concentration under General Syrovy, Inspector-General of the Army. Elsewhere Polish troops had moved up to Teschen on the Polish-Czech border. The Hungarian government had been encouraged to make moves also after meetings with Göring at Rominten on 20 September and had ordered mobilisation, doubling the strength of the Hungarian army.

The Czech General Jaroslav Fajfr spent three days in Moscow negotiation the transfer of 700 Soviet military aircraft. Soviet engineers were sent to Czechoslovakian airfields such as Spiška Nová Ves to prepare for the transfer. In all 123 light bombers from Belorussia, 62 from Kiev and 246 from Kharkov together with 151 fighters from Belorussia and 151 from Kiev were put on standby on 28 September ready to go 'in case of necessity'.[4] All declarations of help were hedged with caution and there would be a limit on Soviet aid, however. For instance, there was never any possibility that they would allow themselves to be left to fight the Germans over Czechoslovakia while Britain and France watched from the sidelines.

In March 1936, the Soviets had argued against an armed response to the German reoccupation of the Rhineland but at the time of the *Anschluss*, when German ambitions had manifested themselves ominously closer to the Soviet border, they had modified their policy and had urged collective action to 'remove the growing danger of a new worldwide carnage'.[5] When it was clear that the Sudetenland crisis was inviting further German expansionism, a top-level meeting at the Kremlin, chaired by Stalin, authorised a message of substantial Soviet support for the Czechs but it was made clear that it was not the issue of the Sudetenland, which the Soviets saw as a purely internal matter and one which had emanated from Versailles for which the Soviet Union bore no responsibility, but the possible subjugation of the whole of Czechoslovakia by Germany that concerned them. Indeed, Litvinov went further and told the German ambassador in Moscow, Count Friedrich Werner von der Schulenburg, that it was even more than the fate of one country but was an issue of 'the power of National Socialist Germany in her violence and desire for attack'.[6] If the Germans took military action against the Czechs, the Soviets expected an armed response from Britain and France in which case it would also 'keep her word to the Czechs'.

Such expectations, however, were voiced with considerable scepticism. Litvinov had called the preservation of Czechoslovakia a 'hindrance to the Hitlerite drive' but had become resigned to the fact that the Western Powers would pursue their own ambitions without the assistance of the Soviet Union; indeed, history shows that Chamberlain would pursue his ambitions without the assistance of anyone at all.

On 13 September 1938 the French Premier Édouard Daladier had made a fruitless plea to Britain, in whose hands he placed all authority to negotiate with Hitler, for a meeting with Germany to reduce tensions over the Sudetenland. Chamberlain had no interest or confidence in the French position and took little notice of it as long as it did not hinder his new initiative for a face-to-face meeting between himself and Hitler when he believed his conciliatory approach and diplomatic skills would bring the German leader to his senses. Daladier, along with much of the British Cabinet, found himself outside the loop on this and was relegated to playing a minor supporting role in the ensuing piece of political theatre. Chamberlain reminded him that it was the French who actually had a treaty with the Czechs, not the British, implying that he was having to step in clear up the mess that their arrogant diplomacy of the 1920s and early 1930s had landed them all in. Although he was to play little part in negotiations, Daladier was at least invited to the Munich Conference which was more than could be said for Beneš who, meanwhile, had shown his willingness to concede three areas of north-west Bohemia to Germany leaving the Czechs' defences intact. He had made this concession to Daladier on 17 September but when it was relayed to Chamberlain on the eve of his flying visit to meet Hitler at the Berchtesgaden it was not welcome news and he withheld knowledge of it from his Cabinet.

Aleksandrovsky met Beneš on 21 September and assured him that Soviet troops would come to the Czechs' aid if Germany attacked and would not hesitate to pass through the territories of Romania, whom they considered to be part of the anti-German bloc, or Poland, who was perceived as pro-German and therefore hostile. It was assumed by both men that French refusal to help was a bluff to pressure Beneš to negotiate and that they would stand up and fight if it came to the crunch. Soviet activity became intense. The Kiev Special Military District mobilised on the same day and infantry divisions called up 8,000 reservists. The Byelorussian Special Military District mobilised two days later and Soviet fighter squadrons were moved to forward bases. Troops of the Kalinin Military District were moved up to the frontier and in Leningrad, Kiev, Kharkov and Moscow anti-aircraft forces were put on alert. Emeritus Professor of History at the University of Alabama Hugh Ragsdale has presented copious evidence to show that the Soviet Union was getting ready to 'discharge its alliance obligations to Czechoslovakia and France'.[7] When the Czechs mobilised on 23 September, Aleksandrovsky hailed it as proof of a world coalition against fascism and that 'justice would ultimately prevail'.

If the Soviet intention was to send military aid to Czechoslovakia, their forces would have to cross Polish territory and the Poles were having none of that. As well as preparing their own forces along the Czech border ready to exploit the situation if Germany attacked, they had responded to the Soviet move by massing their own forces along the Soviet border. For their part, Britain and France assiduously ignored the overtures of the Soviet state which was held by many in those countries to be more of a threat to their own interests than Germany. Seeing German influence bleed across Europe to the east was in many ways a comfort when viewed against the alternatives that might result from direct confrontation in the west.

The Soviet Union had not been invited to attend the Munich Conference in September 1938; indeed even Czech delegates were excluded from the conference room where Chamberlain and Daladier had allowed themselves to be deceived over German intentions and where Hitler had gracelessly acceded to Mussolini's restraining influence as the inevitable was put on hold. Daladier's lamentable contribution to the conference saw France lose all credibility as a restraining force on Hitler. Stalin was well aware that Munich meant it was only a matter of time before Germany attacked the Soviet Union and when that happened it was clear that they could expect no help from either Britain or France. A strategy for defence of the country now depended on creating an occupied zone beyond the Soviet border to provide a buffer against such a German attack. This was to be achieved at all costs.

Three weeks after the signing of the Munich Agreement, Hitler, infuriated by Britain and France 'meddling' in his affairs, issued a directive preparing the Wehrmacht for liquidation of the rump Czech state should it 'pursue an anti-German policy'. The justification for such a move would not prove difficult given Hitler's total power to define what the provocation might be. Hitler knew that the directive would increase Poland's sense of insecurity and so in a speech he tried to reassure them that his real target was the Soviet Union by reference to his Anti-Comintern Pact with Japan. The Soviets needed no reminder and Poland saw through the misdirection but, sitting right in between the two juggernauts, muted any objections hoping beyond hope that the blow would not fall on them yet still refused to discuss a mutual defence agreement with the Soviets.

Meanwhile, Hitler was under no illusions that the Western Allies were his implacable opponents and urged an intensification of Germany's rearmament programme that Göring called 'a gigantic programme, compared to which previous achievements are insignificant'.[8] This, however, brought with it huge inflationary pressures on the German domestic economy with a massive increase of 40 per cent in the amount of currency in circulation compared to a year previously. When the head of the Reichsbank, Schacht, pointed out the inadvisability of continuing with such a reckless fiscal policy Hitler sacked him but it was not so easy to ignore the obvious requirement of raw materials from the Soviet Union to sustain the armaments manufacturing industries. It was clear now, even to economical illiterates such as Hitler and Göring, that a crisis point was approaching which could not be managed by traditional peaceful means. The only option that their limited conceptual understanding of economics allowed them to choose was to force the issue through destabilising the whole economic structure of Europe and re-aligning it in Germany's favour. For Hitler, though perhaps not so much for Göring, the obvious vehicle of chaos was a limited war in which a quick victory with territorial gains would give Germany hugely increased access to the necessary raw materials and workforce that would stabilise its economy.

Such a bold move required careful management if it was to deliver the desired outcome without engulfing the whole continent in uncontrollable conflagration. Hitler wanted war on his own terms which meant limited, achievable goals won against limited, conquerable opponents. Perhaps he could encourage the Soviet Union to resist the temptation to take advantage of a war in the East and maintain its deliveries of raw materials by inveigling it into a deal in which it might profit in equal measure. With the Ukrainian wheat fields and Romanian oilfields in his sights, Hitler needed first to eliminate the threat of attack from Poland, which, with French help, might not be able to resist the temptation to open a second front if Germany forged ahead in south-east Europe. Diplomatically, he ramped up his demands of Poland especially in relation to handing back control of the Danzig Corridor, which he hoped was the least controversial of them, in return for a 25-year guarantee of Poland's other borders with Germany. In October 1938, Ribbentrop was tasked with bullying Ambassador Lipski, a role that came naturally to him, by insisting on immediate Polish acquiescence but disingenuously sugared the pill with assurances of a joint German-Polish military alliance against the Soviet Union if they agreed.

Joachim Ribbentrop was a hugely ambitious man who had worked as a champagne salesman and ingratiated himself with Hitler as early as 1933. He had travelled widely and perceived himself to be a man of the world. In this he was able to impress Hitler who came to value him as someone whose vision coincided with his own and as such was a relief from the usual carping of the professional diplomatic corps which had been a constant irritant to Hitler. He valued Ribbentrop's opinions on foreign affairs to the point where Ribbentrop was appointed Foreign Minister in February 1938 which Hitler saw as a personal victory by both insulting the Foreign Ministry and reducing his reliance on them. Ribbentrop's appointment was met with derision by the majority of the Nazi hierarchy who were embarrassed by his sycophancy to Hitler and who often referred to him as 'the twitching wine waiter'. Ribbentrop married an heiress and adopted the title of 'von' which normally indicated noble lineage in Germany. Joseph Goebbels said of him, 'he bought his name, he married his money, and he swindled his way into office'.

On 26 October 1938, von der Schulenburg sent a memorandum to the *Auswärtiges Amt,* which outlined his plan to extend the Soviet-German trade agreement up to the end of 1939. This would allow Germany to maintain access to Soviet raw materials while solidifying its relations with the country, which had continued to negotiate with the Western Powers. Despite German enthusiasm for a longer agreement, negotiations only resulted in the extension of the March 1938 trade agreement through to the end of 1939. The agreement was signed on 19 December 1938.

Litvinov had made clear his preference for an Anglo-Franco-Soviet alliance having earlier been open about his dislike of Soviet-German economic relations. 'So many German technicians,' he said, 'meant so many German spies', but he warned British and French governments that if they continued to duck the issue, the Soviet Union might be forced to come to terms with Germany. He was, however, feeling a little insecure having sensed a mood change in the Kremlin against his particular views and was acutely aware that those of similar views were a diminishing group slimmed down by recent purges. He mellowed sufficiently to give favour to Halifax's suggestion of a four-party agreement including Poland, and the French urged that the strongest pressure be brought to bear upon Poland, even to the extent of threats, to secure her collaboration but the Polish Foreign Minister, Jósef Beck, whom Litvinov considered to be a 'Nazi pimp',[9] was not interested. It was still the Polish position that they would not permit the Red Army to cross Polish territory even as an ally in the event of war and this was to have the most far-reaching consequences.

Meanwhile, German pressure on Poland had intensified in January with an invitation to Beck to meet Hitler at the Berghof. Here he was offered a share of the Ukrainian cake as a distinctly junior partner but he did not trust Hitler's motives and left without agreement. Hitler's ambition to take the Danzig Corridor back under German control had been made clear and was an issue that he was never going to let go of and one on which Poland would never compromise. When German troops marched into Prague a few weeks later, Polish reticence was vindicated but it had markedly upped the stakes for Beck who could see that nothing now stood between Hitler and Poland, the next piece of the European jigsaw to be reshaped.

On 20 January 1940, Schnurre had been due to travel to Moscow to discuss the future of German-Soviet trade policies but Ribbentrop peremptorily and unilaterally cancelled the trip which had devastating effects on negotiations in the short term. Molotov told von der Schulenburg that German economic negotiations were misguided and underlain by a fundamental distrust on the political level and that Germany was not serious about rapprochement. 'The Soviet government,' he said, 'could not agree to the resumption of negotiations unless the necessary political bases had been established.'[10] Even though the idea of a non-aggression pact to accompany the trade deal was first mentioned in April, Molotov found it convenient to use the cancellation of Schnurre's trip as a way to stall negotiations while Soviet diplomats evaluated results from the ongoing simultaneous talks with Britain. The renowned Polish-American historian Anna Maria Cienciala has asserted that 'Stalin always preferred a pact with Germany, and that he used negotiations with the Western Powers to pressure Hitler into an agreement'.[11] Walter Krivitsky, the head of Soviet Military Intelligence in Western Europe before 1937, claimed that Stalin had contemplated a strategic agreement with Germany as early as 1934 and his policy of building economic ties was a way to ensure that war with Germany would be impossible because of opposition by powerful business interests inside Germany.[12] The problem with this testimony is that Krivitsky was a relatively low-level functionary and would not have been privy to Kremlin policy-making then or at any future date. The theory was also alluded to later in May 1939 by Soviet Chargé d'Affaires Georgei Astakhov who claimed that a German-Soviet alliance had been mooted at the same time as the Franco-Soviet agreement in 1935. Molotov is reported to have said in May of that year that, following on from the deal with France, improved German-Soviet relations were 'desired above all things [and were now] considered possible'. Feelers were put out through Schacht at the time but Hitler was not prepared to consider it, commenting that its time 'had not yet come', but left open the possibility of revisiting the concept when Stalin showed himself to be 'master of Russia'.[13] Gabriel Gorodetsky, by contrast, asserts that the weight of evidence shows that Stalin's strategy was always to promote collective security against the Nazi menace with the Western Powers and that this was not simply a smokescreen behind which overtures to the Germans were orchestrated. The level of expenditure of vast political and diplomatic efforts in pursuit of agreements with Britain and France outweighed all those devoted to similar ends with Germany.[14]

The German annexation of Bohemia and Moravia, the previously unoccupied areas of Czechoslovakia, on 15 March 1939 had finally convinced London and Paris that Germany was beyond appeasement and both capitals went flat-out to prepare for war. On 18 March, the

Soviets proposed a conference of themselves, Britain, France, Poland and Turkey to clarify their common response to German aggression. Britain, still viscerally opposed to any suggestion of Soviet leadership in negotiations, rejected the proposal as 'premature' but invited them instead to tripartite talks with Britain and France aimed at giving guarantees to Poland. Poland, however, made it abundantly clear that it wanted nothing to do with Soviet guarantees and scuppered the talks.

Britain now found itself backed into a bit of a corner and, still smarting from the humiliation of Hitler's unilateral trashing of the Munich Agreement, stood up, pushed back its shoulders, looked Germany in the eye and extended its guarantee to Poland. On 31 March 1939, Chamberlain told the House of Commons that 'in the event of any action which clearly threatened Polish independence, and which the Polish Government accordingly considered it vital to resist, His Majesty's Government would feel themselves bound at once to lend the Polish Government all support in their power'. The French government endorsed this pledge. Abwehr chief Wilhelm Canaris reported that news of Chamberlain's pledge caused Hitler to 'fly into a passion with features distorted by fury [as he] stormed up and down his room pounding his fists and spewing forth a series of savage imprecations'.[15]

The news that Britain was hardening its stance was met in Berlin by a reversal of its own policy towards the Soviet Union and galvanised it into rescuing negotiations. Göring was first to suggest a 'temporary association with Moscow' and Hitler warmed to the idea, instructing Ribbentrop to 'pursue negotiations.' Ribbentrop was knocking at an open door when he put it to Molotov that Britain's whole foreign policy revolved around pushing Germany into a war with Britain's true *bete noir*; the communists. Stalin's innate sense of paranoia supported the idea and he had interpreted Chamberlain's guarantee as a purely hostile Anglo-Polish move against them. Ever since Munich, Germany had been pushing for a strengthening of economic ties with the Soviet Union that had been underpinning German-Soviet relations since the collapse of Lipetsk and it was by building on this that they hoped to conclude a mutually advantageous deal that would stabilise political relations between the countries while the Polish question was resolved. Talks began again on 17 April and had progressed sufficiently by mid-May for Molotov, now the Soviet Foreign Minister, to declare his satisfaction, but he wanted an economic deal to precede any political declaration. Well used to Soviet ploys and machinations whose ultimate purpose was shrouded in obfuscation, the Germans hesitated while trying to decipher Soviet motivations.

Hoping to impress the newly-installed Molotov, on 5 May Schnurre tried to progress the talks by promising that previously blocked Soviet orders from the Czech Škoda works, now under German control, would be expedited. This was not a matter of great urgency but rather a gesture of German willingness to expand economic relations. The Soviet Chargé d'Affaires Georgei Astakhov, however, showed little gratitude by pointing out that it was German hostility that had blocked the deal after 15 March and it was they who had been responsible for the deterioration in relations in the first place. At this stage the German advances were not taken sufficiently seriously for them to be brought to the attention of Stalin. When Ernst von Weizsäcker, State Secretary at the *Auswärtiges Amt*, followed up by tempting Astakhov with a list of desirable items that would become available to the Soviets if trade was improved, the matter did reach the Kremlin but Molotov was quick to damp down expectations of a favourable Soviet response. Should any enthusiasm for closer German ties shown by Astakhov become known it could be dismissed as his own private initiative, leaving the Kremlin free to distance itself from any accusation of double-dealing while it was negotiating with the British and French although it was well known that Soviet diplomats worked within strict constraints.[16] This allowed the Kremlin to sound out German intentions without committing itself and gave people like Ribbentrop a direct, if unofficial, line to Molotov.

Trade between Germany and the Soviet Union in early 1939 had already been extensive but clearly the German initiative was about more than the export of consumer goods. The Soviets could potentially supply cotton, manganese ore, chrome arrant, phosphate, asbestos and wood as well as wheat and oil, all of which would be denied Germany from elsewhere through naval blockade in the event of war with Britain. In return German industry had access to the Trans-Siberian railway for transportation of their exports to and imports from the Middle and Far East. There was a multitude of business and political contacts at every level of government and commerce. The Soviet economy underpinned that of the whole of Germany's, in much the same way that the US underpinned that of Britain, and Stalin seemed eager to support the German economy throughout the anticipated long duration of its conflict with the West. It seemed logical to support the Germans which would even up the balance of economic and military power and thereby prolonging any war that might break out between them and Britain and France.

The British Chiefs of Staff had reacted to the German occupation of Prague by making an inventory of British commitments and comparing it with their military capabilities. The conclusions of their report to Cabinet highlighted major disparities, especially if conflicts were to break out in multiple theatres. Their advice to government was to pursue the triple alliance idea between Britain, France and the Soviet Union against Germany. The French had been informed by their ambassador to Moscow, reacting to the breakdown of Soviet-German talks, that the Soviets might be tempted to retreat into isolation with the next most likely move as coming to an understanding with Germany 'on the basis of a partition of Poland and the Baltic States'.[17] The Soviets, for their part, were suspicious of every move the Western Allies made since the Rhineland Crisis of 1936 which had convinced them that their sole agenda was to keep Hitler's focus on Eastern Europe with the unspoken assumption that it would lead to an inevitable showdown between Germany and the Soviet Union. The strategic incompetence of the Western Allies had been further highlighted by the fact that they had rejected the possibility of holding Germany on a well-defended Czech border only to throw down the gauntlet to Germany months later with a guarantee to Poland which found them in a hugely inferior position militarily.

The German diplomats continued their efforts to placate the Soviets by succeeding in lowering the level of all anti-Bolshevik rhetoric and propaganda in Germany in an effort to regain their trust. In May von der Schulenburg told von Weizsäcker that he believed the Soviets were holding out for something more than a trade deal and that, in order to progress talks, a political gesture was required. He was concerned about the Soviets using any political proposals as a bargaining tool to play off Germany against the Western Allies. For the Soviet Union there was little to choose between Germany and the Western Allies both politically and in terms of which to choose as the best hope for the security of its borders. Ideally Stalin would like to sit back and watch Western Europe fall apart in war while he waited to step in later and pick up the pieces. Only through chaotic readjustment of the status quo could he achieve his goal of pan-European communism.

Moscow had low expectations of Britain but, watching Göring's man Birger Dahlerus' to-ing and fro-ing between London and Berlin, its confidence that Britain would oppose Hitler almost disappeared completely. It fed into the enduring Soviet suspicion that Britain, especially, was trying to 'prod Germany to take action against the east [and] direct aggression exclusively against [the Soviet Union]'. It was this fear that caused the Soviets to continuously escalate their demands for ever-higher levels of military commitment and abandonment of the appeasement strategy. Gorodetsky asserts that the single most important aspect of Soviet policy after 1933 was to counter the threat of a combined British, French and German offensive against it and this underpinned its every diplomatic twist and turn as it tried to promote divisions within the ranks of its opponents.[18]

In early August, Hitler decided to outbid Britain for the Soviets' affections and opened talks, led by the German ambassador von der Schulenburg, a keen advocate of Bismarckian diplomacy, to negotiate a declaration of Soviet neutrality in the event of a German attack against Poland. Stalin had little faith in assurances given by either Germany or Britain and reverted to a policy of '*peredyshka*' which has a range of meanings in translation but essentially meant 'finding time and space to take stock of the situation and prepare for action'. Time, in this context meant putting off the inevitable for as long as possible by whatever means were at hand, space meant a territorial barrier against Germany and preparations centred around boosting military production. Negotiations with Germany had been given a fillip at a critical moment by the appointment of Molotov in place of the anti-German Litvinov. When the succession was announced on 3 May, a circular had gone out from the Kremlin describing the 'serious conflict between . . . Molotov . . . and Litvinov'.[19] Molotov and Litvinov, who often called his successor a fool, had harboured an enduring loathing for each other but it was Molotov, with an almost brutal commitment to hard work and fundamental Bolshevik principles, who was closer to Stalin and would now play an essential role in relations with Germany. He was one of the few members of the Politburo who was able to stand up to Stalin and calmly hold fast to his argument in the face of his bullying.

The French abandoned any hope they might have had for Polish acquiescence to cooperation with the Soviets and this was confirmed by Litvinov who thought Poland would not change its attitude until it 'received a direct blow'.[20] Daladier was rapidly losing patience with Poland as he saw France being impaled on its hasty approval of Chamberlain's 31 March guarantee. He angrily declared that the Poles were leading France 'to ruin' but there was even less confidence that the Soviets would 'draw other people's chestnuts out of the fire' as Stalin had put it on 10 March. Even so, the French press toned down its criticism of the Soviets to allow space for some improvement in relations as war clouds darkened. The French Foreign Minister Georges Bonnet offered immediate aid and assistance 'if the Soviet Union, in support of Poland and Romania, were attacked by Germany' which caused nothing but consternation in London. Things went from bad to worse when Litvinov was removed. It was read in the West as, at best, a move towards neutrality or, at worst, a realignment of Soviet foreign policy in favour of Germany. In reality, it is just as likely that his demise was to do with domestic Kremlin politics as it was about his foreign policies but, it is clear that with Molotov's appointment, Stalin was taking a more personal role in negotiations. Whatever the case, Molotov was quick to reassure the British and French that his appointment did not signal any change 'unless other states changed [their policies]'. There was certainly no immediate change in Soviet foreign policy. Even though Germany continued to ply Moscow with entreaties of friendship there is no record of any noticeable change in Moscow's responses to it at least until August.

On 17 April, the same day that Litvinov presented his plan for a Soviet-French-British alliance against Germany, the Soviet Ambassador to Berlin, Georgei Merekalov, and von Weizsäcker met and their discussion throws light on when Stalin had made up his mind to strike a deal with Nazi Germany. The suggestion is that Stalin was playing a double game by tempting Germany into a deal while offering the Western Allies a different solution. Von Weizsäcker's memorandum of the discussion is said to have argued strongly for a broad rapprochement between Germany and Soviet Russia but this may have been little more than wishful thinking on the part of German diplomats and an attempt to nudge Hitler and Ribbentrop towards an alliance since Merekalov, in his telegram to Moscow covering the discussions, says only that 'there exists for Russia no reason why [Germany] should not live with us on a normal footing' and his account focusses on the release of arms from the Škoda factory.[21] It is clear, however, from other documents that Merekalov held a brief for promoting German-Soviet trade and reinvigorating negotiations in light of the cancellation of Schnurre's January trip but there is insufficient corroborating evidence to support the claim that the meeting heralded the beginning of a process leading directly up to the signing of the Molotov-Ribbentrop pact in August.

At this point, it is worth looking at what other factors might have influenced Soviet attitudes to Germany in the late 1930s. There is evidence from the Moscow show trials to indicate that as early as December 1935, Trotsky had reached an agreement with Hess, who was a member of the Nazi Party but not a member of the German government, that established a framework for what was to follow. Trotsky agreed on a 'generally favourable attitude' towards collaboration especially in the area of Germany being granted concessions for industrial exploitation of Soviet timber and mineral resources and arrangements for cooperation in 'enterprises of the war industries'.[22] The implication is that, at this point, Trotsky was acting independently of Soviet foreign policy by talking directly to the Nazis and offering arrangements that might become possible if there was a change of leadership in the Soviet Union. This is an example of the complexity of negotiations between the two countries where on the German side there was clear water between the strategies of the Nazis and the *Auswärtiges Amt* while for the Soviets, Stalin's policies were often at odds with the more ideological ambitions of the Soviet Communist Party.

April 1937 had been a time of crisis for the Soviet leadership as a number of high-ranking members of the Central Committee began confessing to their part in the planning of a coup d'état against the government. While it has been commonly held that much evidence in the trials was contrived for political purposes so that Stalin could eliminate his rivals and that all defendants were innocent of the charges brought against them and all confessions were fabrications, there is a great deal presented by the revisionist historian Grover Furr in his book *Leon Trotsky's Collaboration with Germany and Japan* that concentrates on first-hand testimony of Trotsky's collaborators and suggests that there was indeed a conspiracy with Trotsky at its head.[23] He was accused, in absentia, in each of the three show trials of collaborating with German Nazi Intelligence in Spain while others such as Tukhachevsky and Bukharin were charged with conspiring with Germany and Japan. Radek explicitly identified Trotsky as having been the driving force behind the May revolts in Barcelona that were seen as a testing ground for similar actions to unseat Stalin in the Soviet Union.

Giving evidence in trials of 1938, Krestinsky, a former ambassador to Germany, claimed that Trotsky had formed an illegal organisation as far back as 1922 that had clandestine negotiations with von Seeckt to offer espionage and intelligence services in return for 250,000 gold marks a year as financial support for his factional battles within the Soviet Communist Party. A number of other accused at the trials corroborated Krestinsky's evidence which, if taken at face value, confirms that Trotsky had been secretly working with the Germans, and indeed the Japanese, against the Soviet government for many years. From his Mexican exile Trotsky, a careful and calculating operator, must have been confident that Stalin was vulnerable and that change was possible in the Soviet Union because, in June 1937, he sent a telegram to the Soviet Central Executive Committee challenging its members to reject Stalin's leadership and offering himself as a new leader. When Stalin was shown the telegram, he scrawled over it 'Ugly Spy' which, again if take at face value, indicates that Trotsky's collaboration with the Germans was well known to him.

During his trial in 1937, Tukhachevsky admitted to the judge Budyonny that Trotsky had called on him to organise an armed uprising in Leningrad and that the German Luftwaffe would support him. Milch is reputed to have confirmed this by telling him that he could 'count on serious help from our side'.[24] Radek claims that he received a letter from Trotsky in April 1934 in which he wrote that 'the advent of fascism to power in Germany basically changes the whole situation. It means the near prospect of war.' Trotsky had no doubt that war would result in defeat for the Soviet Union and, said Radek, welcomed that end as the means of creating the conditions for counter-revolution.[25]

On 25 May, to test the new Soviet negotiator, the British and French offered the Soviets a limited mutual assistance pact which they privately thought to be sufficiently nuanced to avoid any real commitment but Molotov rejected out of hand this 'paper delusion' and a week later presented his own ideas for 'well defined commitments and . . . guarantees for all the states between the Baltic and Black Sea [and] the conclusion of a military agreement within the shortest possible time specifying in detail the commitments of the contracting parties'.[26]

British negotiations with the Soviet Union were severely compromised by Francis Herbert King, a cypher clerk in the British Foreign Office. King's role was to encrypt communications between London and foreign diplomats, the contents of which would inform exchanges between governments but which necessarily contained information that was extremely confidential. King was a paid informer for the Soviet Union which then passed on selected intelligence to Berlin as it saw fit. It may be said that in some cases, British government strategy was available to Moscow and Berlin through their 'reliable source' before it had even left London. Naturally, having access to British government negotiating positions, both the Soviet Union and Germany were well placed to engineer their own strategies to counter them. King had leaked details about the Anglo-French proposals to the Soviets as early as 19 April.[27] This arrangement also allowed Moscow to feed misinformation to Berlin on the strength of it having been received from their 'reliable source' which they had done by suggesting that Romania had agreed to allow passage of Soviet troops in time of war in exchange for confirming Romanian possession of Bessarabia. The lack of any documentary evidence for such an agreement suggests that it was a ploy by Moscow to encourage Berlin back to the negotiating table.[28]

The British ambassador in Moscow, Sir William Seeds, and his French counterpart, Jean Payart, presented Potemkin with a joint proposal, much favoured by Chamberlain, based on the League of Nations Article 16 which stated that 'Should any Member of the League resort to war in disregard of its covenants under Articles 12, 13 and 15, it shall *ipso facto* be deemed to have committed an act of war against all other Members of the League'. Moscow rejected the proposal and came back with their own based on guarantees to the Baltic states and Soviet demands for the right to intervene militarily if there was a perceived threat to Soviet security. Chamberlain saw this as sacrificing the Baltic States to Soviet control which would not play well in Washington. This issue of 'indirect aggression' came to the fore in June when Germany signed non-aggression pacts with Estonia and Latvia. Halifax was getting quite annoyed with Soviet attitudes and claimed that the 'Russian business . . . frays everybody's nerves'.[29] Eventually Britain agreed to a secret protocol that would meet Soviet demands and agreed to send a military mission to Moscow for talks.

On 15 June Britain sent Robert Strang, who had been the British chargé in Moscow in the early 1930s, to act as Seeds' unofficial ambassadorial assistant to negotiate directly with Moscow but it was soon clear that he had gone with instructions not to give ground but to actually take back concessions made in earlier talks. The proposal included Article 16 of the League Covenant and it is no wonder that Stalin stood firm against such terms. Strang's visit may well have been the catalytic moment in which Soviet policy turned decisively in favour of Germany. Stalin replied to Strang by demanding a free hand in the Baltic in return for a guarantee to Poland and Romania. As early as April, France had indicated that it was willing to consider such an arrangement but Stalin knew that none of these terms would be acceptable to Britain. While Chamberlain still saw an alliance with the Soviets as vital to prevent them lining up alongside the Germans, the Baltic States would never agree to submit to what would, in practice, be Soviet domination and both Poland and Romania would refuse point blank to allow Soviet troops across their borders under any circumstances. Molotov, however, left open the door to further talks but these dragged on endlessly, bogged down in arguments over detail with the Soviets now firmly in control of the agenda. Taking fright, Estonia and Latvia signed non-aggression pacts with Germany who immediately moved in and began fortifying their borders.

In tandem with Strang's mission, Stalin was also negotiating with Germany. He offered neutrality in the event of a German attack on Poland if he could be allocated a share of the spoils. Any sort of agreement with the Soviets was unpalatable to Hitler, but he was forced into it out of necessity and whilst it did not diminish his antipathy, he chose to distance himself from direct involvement and, even amongst his close confidants, rarely discussed the subject of economic relations with the Soviets. The negotiators, however, had powerful allies. Both Göring's Luftwaffe and Admiral Erich Raeder's Kriegsmarine were hungry for all the Soviet pig iron, chrome, and manganese that satisfied their near-insatiable appetite for steel, and manufacturing industry was doing very nicely selling the Soviets outdated products which, because of their antiquity, could not be easily sold elsewhere. The continuing supply of Soviet wheat to counteract any Western naval blockade was a powerful incentive to Germany. Ribbentrop was pleased to find himself at the forefront of European diplomatic affairs passing back and forth between Berlin and Moscow which fed his voracious ego.

In his role as Foreign Minister Ribbentrop had developed his own concept of foreign policy that complemented that of his Führer. He would make those uncomfortable decisions that Hitler knew had to be made but could not bring himself to. For Ribbentrop, the great obstacle to German ambitions was Britain and his focus became the creation of a wide-ranging bloc, including Italy, Japan and even the Soviet Union, that excluded it. Only by isolating Britain, he believed, could Germany achieve its goal of becoming a world power. The coaxing of the Soviet Union into a pact with Germany was one part of this overall strategy. Often derided as a cipher and sycophant and mocked for his unbearable arrogance, Ribbentrop was much more subtle and able than he has been given credit for. His strategy towards the Soviet Union was aimed at thwarting Britain's traditional efforts to play its 'balance of power' game in Europe and thereby bring pressure to force concessions to Germany's colonial ambitions. At the same time his diplomatic initiative, pursued without any consultation with the Wehrmacht, would please Hitler by further establishing political supremacy over the anti-Bolshevik General Franz Halder whose opposition to Hitler's wider ambitions was irksome to say the least.

Elsewhere, on 15 Jube Astakhov had met with Herr Dragunov, the Bulgarian Minister, when their discussions touched on the possibility of a Soviet non-aggression pact with Germany. This may have been another deliberate ploy by Astakhov to send an unofficial but meaningful message to Berlin from Moscow in a roundabout way or it may have been no more than his own personal initiative to gauge the German response but, in any event, Dragunov did relay that information to the *Auswärtiges Amt*. Von der Schulenburg impressed upon Molotov on 28 June the desire of Germany to improve relations but while Molotov listened attentively there was still no official response. It was not until 24 July when Schnurre, Foreign Office Official Walther Schmidt,

Astakhov and Evgeny Babarin, the head of the Soviet Trade Delegation, eventually discussed economic ties that would pave the way for future political alliances. Schnurre proposed a three-stage programme for the normalisation of relations alongside trade, credit, cultural and political discussions. Astakhov reported that Schnurre had assured him that Germany was willing to come to an understanding 'on all questions'.[30]

Evidence suggests that it was not until July 1939 that both Germany and the Soviet Union began to plan seriously for closer ties. On the 7th of that month, in a move that signalled a crucial German commitment to rapprochement, they offered 200 million Reichsmarks worth of credit to finance a Soviet-German trade agreement which Trade Minister Anastas Mikoyan received with 'great interest'.[31] All the impetus for agreement was now coming from the German side while the Soviets calmly waited to see what else might be on offer. They responded by agreeing to more trade talks in Berlin which Ribbentrop used as an unofficial channel to Moscow.

As a dominant leader in an authoritarian regime, Stalin might have assumed that Hitler used his position to control all aspects of German policy just as he did with Soviet policy but in reality, and it was something that Stalin did not appreciate until it was too late, there were two forces vying for control of German foreign policy. Hitler was either unable or thought it too much trouble to challenge the position of the *Auswärtiges Amt* in relation to trade negotiations with Moscow which was one of the reasons that German political and economic strategies were often out of alignment. When Molotov spoke with Schnurre he was assured by the German that he spoke for Hitler and Ribbentrop but that was far from the case. This was mirrored to some extent by Astakhov appearing to show enthusiasm for closer ties with Germany which was some way from the official Kremlin position. Schnurre, however, had laid the foundations for closer ties between the two countries and Astakhov was clear that the Germans would take every opportunity to 'let us understand their readiness to change their policy towards [the Soviet Union]'.[32]

During the years since Hitler's elevation to the Chancellorship of Germany, Soviet foreign policy had been directed towards reaching an agreement with the Western Powers to contain German expansionism but the eventual collapse, in August 1939, of negotiations to create a triple alliance would demand a rethink of that strategy. Just how serious the three countries had been about forging the alliance has been debated at length. Soviet documents indicating a real desire on their part for a deal are supported by French diplomatic cables from their Moscow embassy at the time[33] but Britain and France had, at

163

no time since the October Revolution, pursued anything other than a confrontational attitude to the Bolshevik regime despite occasional trade agreements. When it came to discussions in the summer of 1939, the British were a little more inclined towards cooperation but hesitated to get down to details because, as Sir Alexander Cadogan put it, 'we should very soon have to disclose the emptiness of our cupboard'.[34] Sir Robert Vansittart, however, argued that British, French and Soviet interests were identical. His view was that if they were not careful Hitler would pick them off one after the other and it was time that the policy of appeasement came 'to a deservedly inglorious end'. He realised the urgency when he wrote 'we practically boycotted [the Soviets] during 1938. We never . . . endeavoured to establish close contact with them, and this fact accounts for the gradual drift towards isolation that is going on in Russia. That fact and that tendency we ought to correct and correct soon.'[35] The British sought to place the blame for failure of the talks on the Soviet Union but it was clear from their own analysis that the Soviet side had made serious alliance proposals with precise, reciprocal undertakings which the British government was reticent to entertain. The French were annoyed by British failure to acknowledge that they had been more receptive to Soviet proposals.[36]

What were the Soviets to make of it all and on which side would they come down? Molotov thought the Anglo-French negotiators 'crooks and cheats', but, at the same time, did not really know what to make of the new German initiative.[37] He was new to the job and careful not to make any mistakes that might cost him his life. Both the Axis Powers and the Western Allies would have to consider the position of the Soviets very carefully in any future decisions, and both held out the hand of friendship to them. Firstly, however, Germany tested the water with Britain by sending Helmuth Wohlthat to see Sir Horace Wilson in London on 26 July to see if the British would be interested in a non-aggression treaty. The British were, indeed, interested in talking about the subject. Their terms would be a German hands-off policy towards the British Commonwealth and a continuation of trade and in return they would withdraw their interest in the Danzig question, in effect abandoning Poland. Wilson insisted that all discussions would have to be conducted in strict secrecy because, after Prague, British public opinion would not stand for any further exhibition of appeasement. The British Foreign Secretary, Lord Halifax, sent a message to Hitler via the Swedish go-between Birger Dahlerus to say that Britain would urge the Poles to exercise restraint but made no such request of Hitler. Naturally nothing constructive came of these talks with neither side taking them at all seriously. They did, however, have a galvanising effect on Stalin when news of the talks was leaked to the press.

Molotov chose to play his cards very close to his chest and waited to hear what each of his suitors had to say. He was not so easily convinced and did not immediately accept the proposed plan preferring to continue talks with both Germany and the Western Powers but by 28 July he had started to show a preference for the Germans. He welcomed an improvement in economic relations but only if it could be shown that they were sincere and really want to improve political relations with the Soviet Union.

The Western Allies had belatedly roused themselves to make some effort to influence events and sent a joint Anglo-French delegation to Moscow in August headed by the extravagantly named Admiral Sir Reginald Aylmer Ranfurly Plunkett-Ernie-Erle-Drax with the French General Joseph Doumenc. They landed from the steamship *City of Exeter* at Leningrad on 10 August. The Soviets were neither impressed by names nor by the total lack of authority of any of the delegates to enter into meaningful negotiations. The mission had been designed to be no more than a show of Western solidarity by the British and Drax had been instructed by Chamberlain to 'go very slowly . . . watching the progress of the political negotiations and keeping in very close touch with [London]' and drag out the talks and do no more than disrupt the Soviet-German negotiations since the 'House of Commons had pushed him further than he had wished to go'.[38] The French, by comparison, had been sent to Moscow with full negotiating powers and instructed to return with a signed agreement.[39]

The British-French military mission arrived in Moscow on 12 August and Stalin instructed Voroshilov how to handle them. 'Ask them whether they have full powers to sign a military convention,' he said 'and if they say no ask them why they have bothered to come at all.' If the delegates answered yes then Voroshilov was to ask them what their plans were to defend their allies against German aggression. If there were plans then it would be necessary for the delegates to explain how they would guarantee the passage of Soviet forces through Poland and Romania because if that was not agreed upon then they should be under no illusions that the whole strategy was 'doomed to failure'. Under no circumstances was Voroshilov to permit the delegates to inspect any Soviet defence installations. Stalin had made sure that the talks would fail by making demands that were certain to be rejected. He was convinced that the Germans were now willing to give him what he wanted in relation to Poland, the Baltic States and south-east Europe. Most analysts of Stalin's strategy now believe that his dealings with the British and French were designed simply to exert pressure on Hitler to expedite his agreement to a non-aggression pact and, indeed, evidence suggests that it achieved exactly that.[40]

The delegates met Voroshilov on 14 August but the first thing the Soviets wanted to know was whether the Poles would agree to allow the passage of Soviet troops and, of course, despite prevarication, obfuscation and vague expression of hopes that the matter could be sorted out in due course, the answer was clearly 'no'. When Voroshilov realised that the delegation had come empty-handed it was a simple matter to embarrass them by asking Drax for details and assurances they knew could not be given and so were able to wind down the talks and adjourn them 'indefinitely'.[41]

Berlin had been apprised of this mission as early as 21 July, long before it had set out, through its 'reliable source [King]' even before Seeds, who received his instructions on the 25th. As a result, the Germans stepped up their own negotiations with the Soviets that were taking place in Berlin ostensibly over a trade-credit arrangement. Eager to conclude a wider deal, Berlin made significant concessions over territorial issues in order to outbid Britain and France for the prize of a Soviet alliance. In early August the Germans insisted to Moscow that they had limited interest in the Baltic or Ukraine and even said they would be ready to see eastern Poland come under Soviet occupation but progress with any discussion on these matters could only be made as long as there was no military or political agreement between the Soviet Union and the Western Powers. The pressure for a Soviet-German agreement at this stage was all coming from Berlin and all Molotov would say was that Moscow was 'interested', no doubt waiting to see what further inducements Berlin might be ready to offer.[42] Berlin knew from their 'reliable source' that Chamberlain had moved his position on the vital issue of 'indirect aggression', a notoriously vague concept that allowed for a range of interpretations and one that Seeds had tried to clarify in a telegram to Halifax on 29 July. They were therefore able to modify their own approach and move smartly when von der Schulenburg met Molotov on 15 August. Previously, on 7 August, Stalin had learned of rumours circulating in the German military that plans had been laid down to invade Poland on any day after 25 August and of Hitler's attempt to make personal contact with Chamberlain, this intelligence coming probably through the German diplomat and Soviet agent Rudolf von Scheliha who had extensive contacts in the higher echelons of the German military and government and worked in the German embassy in Warsaw. While this report emanated from gossip rather than any leaked official decision, it prompted the Soviets to take a more urgent approach to talks.[43]

Having finished his military plans for the invasion of Poland, Hitler was anxious to conclude both an economic and a political pact which would forestall any Soviet military intervention. Ribbentrop met Astakhov on 3 August and insisted that Germany was serious about a deal but first required a firm official statement from Moscow that it was equally committed. In a memo dated 10 August Schnurre wrote 'We had noted with satisfaction that the Soviet Government was anxious to continue the conversation regarding the improvement of Soviet-German relations'. He assured Astakhov that even in the event of a solution by force of arms German interests in Poland were quite limited, and they did not at all need to collide with Soviet interests of any kind. As a gesture of goodwill, however, Moscow would also have to immediately cut off all ongoing talks with France and Britain. The Soviets took their time to respond but eventually did so by terminating talks with Drax and Doumenc. It was not a difficult decision since Ribbentrop had made it clear that the Soviets would be amply rewarded by territorial gains in the Baltic and eastern Poland and all questions could be settled 'to the complete satisfaction of both parties'.[44] Hitler sent a telegram to Stalin saying that Ribbentrop would come to Moscow personally to discuss the details with Molotov. When Stalin replied enthusiastically in the affirmative, Hitler at the Berghof slammed his fist on the table and cried 'I have them! I have them!'[45]

Molotov, having concluded that the Germans were under extreme time pressure and so playing a weak hand, demanded three conditions. Firstly, both parties had to settle a trade and credit agreement, secondly, they must conclude a non-aggression pact and finally, they must create a secret protocol that laid down the interests of each party. Existence of this secret protocol were first revealed by one of the German negotiators, Friedrich Gauss, at the Nuremberg Trials and the original documents were uncovered in the Soviet archives in 1989.[46] In terms of a trade agreement, which the Soviets wanted before anything else, Germany was cautious and tried to extract terms that furthered their rearmament goals by initially exporting only those machine tools and equipment that would expedite production of the raw materials they wanted to import and only afterwards did they want to supplying goods and materials of direct benefit to the Soviet economy.

On 16 August Ribbentrop told Molotov that Germany was ready to sign a Non-Aggression Pact, contingent upon the completion of the economic agreement. This effectively ensured that the negotiations with the British and French would not be resumed. Schnurre and

Babarin duly signed an economic treaty in Berlin three days later that, in terms of the volume of goods traded, was nine times greater than the deal struck in 1936. At first sight it appeared that the agreement was hugely in favour of the Soviet Union which questioned why Hitler would have agreed to such a one-sided deal. The Soviets agreed to supply 180 million Reichsmarks-worth of raw materials on payment for 120 million Reichsmarks-worth of German industrial goods to be supplied over a two-year period. They would get, in addition, 200 million Reichsmarks of credit, repayable over seven years at 4.5 per cent interest, to cover the difference in raw material purchases and for factory equipment, installations, machinery and machine tools, ships, vehicles and other means of transport.

The credits, however, were not quite as generous as Molotov liked to boast, given that they did little more than balance out the repayment of credit owed to Germany from the 1936 credit agreement. Despite Stalin's view that the Soviets would dictate terms to Germany, it was the Germans who benefitted the most from the agreement. Much of the industrial machinery sold to the Soviets, who had been unable to trade in it with other industrialised nations since 1932, benefitted German manufacturers since it allowed them clear out redundant and outmoded machine tools and replace them with the next generation of technology. The coal from the Ruhr coalfields was actually surplus to German requirements and unsaleable elsewhere so again was handed over at little cost to the German economy. Almost as soon as the ink was dry, Schnurre proposed a rescheduling of the terms, postponing German payments which allowed it to make more investment in its own arms manufacturing industries and in return, Germany would aid in the construction of new industrial plants in the Soviet Union over a five-year period. The economic agreement of 1939 and the continuing trade negotiations and treaties were actually of more significance to the German war effort than the Non-Aggression Pact that followed. In 1939, Germany was self-sufficient only in coal and food. It produced only about one third of its oil, one of the most important wartime resources, and the deal stipulated 90,000 tons of Soviet mineral oil each year.

As a last-gasp effort, the French agreed not to oppose the passage of Soviet troops across Poland but they had got news from Warsaw on 19 August that their attempts to persuade the Poles to agree had failed. It is believed that a telegram conveying this to Voroshilov was deliberately delayed by Soviet Intelligence. When Vorishilov received it on 22 August, he knew that it was too late, with Ribbentrop already on his way to Moscow. He replied that the Poles showed contempt by refusing to take part in talks and the absence of any guarantee from them implied a denial of passage. Neither had he heard anything definite from the British about the issue. He did, however, send another note to say that 'Polish-Soviet cooperation would not necessarily be excluded' but that was never going to be enough.[47] Seeds went to speak to Molotov on 22 August but met only bad-tempered accusations of British meddling in Soviet affairs and negotiating in bad faith. He might have been more inclined to stay and argue his case if a vital telegram emanating from Washington had not been delayed. The US Embassy in Moscow had learned of Ribbentrop's impending visit which obviously suggested that a German-Soviet deal was close and told London on 18 August. Unfortunately, this information had come across the desk of Francis King and he was able to delay its transmission to the Moscow embassy until after Seeds' meeting with Molotov.

Having played both sides against the middle, the Soviets had made their choice. British and French negotiators were humiliated. On 22 August Chamberlain proposed that the British Parliament pass an Emergency Powers (Defence) Bill and sent a note to Hitler explaining that 'These steps were rendered necessary by the military movements which have been reported from Germany, and by the fact that apparently the announcement of a German-Soviet Agreement is taken in some quarters in Berlin to indicate that intervention by Great Britain on behalf of Poland is no longer a contingency to be reckoned with. No greater mistake could be made.' He called for direct negotiations between Germany and Poland. Hitler replied that 'Germany was prepared to settle the problem of Danzig and of the Polish Corridor by a very generous proposal, made once only, and by means of negotiations' and in reference to British military mobilisation, he added that 'in the event of such military measures being taken, I shall order the immediate mobilisation of the German armed forces'. The Soviets had seen enough. Long had they warned the British and French that there was another option on the table and now was the time to show it. On the following day, two Luftwaffe Fw 200 Condor aircraft left Berlin with a high-powered delegation on board.

On 23 August 1939, Ribbentrop, accompanied by about forty officials, advisors, photographers and translators, landed at Moscow's Khodynka airfield to a spectacular welcome before being driven to the former Austrian legation building which had been allocated to them during their stay. Very soon, Ribbentrop and von der Schulenburg were driven to the Kremlin where they were met by Stalin and Molotov. The importance of the meeting was clear to von der Schulenburg who, during the whole of his five years at the Moscow embassy, had never before laid eyes on the Soviet leader. Talks between the four men began immediately. Stalin believed that he held the stronger hand and opened with questions about 'spheres of interest'. Ribbentrop immediately conceded that Eastern Poland, Bessarabia, Finland, Estonia and half of Latvia would fall within the Soviet sphere. Stalin could hardly believe that he had got so much so soon and naturally asked for more. He called for the ports of Libau and Windau to be brought within the Soviet sphere of influence which essentially delivered the rest of Latvia. Ribbentrop had been given full negotiating powers but chose to consult Hitler. He returned to the table within half an hour and agreed. In a matter of minutes Stalin had been given the opportunity to regain almost all Soviet territories lost at the end of the First World War.

The rest of the talks dealt with the German position with Japan and the perceived weakness of Britain. Stalin said Britain 'was weak and only wished to have others fight for it'.[48] Other terms were agreed but an overenthusiastic preamble hurriedly concocted by Ribbentrop was watered down by Stalin who reminded the German that public opinion in both Germany and the Soviet Union would have to be carefully prepared to receive news that the two countries that had been 'for many years . . . pouring buckets of shit on each other' had now made up.[49] Talks ended with an alcohol-fuelled reception at which Stalin toasted Hitler's health and said that 'the Soviet Union would not betray its partner'. With that the Pact was signed. Its clauses included a guarantee of peace between both countries and a commitment that neither government would ally itself to or aid an enemy of the other. In addition to the publicly-announced terms, the treaty also included the Secret Protocol which defined the borders of Soviet and German spheres of influence.

The secret protocols of the Molotov-Ribbentrop Pact were actually known to many only days after the signing although their existence was initially denied by the Soviet Union. They were first mentioned in public at the trial of Rudolf Hess in March 1946, although Soviet objections meant that they could not be used as evidence, and published in the *Manchester Guardian* at the time but it was not until the original documents were released from Soviet archives in 1992 that their existence was admitted by Moscow. The Estonian military and Latvian diplomatic corps were aware as early as 26 August 1939 that the Pact had divided up the Baltic States into German and Soviet spheres of control although details were scarce. In early October, Stalin and Molotov actually told the Lithuanian Foreign Minister Juozas Urbšys and General Stasys Raštikis, the commander of the Lithuanian Armed Forces, about the secret terms in order to pressure them into accepting a mutual defence agreement with the Soviet Union. This may have been a mistake or just part of another Machiavellian Stalinist plot to keep the Germans on their toes but soon afterwards Molotov apologised to Ribbentrop for the indiscretion. It is hardly possible that rumours of the secret protocols did not reach Paris and London.

News of the Molotov-Ribbentrop Pact and the matter of the delayed telegram now brought to light the earlier intelligence supplied by Krivitsky, now a defector living in the US, that had predicted the Molotov-Ribbentrop Pact and was dismissed at the time as 'twaddle' and 'directly contrary to all our other information'.[50] When interviewed about his predictions, Krivitsky, who was listened to much more closely now, gave enough information for the British to identify King as a Foreign Office spy. King was arrested a few weeks later in September.

When the Anglo-French mission requested an urgent meeting, Voroshilov did not respond until 25 August when he apologised for the delay because he had been on a 'duck hunt' and regretted to inform them that talks could not continue because 'political conditions had changed'.[51] On the same day the Anglo-Polish Mutual Assistance Treaty was signed in London that contained promises of mutual military assistance between the nations if either was attacked by some other European country. It carried a secret protocol specifically stating that Britain would give assistance to Poland if attacked by Germany, but in the case of attack by other countries, the parties were required only to consult together on measures to be taken in common.

Within Hitler's overall scheme, the conclusion of the Russo-German Non-Aggression Pact represented the necessary precondition which enabled him to conduct his war against an isolated Poland but that was not necessarily his intention. The signing of the Pact was designed not to provoke war but a means of exerting pressure on the Poles to compromise on the Danzig question. Immediately after the Pact was signed, Germany sent a number of requests to Moscow, firstly to send a Soviet military mission to Berlin and, secondly, to place strong Russian troop concentrations along Poland's eastern frontier so that pressure from both east and west would coerce the Poles into realising the hopelessness of their position and accepting the German proposals.[52] The Soviet government had seen only two options: fight Germany now or fight it later. Stalin chose to fight later. It was not a question of whether Stalin trusted Hitler more than the Anglo-French; Stalin trusted no one. It was simply a question of buying time, which is exactly what Chamberlain had done at Munich.

Debate rages over whether it had been Stalin's strategy to form an alliance with Hitler from as early as the German-Soviet credit agreement of April 1935. Litvinov was clear when he had told von der Schulenburg in May 1935 that he hoped for a non-aggression treaty between Germany and the Soviet Union along the same lines as the one the Soviets had signed with France. However, if Stalin had always intended to form an alliance with Hitler, it does not explain why, in 1937, he eliminated those very elements, like Krestinsky and Karakhan, the Soviet ambassador to Turkey, most closely identified with a pro-German orientation of Soviet foreign policy while sparing those like Litvinov whose hostility to the Nazis was legendary. Neither does it explain why he also purged those Red Army officers who, according to their indictments, had been too close to the Germans. On the other hand, however, it was quite illogical for Stalin to endanger national security by purging the Red Army High Command if he had been contemplating war with Germany. It must be concluded that in 1937 Stalin had feared his internal enemies far more than his external ones, which left his policy towards Germany in something of a muddle. It was no clearer when faced with the reality of Germany's threat to Poland in the summer of 1939 that he had made much progress in this regard and it might be argued that it was, in fact, the abrupt realisation of the failure of his decade-long strategy of collective security and the catastrophe of his paranoid fears that had forced the Molotov-Ribbentrop Pact upon him.

The Soviets had finally abandoned all hope of collective security and struck a deal which they thought allowed them to make the most of their situation while keeping a number of options open. Hitler's true intentions could still not be known but if he chose to attack Poland and was successful without interference from the Western Allies then the Soviets were well placed to extend their influence west at minimal cost. If a wider conflict engulfed Europe, they would be able to remain neutral and would in the words of Molotov, '[pursue] new possibilities of increasing our strength, further consolidation of our positions, and further growth of the influence of the Soviet Union on international developments'.[53] Much would depend on the outcome of a German-Polish war.

In the early morning of 1 September 1939, sixty German divisions invaded Poland with an advance force consisting of more than 2,000 tanks supported by nearly 900 bombers and over 400 fighter planes. From East Prussia and Germany in the north, and Silesia and Slovakia in the south, German units quickly broke through Polish defences along the border and advanced on Warsaw in a huge encirclement attack. After some hesitation, Britain and France stood by their guarantee of Poland's border and declared war on Germany on

3 September 1939. Despite fighting tenaciously and inflicting serious casualties on the Germans, the Polish army was defeated within weeks. On 17 September the Polish government fled the country and after heavy shelling and bombing, Warsaw surrendered to the Germans on 27 September 1939.

The division of Poland was not the first article in the secret protocols on the Molotov-Ribbentrop Pact and in the last days of August some Red Army troops had actually been withdrawn from the Polish border, much to the consternation of Berlin. This suggests that, at the time, the Soviets had made no decision about moving into Poland. It was events that caused a shift in their attitude, especially a note from Ribbentrop to Molotov on 3 September virtually inviting the Soviets to occupy those parts of Poland that were within the Soviet sphere of influence as laid down by the Pact to prevent Polish forces from establishing a stronghold there.[54] However, this request, together with mounting evidence of a rapid Polish military collapse and lack of response from the Western Allies over the next few days, brought only a slow and tentative response. It was only on 9 September that Molotov announced that Soviet moves might be expected 'in the next few days'.

It was not at all clear to Moscow that occupation of eastern Poland was the correct action. If they marched in would the Western Allies, in the heated political atmosphere of war, having declared war on Germany go on, in a fit of righteous anger, and declare war on the Soviet Union also? They were still hedging their bets against a future war with Germany by hoping to avoid an irreversible split with the Western Allies. Having given a commitment to act, it was still another eight days before the Red Army actually crossed into Poland during which time the Soviets had removed the risk of Japan taking advantage by concluding an agreement with them to end their war in the East. There was still the small matter of justification for the attack, something that the Soviets felt necessary to explain to communist movements worldwide who might otherwise not understand an act of naked aggression in concert with fascist invaders. Molotov announced on Soviet radio on 17 September, '. . . the Polish state . . . has ceased to exist. Treaties concluded between the USSR and Poland have thereby ceased to operate . . . The Soviet Government can no longer [remain] neutral . . . Ukrainians and White Russians [in Poland] are left without protection.'[55] Given the destruction of Polish forces and the collapse of morale in the country, the Soviet occupation of all Polish territory east of the rivers Narew, Vistula and San was completed in less than a week. German and Soviet forces now faced each other across a common border which made it imperative that the Soviet Union

173

strengthen its defences. Central to this strategy was Lithuania which had an extensive border with East Prussia. A second Nazi-Soviet pact (the German-Soviet Boundary and Friendship Treaty) was signed on 28 September recognising the demarcation line separating the ethnic Polish regions from the predominantly non-Polish ethnic areas bordering the Soviet Union. This involved the transfer of some Soviet-occupied areas to Germany in return for Soviet control of Lithuania.

Chamberlain spoke of learning 'with indignation and horror' of the Soviet action but, despite Polish insistence, made no formal protest to Moscow. Both the British and French had found welcome relief from the exact wording of the Anglo-Polish Agreement of 25 August that had restricted Britain's commitment to Poland only in relation to an attack by Germany. Nothing in the agreement made reference to the Soviet Union. The French were quick to support a British decision not to declare war on the Soviet Union since all decisions should be 'determined by which would help most to achieve the common end of defeating Germany'. Now that a common border existed between Germany and the Soviet Union it was, in the opinion of Ambassador Seeds, 'only a matter of time before friction between them developed.' Churchill argued for renewed and strengthened relations with the Soviets.[56] This left the primary Allied war aim of protecting Poland devoid of any relevance since to pursue it would mean war with the Soviet Union.

As part of the September commercial agreement, around forty Soviet delegates went to Germany in October 1939 with a shopping list of technological goods. They were shown round by Ernst Udet, the Luftwaffe's Chief of Procurement and Supply, and Göring personally but not all were impressed by what was on offer. General Dmitry Gusev thought that, for instance, they were only being shown aircraft that were a generation behind those that the Luftwaffe were currently using. Apparently Udet was indignant at the suggestion and basically told the Soviets that if they didn't like the goods they could look elsewhere. At the Krupp works in Essen large areas of the factory they visited were shielded by huge tarpaulins and despite visiting all the major aircraft manufacturers they were not given access to jet-engine technology currently under development. It would have been clear to the Soviet delegates that they were being short-changed since their own aircraft industry was, in some instances, producing more advanced aircraft than the ones they were being offered.[57] The Soviets, evidently feeling not a little insulted, requested greater access to shipyards to see the latest in battleship design. It was clear to the Germans, however, that their own delegates in the Soviet Union were getting even less cooperation so there was little incentive to extend their hospitality. The much-anticipated supplies of food, especially, were very slow to materialise. Oil imports as well were far below the level agreed which spawned fears that grain supplies that would be vital for the German economy in 1940 could not now be relied upon.

At this point the Germans decided to re-focus attention on the trade agreement which did not seem to be working as planned. They proposed an increase in the volume of raw materials coming both from the Soviet Union and across its territories from third countries. In return they offered enhanced economic planning facilities, greater transfer of new technologies and more help with expanding the Soviet manufacturing base. When Schnurre went to Moscow, however, he was told that the Soviets wanted much more in the way of military hardware and access to the latest naval designs. This was an impossible demand given that Germany's military manufacturing industries were already working flat out producing equipment for the Wehrmacht.

A major stumbling block was over the cruisers *Lützow*, *Seydlitz* and *Prinz Eugen*, currently under construction in German shipyards, which the Soviets wanted to buy. Hitler agreed only to the *Lützow* sale but Göring put a price on it that was immediately rejected. Eventually an agreement would be reached at which point Stalin pointed out that he had effectively bought two cruisers. It is clear from his observation to the effect that he would have one extra ship and the 'expected enemy' would have one less that he was under no illusions as to where events were inexorably leading. Any further progress on the other two ships would depend on the Soviets sticking to the volumes of raw materials and food supplies agreed the previous September but the Soviets were digging their heels in over what they saw as the excessive cost of all industrial imports itemised in the same agreement.

A further agreement was reached on 11 February 1940 whereby the Soviet Union would send Germany 650 million Reichsmarks-worth of raw materials in exchange for 650 million Reichsmarks-worth of machinery, manufactured goods and technology. Transit rights were agreed for traffic on Soviet-controlled railway lines to and from Romania, Iran and Afghanistan. The Soviets would get the *Lützow* and plans of the battleship *Bismarck* and a large quantity of other naval weaponry. The new agreement, however, looked much more impressive on paper than it did in reality. As an example of how it worked in practice, the *Lützow* was delivered incomplete to the Leningrad shipyard in April 1940 where she was renamed the *Petrovpavlovsk*. With half of her guns missing and much of her superstructure incomplete she was not seaworthy until 1942 when she was peremptorily sunk in shallow water outside Leningrad harbour by German artillery. She would be raised a year later to take part in the final stages of the Second World War.

There is no evidence to show that, for Hitler, the Soviet Union posed a problem in the short term although there is ample evidence to indicate that a showdown with the communists on the Eurasian plains was the central tenet of his long-held ambitions. Up until the summer of 1940 it had been Western Europe that dominated his agenda and no offensive plan against the Soviet Union existed in the German General Staff. It was Halder who first raised the alarm on 23 May with reports of strong Russian troop movements in the Baltic States and to the south, opposite Bessarabia, and Wehrmacht chief General Alfred Jodl, echoed that concern a day later by noting in his diary that 'Russian troop assembly position in the east is threatening'. Hitler seemed unconcerned, believing that the Soviets would restrict their activities to Bessarabia, but he was wrong. From 25 May onwards the Soviets orchestrated a series of crises with Lithuania, Estonia and Latvia, all three of which were occupied and incorporated in the Soviet Union on 21 July 1940 precisely at the moment that Hitler had ordered a drastic demobilisation of the German army to return men to manufacturing industries.

Trade negotiations were clouded also by the Soviet Union's constant nibbling away at the geographic boundaries of influence laid down in September 1939. Every small encroachment seemed insignificant in itself such as the annexation of a strip of Lithuania along the Šešupė river and such incidents, whilst incurring swift rebukes from Berlin, seemed insufficient to risk a complete breakdown of relations but the accumulated effect was to slowly increase Soviet power in the Baltic at Germany's expense. The Soviets had concluded a Mutual Assistance Treaty with Lithuania in October 1939 which allowed 20,000 Soviet troops to be stationed in the country. On 14 June 1940, however, the Soviet Union accused Lithuania of violating the treaty and took control of its government departments, thereby incorporating the Lithuanian Soviet Socialist Republic into the Soviet Union. The Molotov-Ribbentrop Pact had stipulated that the area along the Šešupė would be within the German zone of influence but the Soviets swallowed it up along with all the rest of Lithuania and despite the Soviets offering Germany compensation, the matter became a running sore that defied resolution.

Further south, it was almost too much for the Germans to accept the Soviet occupation of Bessarabia and Northern Bukovina, between Romania and Ukraine, but the Soviets argued their historic claims to these areas above all else. It had been the possibility of Britain agreeing to peace with Germany after the rapid and unexpected collapse of France and the debacle of Dunkirk that focussed Stalin's mind on the likelihood of Hitler turning his attention east. It was therefore suddenly of the utmost importance to push the Soviet frontier as far west and south as possible. Stalin, too, anticipating an end to the war in the West, was preparing the ground for a new agreement with Germany over spheres of influence in the Balkans. To soften the blow of these annexations for Hitler, Stalin ordered a temporary increase in Soviet exports to Germany at reduced prices. Here again, Stalin misread the situation by thinking that trade deals influenced Hitler's strategic decisions. Far from creating a platform for peaceful renegotiation, Stalin's moves in Lithuania and the Balkans deepened Hitler's hostility to what he saw as a looming threat. The Balkan theatre now became the focus of a power struggle between Germany and the Soviet Union.

Romania had felt the effects of the capitulation of France who with Britain had been joint guarantors of its security, when on 26 June 1940 Molotov demanded the cession of Bessarabia, to which it had a long-standing claim, and Northern Bukovina. The Soviets were inching their way closer to the Bosporus and the Dardanelles. Romania panicked and threw itself at the mercy of Germany, asking for a security guarantee, but Ribbentrop advised them to accept the Soviet demands to avoid the situation spiralling out of control. The question of Bukovina was outside the 23 September agreement and was a serious provocation to Germany that Halder was quick to point out and Ribbentrop made representations to Molotov to protest. Northern Bukovina, he said, was too close to the Romanian oilfields and it was essential to scale down the provocation to 'prevent those area from becoming a theatre of war'.[58] Hitler, however, chose to tacitly accept the Soviet move, although not without serious reservations, in the interests of maintaining peace but it was probably the single most important incident that now alerted Hitler to the acute dangers posed by Soviet expansionism in the Balkans and he began to devise a strategy to counter it. While the Soviet occupation of Bessarabia went off without incident, Hungary chose now to press its claim to Northern Transylvania, resulting in a border stand-off between Romanian and Hungarian troops. Britain was helping to stir the pot by making a further move to engage the Soviets by offering talks over Iran. Germany felt the need to send a warning to Hungary and Bulgaria to back off Romania but the Balkans were now coming to the boil once again and the only victor there would be Britain, watching from the sidelines as the whole region threatened to go up in flames.

With a German invasion of the British Isles looking ever less likely, the immediate priority for Germany was for a peaceful reconstruction of the occupied countries, France, Belgium and the Netherlands, compared to which Soviet moves were seen as no more than an inconvenience and a minor threat to some raw material supplies especially from Finland. When the Soviets had invaded Northern Bukovina on 28 June 1940 there had been no response from Hitler to suggest that at that point a campaign against the Soviet Union was in the planning stages even though the move cut off German access to the Baltic countries. In fact in a review of military spending priority was given to the Luftwaffe and the Kriegsmarine which suggests that an attack against the Soviets was not on the agenda given that such a campaign would require preferential investment in the armoured land units. However, on 21 July 1940, Hitler concluded that British refusal to enter into peace talks was underpinned by the expectation of military aid coming from the US and the hope of the Soviet Union eventually switching allegiances and threatening Germany from the east. As a result, he asked Field Marshal Walter von Brauchitsch, the Commander-in-Chief of the Army, to submit plans for a campaign against the Soviet Union that would immediately seize enough territory so that the armaments plants in eastern Germany and the Romanian oil fields would be beyond the range of Soviet bombers. At the same time the German ground forces would be required to advance far enough to bring important production centres of the Soviet Union within striking distance of the Luftwaffe. The tentative invasion date was set for May 1941 and all plans were to be prepared under the utmost secrecy.

The first task directive, *Aufbau Ost* (Build-up East) called for a rapid concentration of forces in western Poland that would attack the Soviet Union regardless of the military situation in the West. It was vital that the Soviet Union was 'smashed in one fell swoop' which required that victory was achieved before the Russian winter set in. Two lines of attack were envisaged either side of the Pripyat Marshes. The first would be towards Kiev and the other across the Baltic States towards Moscow. A secondary operation would occupy the Baku oil fields. The Marcks Plan of 5 August stipulated that the focus of the attack was the food and raw-material producing areas of the Ukraine and the Donets Basin as well as the armament-production centres around Moscow and Leningrad. The principal objective was Moscow, the fall of which would lead to the disintegration of Soviet resistance.

During October 1940 the Operations Division completed a strategic survey which noted that the Red Army's numerical strength, the vast terrain to be covered, the adverse conditions of the Russian theatre and the necessity of defeating the Soviet Union with a minimum of delay raised a series of problems for which in many instances no fully satisfactory solutions could be found. On the other hand, ever since the Red Army had performed so badly during the campaign against Finland in the winter of 1939–40, the average German General Staff officer had a low opinion of the military potential of the Soviet Union.

At the end of June 1940, Hitler had instructed his staff to examine the possibilities of a campaign against the Soviet Union, but it was a full three weeks before he showed any interest. The Non-Aggression Pact had a clause that called for discussion of issues that were of mutual interest but Hitler had ignored that when he had launched his attack in Norway and Denmark in April 1940. Ribbentrop had managed to wriggle his way out of that one and persuaded the Soviets to restart the supplies of grain and oil that they had halted in protest but it was becoming an uncomfortable reality that the raw material supplies coming either from the Soviet Union or Soviet-controlled areas were vulnerable to Soviet 'blackmail'.

The Romanian Ploesti oilfields were a major worry for Hitler since supplies from there represented the mainstay of Germany's oil imports meaning that security of that region was of paramount importance and Britain would have to be prevented from establishing bases which could be used to launch air raids against the oilfields or gain a foothold in the Balkans to mount a land operation in that direction. In this regard the Soviet Union occupied a crucial position both as a supplier of oil itself and as the power nearest to Romania. Romania itself was at risk from Bulgaria, Hungary and the Soviet Union, all of whom were keen to take back those areas taken from them and incorporated into Romania at Versailles, and sent desperate pleas for German guarantees of help to which Hitler did not even reply. Hitler requested that the Soviets scale back their designs on Romania while Britain sent Sir Stafford Cripps to Moscow. The Romanians took stock and acquiesced to Germany terms for a new oil deal for which they had been clamouring.

The Soviet occupation of Northern Bukovina meant that exports from the Baltic upon which Germany depended were now also at risk. The Soviets had taken the terms of the Molotov-Ribbentrop Pact very seriously indeed and interpreted them in the fullest manner. Ribbentrop then had to make the best of seeing Rome and Moscow exchange ambassadors with the risk now of Italy flexing its muscles in the Balkans with consequences that could not be foreseen but which would probably be another destabilising influence that Germany could do without. It was clear from the start, however, that Molotov, with a

179

hundred Soviet divisions on his western borders, was going to play off Italy against Germany by seeking Italian support for the resolution of all Hungarian, Soviet and Bulgarian claims against Romania. Halder immediately increased the number of German divisions in the East.

It was at this point that it occurred to Hitler that Britain was actively provoking the unrest in the Balkans with the ambition to break the German-Soviet bonds. He had long pondered the question of why Britain had continued to fight after Dunkirk and concluded now that it was holding out with its last breath in the hope of drawing the Soviet Union into an anti-fascist alliance. For the first time, Hitler was not in control of the agenda. The situation was such that he could not see a clear way of attaining his next objective. Was Britain an enemy to be crushed or a weakened foe to be simply ignored? Expansion in the East remained his overriding ambition but a still-active and belligerent Britain threatened a war on two fronts which Hitler had been at such pains to avoid up until this point. His half-hearted threats to invade Britain never really came to anything after Göring's Luftwaffe, taught a lesson in aerial warfare by the RAF, changed its focus towards strategic bombing just at the moment it had gained a potentially decisive advantage in the fighter battles and let Britain off the hook in September, giving it just enough time to recover and continue its resistance.

Much given to favouring quick solutions to his problems, Hitler was not happy about the prospect of a long-drawn-out war with the British Empire and chose to believe that it could be brought to its senses and the peace table by stripping it of the only thing that was keeping it going. As long as the US could be kept out of the war, Britain's only hope was to make an alliance with the Soviet Union. This precipitated a decision that Hitler had not wanted to make at this time but one which he could no longer avoid. After consideration, he saw two alternatives. The first was to reinforce the relationship with the Soviet Union and endorse Ribbentrop's ambition of a continental bloc against Britain or alternatively smash the Soviets in a swift Blitzkrieg and deprive Britain of its last hope for salvation. The first option was becoming less attractive daily as the Soviets continued to manipulate the situation in the East whereas the second appealed immediately to his basic character that craved war but that would bring about the two-front war he feared.

Cripps went to Moscow in early July to try and persuade the Soviets to take control of the whole Balkan region to maintain the status quo there. It was a subtle move that appealed to Stalin. Hitler now responded positively to Romania by taking the initiative and control in the region by offering to guarantee its borders minus a few bits hived off to keep Hungary and Bulgaria quiet. He also brought a new piece onto the board by making overtures to Japan in the hope of distracting Britain by threatening its Far Eastern interests. In August, Molotov expressed satisfaction in improved relations with Britain and looked forward to unspecified 'successes' which, to German ears could mean only one thing: the Balkans. Still Germany did not refocus its armament programme towards land forces which suggested that it was not yet in the final stages of planning at attack against the Soviet Union.

When Italy let it be known that it harboured ambitions in Greece and Yugoslavia, the whole stability of the Balkans was once again put under extreme pressure and Germany gave the highest priority to preventing that. Hitler managed to divert Mussolini's attention towards North Africa which, for the moment, lowered the temperature but just as Italian meddling was averted, Hungary and Romania had another spat. Hitler forced them to the negotiating table but talks broke down after just eight days as Soviet troops roused themselves in Bukovina. Halder sent another ten divisions east with a view to eventual occupation of the Romanian oilfields. For the first time Soviet bullying in the region was met with a serious intent to oppose it as Soviet-German relations turned decidedly cool. And in the cold, dark forests of Scandinavia the temperature was poise to plummet.

Germany was desperate to preserve access to its source of nickel from Petsamo in Finland but Soviet troops were massing on the Finnish border. If war broke out between the Soviet Union and Finland the supply of nickel, almost as important to the German war economy as Romanian oil, would be interrupted. Hitler personally sanctioned the supply of arms to Finland and German alpine troops were despatched, ostensibly in transit to occupied Norway, but in reality to be in readiness to occupy Petsamo if necessary. Ribbentrop was furious about the Soviet menace to Finland and let Molotov know but he rejected Ribbentrop's complaints both over Finland and the Balkans with some disdain, signalling the beginning of the end of the relationship so loudly proclaimed by both men only months before. While Germany was still fighting the 'Battle of Britain' the Soviets were tirelessly nibbling away at German interests in the East. It was now a matter not of 'if' but 'how soon' Hitler would lose patience but winter was coming and the campaign season was ending. The Soviets, however, did not see it that way. They demanded a greater share of the Petsano nickel exports. Meanwhile Romania begged Germany for a division to be sent but Hitler would send only enough forces to protect the oilfields. Hitler turned to Spain and Vichy France for support against Britain but, fearing British reprisals, neither would commit.

Romania was experiencing a loss of territory that amounted to a third of its lands and resulted in the abdication of its ruler King Carol. German troops occupied the oilfields in October but crucially they did so without informing the Soviet Union and so had acted in violation of Article 3 of the Molotov-Ribbentrop Pact. The move also infuriated Mussolini who had his own plans for the region. The match had been struck.

The Italian invasion of Greece began on 28 October but within days the Italian army suffered reverses which saw Greek forces move deep into Albania, making it inevitable that Germany would be drawn in to rescue its ally. Britain now saw its chance to stake a claim and occupied Greek airfields, putting the Romanian oil fields within range of RAF bombers. Bulgaria now took on a more central role. With German troops in Romania the road to Greece now lay through Bulgaria but the Soviets would object strongly to German forces in that country. The whole situation was slipping out of Hitler's control. Responding to rumours of RAF aircraft at Lemnos airfield, he ordered two divisions, soon to be increased to ten, to prepare to advance through Bulgaria to Salonika. Hitler signed Directive No. 18 on 12 November hoping for Yugoslavian acquiescence and based on the assumption that Bulgaria would not obstruct German plans. Nothing much was expected to happen until the spring and the Italians were left to their own devices and suffer the consequences of their failure.

Things had only got worse after Mussolini had invaded Greece, which forced the British to send forces to Greece and Crete. This was now a far cry from the days when Hitler could devote all his attention to poring over his maps and planning relatively straightforward campaigns against known entities in direct battles. In September 1939 and May 1940 arrows on the map and sweeping manoeuvres were much easier to understand and Hitler must have craved a return to the days of lecturing his generals and giving them the benefit of his military genius. Balkan intrigues and multiple agencies at play in sporadic, ill-defined circumstances where undefined goals and diplomatic complications defied simple analysis were decidedly not to his taste. What was, however, was the bold initiative, the great strategic move, the employment of massive force with clear intent, the war of manoeuvre and tactical brilliance? That was what Hitler understood above all else and that is what he now planned to break out of the mess and confusion that clouded his ambition.

He ordered the setting up of training bases and storage depots in the East well out of range of RAF bombers and openly moved more divisions up to the Romanian border as a sign to all that he would defend the Ploesti oilfield at all costs. At the same time, the Soviets doubled their forces on their western border. Ribbentrop, meanwhile, was working on forging a stronger relationship with Japan and trying to bring the Soviets into a four-way agreement with Germany, Japan and Italy. The growing military aid now flowing into Britain from the US was making it less likely that Britain would capitulate and it was of vital importance that US attention be diverted from the Atlantic to the Pacific. When the German chargé went to discuss this with Molotov, however, he was pointedly kept waiting while the Soviet Foreign Minister held lengthy discussions with Cripps. Dealing with the Soviets was going to be every bit as difficult and long-winded as it had ever been but Ribbentrop and the German High Command were confident that a common front could be built against Britain.

The Soviets were as restless as ever in pursuing their own agenda and continuing to probe for weaknesses to exploit. They found one by sending forces to occupy the mouth of the River Danube, thereby controlling all marine traffic in the area. At the same time they made a point of sending a military delegation to Bucharest to keep a close eye on German diplomatic and military activity there. The Germans now tripled their forces in the East in response to the Soviets, whom Halder said would 'bite on granite' to get their own way.[59] Hitler issued Directive No. 18 on 12 November 1940 stipulating preparations for a spring invasion of Britain which could only be contemplated if the Soviets were contained in the east and the Balkans were kept under control.

The pertinent extracts of Directive No. 18 are as follows;

4. *The Balkans.*
Commander-in-Chief Army will be prepared, if necessary, to occupy from Bulgaria the *Greek mainland* north of the Aegean Sea. This will enable the German Air Force to attack targets in the Eastern Mediterranean, and in particular those English air bases which threaten the Romanian oilfields.

In order to be capable of fulfilling all tasks, and to keep Turkey in check, planning and march tables will assume the employment of an Army Group in a strength of about ten divisions. The use of the railway line running through Yugoslavia will not be assumed in planning the movement of these forces. In order to reduce the time required for the movement, the German Military Mission in Romania will be shortly reinforced to an extent about which I require advice.

In conjunction with the proposed land operations, Commander-in-Chief Air Force will prepare to post air force units to the South-eastern Balkans and to set up an Air Force Signal Service on the southern frontier of Bulgaria.

The German Air Force Mission in Romania will be reinforced to the extent proposed to me.

Requests by *Bulgaria* for equipment for its army (weapons and ammunition) will be met sympathetically.

5. *Russia.*

Political discussions for the purpose of clarifying Russia's attitude in the immediate future have already begun. Regardless of the outcome of these conversations, all preparations for the East for which verbal orders have already been given will be continued.

Further directives will follow on this subject as soon as the basic operational plan of the Army has been submitted to me and approved.

The Soviet-German relationship went from bad to worse as the autumn of 1940 brought it to the first anniversary of the Molotov-Ribbentrop Pact. Optimism and the mood of collaboration was rapidly being replaced by suspicion and hostility. Both sides were openly violating the agreement but clearly still accruing benefits from it and neither was yet ready to denounce the other. Ribbentrop invited Molotov to visit Berlin in October in an effort to breathe new life into the relationship and that seemed to ease the tension. Stalin instructed Molotov to mollify his hosts, avoiding getting too involved in detailed discussions of a new treaty to replace the current one but rather getting a feeling of what German intentions were now that its war against Britain had hit the buffers.

Soviet policy during 1939 had been to neutralise the military expansion of the German Reich which, since Munich, was clearly directed against Hitler's Bolshevist arch-enemy. Stalin had been content to see the Western Allies declare war on Germany in September after which he expected to see the Imperialists wear each other down in a long war eliminating, for the time being, the German threat to the Soviet Union. In the secret annex of the Molotov-Ribbentrop Pact Germany had made territorial concessions in Finland, the Baltic States, Eastern Poland and Bessarabia as compensation for the strategic advantage of non-aggression. For the Soviets this arrangement had extended their buffer against a German attack.

There was no doubt in Hitler's mind that the Soviets had two immediate objectives; the subjugation of Finland and a controlling presence in the Balkans, neither of which was in the interests of

Germany. The Soviet stance left Hitler fearing that the Soviets were not to be deterred and the two countries no longer stood 'back-to-back but chest-to-chest'[60] but Ribbentrop continued to try to paper over the cracks. When Molotov went to Berlin on 12 November 1940 Ribbentrop tried to convince him that the war against Britain was already won and between them Germany, the Soviet Union, Italy and Japan should go about specifying their spheres of influence in the world. The Soviet Union, said Ribbentrop, should look to expand into India and the Persian Gulf but Molotov would not be diverted from his focus on Europe. Even a personal meeting with Hitler, who assured him that Germany was preoccupied with administering lands already under occupation and did not envisage any further incursion in Eastern Europe, failed to move the Soviet Foreign Minister. Germany was only interested in maintaining control over its current assets and raw material sources, said the Führer, and whilst acknowledging that Germany and the Soviet Union were far from compatible politically, they could quite easily live side-by-side in an amicable relationship. Molotov replied that the current arrangement between the two countries served them both very well but where Hitler had painted his canvas with a broad brush, Molotov adopted the pointillist method and highlighted the many small areas of concern that awaited resolution before the Soviet Union could think about joining in any new agreement. Hitler was not remotely interested in details and concluded that Molotov was prevaricating. As a backdrop to the talks on the final evening reception at the Soviet Foreign Ministry, the British, who had become aware of Molotov's visit, sent a small force of RAF bombers over Berlin and the air-raid sirens interrupted Molotov's toast to his hosts reminding them all that, despite Ribbentrop's assertions to the contrary, Britain had not laid down and died.

Based on Molotov's visit, on 15 November von Weizsäcker, State Secretary at the *Auswärtiges Amt*, issued a draft treaty proposal 'on the basis of the treaties concluded last year and resulted in complete agreement regarding the firm determination of both countries to continue in the future the policy inaugurated by these treaties'. Any rumours of a rift in German-Soviet relations were 'conjectures . . . in the realm of fantasy.' Article 1 began; 'In the Three Power Pact of Berlin, of September 27, 1940, Germany, Italy, and Japan agreed to oppose the extension of the war into a world conflict with all possible means and to collaborate toward an early restoration of world peace.'

Germany, Italy, Japan and the Soviet Union undertook to respect each other's natural spheres of influence and recognised the current extent of the possessions of the Soviet Union and would respect it.

Furthermore, the four powers were to undertake to join no combination of powers and to support no combination of powers which was directed against one of the Four Powers. There was attached to the draft a secret protocol outlining the spheres of influence of each power.

On 26 November, von der Schulenburg conveyed to Berlin the Soviet response in what became a turning point in German-Soviet relations. They were only prepared to accept the draft treaty on the understanding that German troops were immediately withdrawn from Finland and 'within the next few months' the security of the Soviet Union in the Straits would be assured by the conclusion of a mutual assistance pact between the Soviet Union and Bulgaria, and by the establishment of a base for land and naval forces of the Soviet Union within range of the Bosporus and the Dardanelles by means of a long-term lease. It was obviously not the reply that Hitler wanted and one is left to imagine his response. The proposed treaty clearly fell right off the agenda because the next reference to it was not until 17 January 1941 in a telegram sent by von der Schulenburg.

Chapter 12

BARBAROSSA

Soviet control of Finland was quite out of the question for Germany and Hitler was growing tired of being played by Stalin. The constant Soviet nibbling away at the understanding reached between Ribbentrop and Molotov at their historic meeting on 23 September 1939 had not actually broken it but, as far as Hitler was concerned, it was becoming worthless as a document on which to base German-Soviet relations. Stalin was no longer to be trusted to any degree and could not be relied upon in a crisis. By 11 December 1940, Brautschitch and Halder had submitted to Hitler the first operational plan for an attack against the Soviet Union and called it *Unternehmen Barbarossa*. Barbarossa (Red Beard) was the name given to the German Holy Roman Emperor, Frederick I (1122—90). His empire had stretched from the North Sea coast to Sicily. Poets embellished his legend and created the tale of the sleeping Barbarossa in the Kyffhäuser mountain cave, waiting for the right moment to return and unite Germany.

On 18 December Hitler issued Directive No. 21 in which he called for all future troop movements in the East to be conducted under strict secrecy. His ideology, subsumed since his accession to power, now found its chance where theory and practice coincided. Both preventive war and ruthless territorial aggrandisement, accompanied by mass enslavement and extermination on a scale which – Stalin apart – no one in Europe had practised in modern times, merged into an orgy of destruction.[1] German policy towards the Soviet Union in 1940-1 was not orchestrated according to a detailed programme conceived by Hitler in his Lansberg prison cell in 1923 but had been forced upon him by events.

Stalin had called a military conference in Moscow during December 1940 when all aspects of doctrine were discussed. The leader did not attend in person but followed proceedings assiduously. The conference may well have been a response to reports reaching the Kremlin from the Soviet ambassador in Berlin, Vladimir Dekanozov, about Hitler's increasingly belligerent attitude. It was a little over a week after its issue that Stalin became apprised of the contents of Hitler Directive No. 21. As the new year turned intelligence reports poured into the Kremlin about German troop movements in Poland towards the frontier with the Soviet Union. An intercepted telegram from Tokyo suggested that full deployment was complete. Stalin could hardly have been surprised by rumours of a German attack but nothing in the current situation had prepared him for the fact that it might happen so soon. His volcanic temper exploded to the point where his Trade Minister Anastas Mikoyan feared that he had become 'unhinged'.[2]

The Soviet armaments industry had grown dramatically during the 1930s but in 1940 it was still very reliant on German industry for both machine tools and technical expertise. A new generation of tanks, the T-34 and KV (*Kliment Voroshilov*), were being planned to supersede the T-26 and BT (*Bystrokhodny tank*) models with new factories going up. Mikoyan placed orders in the summer of 1940 with the German Reinecker machine tool manufacturer for heavy machinery mostly for forging, cutting and pressing steel plate. Production of the Soviet Yak-1 fighter aircraft at the Kirov and Kharkov factories was also reliant on German suppliers for a little under half of its heavy manufacturing machine tools. For the Soviets the German connection was still of vital importance even though Stalin would stretch German patience and forbearance almost to its limit at times.

Soviet supplies to Germany consistently fell below the levels promised in the commercial agreements but Germany was actually much less reliant on the Soviet Union at this time for its raw materials than it had been just a year previously. Romania was supplying vast amounts of oil and Sweden much of Germany's iron ore. Huge quantities of oil had been confiscated from occupied France and domestic synthetic rubber production had soared. It was in foodstuffs and animal feed, however, that the Soviet Union was of greatest importance even though, as has been mentioned, supplies fell far short of the promised levels. When meetings were held to address the delivery shortfalls, they became mired in arguments. The Germans complained of the excessive bureaucracy involved with even the smallest purchase and, above all, the exorbitant prices placed on Soviet goods and grew weary of constant niggling over minor details which seemed to have been a Soviet speciality. On the Soviet side the negotiators, as part of a rigid system of hierarchical control and political constraint, showed little willingness to compromise or deviate from the position dictated from above and that was governed by political directives from the highest levels. Every now and then, Stalin would intervene and castigate his side for intransigence then sweep all obstructions aside in blatant denial of the fact that it was he who had dictated Soviet negotiating tactics in the first place. This was all for show since very soon the old obfuscation and delaying tactics soon re-emerged.

The Soviets, too, had their complaints, mostly to do with the delay between Soviet material supplied and German payments made for the same although the terms had been clearly laid out when the deals were struck. German deliveries fell behind schedule also now that the country was at war and pleaded 'forces beyond our control' when upbraided whereas in fact firms such as Krupp were naturally prioritising orders for the Wehrmacht. There was little evidence of goodwill on either side but, while both the German and Soviet leaders were utterly ruthless in progressing their agendas, it was Stalin, whose political career had been built on chicanery and backroom plots, who was better able to manipulate situations for maximum advantage.

Stalin had taken a personal interest in the details of negotiations but seems to have overlooked a significant fact in that the German negotiating position did not represent the policy of Hitler himself, but the policy of the German Foreign Ministry and German industrialists, supported by Ribbentrop, Göring and Raeder, who could conceive and carry through the policy of cooperation with Moscow almost entirely independently of Hitler who regarded the deal with the Soviet Union to be strictly time-limited. His long-term aims of the destruction of Bolshevism were enshrined in ingrained ideological dogma and was impervious to outside influence.

Stalin continued to believe that Hitler himself directed Soviet policy and Molotov failed in all his dealings with the Germans to see that it was the *Auswärtiges Amt* he was dealing with and not the whole German government. It was the fundamental flaw of Stalin's whole dealings with Hitler up to 1941 that he saw the German governmental system in his own dictatorial image and laid out his policies according to what initiatives the German diplomats presented to him in Moscow which he believed to be those of Hitler himself. Soviet economic support for the German war with Britain appeared to Stalin to be a fundamental requirement of German foreign policy. Even when German troops mobilised on the Soviet border, the Kremlin leadership had to ask themselves what advantages the German Reich would gain from an attack on the Soviet Union which led to a war on two fronts. This would weaken the effort against England and risk the loss of Soviet raw materials. According to the Kremlin's analysis and that of London and Washington at the time Hitler would not attack a state from which he could get a maximum of support under peaceful conditions.

For Hitler it was the way that the Non-Aggression Pact had fitted into his strategic vision for the European war that interested him and he left negotiation of trade issues, which did not, to others. Stalin completely failed to see that the whole detailed negotiations beyond the basic issue of non-aggression did not influence Hitler's decision making. He wrongly assumed that Hitler's war strategy was reliant on the trade agreement and that Germany's reliance on raw-material imports from the Soviet Union made a German attack less likely. Hitler did not see it that way. For him, war with the Soviet Union might halt imports in the short term but a successful invasion would increase German access to Soviet raw materials in the medium term without all the bothersome negotiations over quotas and prices.

Once again the Balkans had become a tinder-box waiting for someone to strike the match. In June 1940 the Soviet Union had resumed diplomatic relations with Yugoslavia. Britain sent its approval of the Soviet annexation of Bessarabia and supported Hungary's claims to Romanian territories while the Italians confided to Berlin its plans to invade Yugoslavia and Greece. Germany assured Bulgaria, Romania, Hungary and Yugoslavia that it had no territorial ambitions in the Balkans. As ever, Hitler's overriding concern was to protect his Romanian oil supplies. On Hitler's strong advice the Bulgarians and Hungarians had begun negotiations with Romania that resulted in southern Drobudja being ceded to Bulgaria but Romania refused to budge on Hungarian demands for Transylvania. The impasse was broken when Germany gave Romania a security guarantee if it agreed to Hungary's claims. This did not please Hitler, who had wanted as little involvement as possible over and above the oil supply, but was necessary to keep a lid on the Balkan disputes.

During November the Army High Command was distracted with preparations for an attack on Gibraltar and the situation in the Balkan Peninsula when Molotov visited Berlin on 12–13 November and offered some hope that Hitler's plans to attack the Soviet Union might be modified by a change in Soviet policy but when the Kriegsmarine chief Admiral Raeder had an audience with Hitler the day after Molotov's departure, he found him still deeply committed. Raeder, ever cautious and protective of his navy, argued that Germany was too weak to open an eastern front and anyway, the Soviets would not pose any threat to Germany for at least three years.

The situation in the Balkans was becoming a troublesome sideshow that could have serious consequences. Hitler now chose to take decisive action to try and regain the initiative. If he was going to launch an attack against the Soviet Union, and that was still his prime objective, it was vital to sort out the mess in the south and secure the Romanian oilfields before anything else. Although the Soviets were firmly in his sights, the timing of any move against them was critical. When Molotov had been invited to Berlin, Hitler had played the part of victor in the West and offered broad discussions on the partition of Europe between the Axis powers. Molotov, however, had not gone to Berlin for entertainment, he had wanted to discuss details, in particular Finland and the Balkans where disputes were far from being resolved. It was vital, said Hitler, to prevent the British from getting a foothold in Greece and that was why he had been forced to take the precipitous step of occupying Romania and preparing to move into Bulgaria. The Soviets too had concerns about the British entering the Soviet Union by the back door and claimed that they had equal reason to station forces in the area. He suggested that the Soviets could guarantee Bulgarian security and slam the door shut on the British which meant that the Germans had no need to go into Bulgaria.

The German answer was to offer a security pact with Spain, Hungary, Bulgaria and Romania but Spain and Bulgaria hesitated. Bulgaria, in particular, was not ready to take sides against the Soviets despite German guarantees to give them access to Aegean ports. Hitler sent a further two divisions to Romania in preparation for a spring initiative to resolve the impasse. Meanwhile, the Soviet Union offered Bulgaria its own mutual assistance treaty. The Bulgarians were between a rock and a hard place and their situation did not improve when Hungary, Romania and Slovakia all signed up with Germany in November which, in reality, was little more than an acknowledgement of the status quo, with German forces already in all three countries. Yugoslavia, another child of Versailles, was something of an enigma for Hitler. He couldn't quite decide what to do about it and he had a keen appreciation of the strength of its fighting forces which, if they were combined with the Greeks, could throw his whole Greek strategy into turmoil. With winter upon the Balkans and no prospect of any sort of large-scale movement of forces until the spring, there was time to sow confusion within the Yugoslav camp where the Croats were pro-German but the Serbs were not, by offering incentives and bribes in the form of a share of the Greek prize, specifically the Aegean port of Salonika together with a German security guarantee. The Yugoslav Foreign Minister Aleksander Cincar-Marković had been invited to meet Hitler and Ribbentrop at Berchtesgaden in late November where he was offered a treaty of friendship but when he took the idea back to Belgrade it failed to get any support.

When the Italian campaign got into serious trouble in Greece and the British looked ever more likely to establish airfields in the north of the country, the mood in Berlin darkened. There was no possibility of making a move against the Soviet Union with the Balkans simmering away in the background and threatening to boil over and all the time reports were coming into Berlin of extensive defensive barriers going up around Kiev and between Grodno and Brest in eastern Poland on the road that traditionally led to Moscow. Stalin was becoming increasingly unnerved by the prospect of a German attack and chose to use the economic relationship to dissuade Hitler from launching a precipitate action. Although he was in no doubt that the blow would fall eventually, it was vital to forestall it as long as possible. All the evidence suggests that he was confident Hitler's need for Soviet food and raw materials was sufficient to deter military action at least until 1942.

In December 1940, Stalin changed his erstwhile policy of running hot and cold over trade negotiations. His habit had been to alternate between deliberate slowing down of supplies and then to step in as the saviour of the day to open up the floodgates of oil and grain again as the mood took him or as his strategy demanded but now he launched into a full-scale 'charm offensive'. Firstly his negotiators quickly agreed to a new Tariff and Toll Treaty in a move that astonished Schnurre with their 'quite cordial [demeanour and] surprising indications of goodwill'.[3] This was followed the next month with a German-Soviet Border and Commercial Agreement that Schnurre called 'the greatest [commercial agreement] Germany had ever concluded'. He had certainly been taken in, as evidenced by his lauding of the deals in Berlin as a 'solid foundation for an honorable and great peace for Germany'. German industry showed confidence in the future as exports to the Soviet Union soared. Here again there is evidence of German industry and the Foreign Office pursuing a different agenda to Hitler who obviously did not have a tight grip on Soviet-German trade negotiations. As exports soared, with the balance of trade very much in Germany's favour and Soviet indebtedness to Germany increased, war with them was starting to make less and less sense but war was now at the top of Hitler's agenda. Unable to curb the flow of German goods to the Soviet Union, he was forced to issue orders to forbid publication of the details of the burgeoning trade. Here again it was clear that Stalin had missed the point if he thought that he could control Hitler by manipulating trade negotiations and it was going to be a harsh lesson for him to learn when he finally faced the truth.

Hitler's decision to attack the Soviet Union was prepared under strict secrecy limited to the highest level of the military until the spring of 1941 but once it was given the green light preparations would soon become apparent giving, in Halder's view, at least four whole weeks of warning to the Soviets. When forces were seen to be massing in the East, however, it would be depicted as dissimulation and a large-scale deception preparatory to launching the invasion of England. The Chiefs of Staff of the three army groups designated for the attack were asked by Halder to study the invasion plans and selected aspects were up for discussion at Army High Command headquarters on 13 and 14 December. Although discussions highlighted a number of problems for which there was no immediate solution, it was also concluded that the Soviet Union would be defeated in a campaign not exceeding 10 weeks' duration. The study was submitted to Hitler who confirmed his original plans. Six days later a Hitler signed Directive No. 21, Operation Barbarossa to 'crush Soviet Russia in a lightning campaign'.[4] The generally-held opinion that the Russian campaign would be of short duration was supported by Section III B of Directive that specifically gave the Luftwaffe primarily a ground-support mission indicating that strategic bombing would be unnecessary. Raeder again tried to persuade Hitler to hold back and concentrate all Germany's military power against Britain but Hitler ignored his appeals believing that the Soviet Union's expansionist policy in the Balkans made it essential that Germany eliminate its last opponent on the European continent before the final showdown with Britain.

Further expansion of Soviet-German economic relations was pushed ahead under the leadership of the *Auswärtiges Amt* and the civil departments concerned, oblivious to Hitler's war plans. Ribbentrop had been kept out of the loop on war preparations and continued to include the Soviet Union in his bid to form a continental block of the Euro-Asiatic powers. Another economic agreement was made with the Soviet Union on 10 January 1941 only weeks after Hitler's secret Directive No 21 had been issued. The willingness of Stalin to enter into yet another trade agreement saw Göring trying to dissuade Hitler from his invasion plans but without success. There now arose the apparently contradictory situation of Göring, with Hitler's authority, issuing orders to German industrialists to give a higher priority to the export of material to the Soviet Union at the same time as the Wehrmacht was preparing to invade the country. The conclusion to be drawn is that Hitler was anxious to lull Stalin into a false sense of security and give him the impression that he had no immediate intention of invading.

Hitler was so convinced that German forces would conquer the Soviet Union within four months from the start of the attack that as early as 17 February 1940 he had discussed with Jodl plans for an invasion of India and Afghanistan to be followed by seizure of British strongholds in the Mediterranean (Gibraltar) and the Near East, by concentric drives from Libya toward Egypt, from Bulgaria across Turkey, and possibly from the Caucasus across Iran.

Mussolini was becoming an embarrassment to the Fascist cause. The debacle of Italian failure in Greece had set in motion a whole chain of events that threatened to send all of Hitler's plans for the Soviet Union spiralling out of his control. He tried to defuse the situation by offering to mediate in the Italo-Greek war and promised the Greeks a slice of Albania if they would cooperate with German forces to expel the British but the Greeks would only promise to restrict the level of British forces in their country, not kick them out completely, and then only if the Germans would agree to keep their forces out of Bulgaria. Agreeing to that, of course, would give the Soviets free rein to go there instead and was unthinkable for Hitler. In January, Halder summed up by saying that Romania was securely under the control of half a million German soldiers, but Bulgaria and Yugoslavia remained problematical. While the winter weather put a block on all large-scale movements, Germany started infiltrating troops into Bulgaria on a daily basis. Despite the appalling state of the roads and bridges German forces were soon everywhere, preparing airfields, building pontoon bridges, repairing the cobblestone roads and generally making all the preparations necessary for the advance of the German army. Germans began to arm the Bulgarians with materiel captured in France and beefed up Bulgaria's coastal defences against possible Soviet attack but the Bulgarians would still not sign a treaty. In February, however, a secret agreement was arrived at whereby German forces would be provided with transportation, but Bulgarian troops would not be called upon to fight alongside them.

There was still the question of Yugoslavia which remained the only potential ally for the Soviet Union and which might be tempted to come in on the side of Greece if the Germans attacked. Britain urged Turkey, Greece and Yugoslavia to come together to invade Albania but to no avail. Again Yugoslavia, despite its almost total subjugation to Germany economically, rebuffed German offers of a treaty for which Hitler blamed Mussolini's fiasco in Greece that had encouraged the Yugoslavs to think that the Germans would fare little better in the

Balkan mountain ranges. In February, the Yugoslav Foreign Minister Dragiša Cvetkovič was invited to Berchtesgaden where Hitler made him several tempting offers alongside veiled threats of economic sanctions. German experts could be sent to manage Yugoslav factories, mines and agriculture and Yugoslavia would get an outlet to the Aegean.[5] None of this was convincing. German promises could not be relied upon and Britain was too far away to give real help but when Turkey and Bulgaria signed a non-aggression treaty the writing was on the wall that both had resigned themselves to the German occupation of Bulgaria. When Bulgaria went further and signed a treaty with German suddenly there were German forces of the Bulgarian-Yugoslav border. The Prince Regent of Yugoslavia, Paul, described by D.C. Watt as a man of 'character, balance, taste and charm . . . which were useless in the present circumstances and in a country where arguments of might are the only ones which count', went again to Berchtesgaden but this time secretly. He made several visits during March after which he was worn down by German pressure and signed an agreement on 25 March the terms of which were far less favourable that those that had been offered a couple of months earlier. This was met with great hostility in Belgrade and the government there was felled only days later by a British-sponsored military coup. The Soviet Union saw its chance as Yugoslav street protests raged against German interference in the country. When Hitler heard he flew into a rage and threatened to destroy Yugoslavia. His paranoia seemed justified when the Soviets signed a Treaty of Friendship with Yugoslavia on 6 April 1941.

The whole Balkan maelstrom had been a massive distraction for Hitler who was now struggling to give all his attention to the invasion of the Soviet Union. There seemed to be no overriding reason why he allowed himself to be diverted from his main goal. Oil supplies from Romania were fairly secure and British air bases in Greece were few and far between. Yugoslavia was troublesome but its army, riven by sectarian divides, posed no serious threat to the Germans and its government would become less confrontational if the Germans eased off their pressure. Hitler's entanglement in the Balkans had come about initially by the Soviet annexation of Bessarabia which had antagonised Hungary and Bulgaria who had then posed a threat to Romania which is where the Germans intervened bringing them into a direct power struggle in the region. When an equilibrium of sorts was established, it was upset by Mussolini's invasion of Greece which turned into a fiasco, letting the British gain a foothold in the Aegean. Hitler was not prepared to allow himself to become embroiled in provincial squabbles when his forces were poised to take the step for which he had been preparing all along and so he chose to settle the matter once and for all in the only way he knew how.

Despite the Soviet treaty with Yugoslavia, Hitler had already issued Directive No. 25 'Operation Strafe', on 27 March, which was a plan of attack on Yugoslavia. Massive Luftwaffe air raids were launched on Belgrade as the Soviet-Yugoslav treaty was being signed on 6 April. Ground forces crossed the border from Romania and Hungary. Italian and Hungarian forces moved in a few days later and Yugoslav resistance collapsed after eleven days. At the same time as Operation Strafe was kicking off, German troops also invaded Greece in Operation Marita across the Bulgarian border, making a second front with the bulk of Greek forces lined up against the Italians on the border with Albania. German troops occupied Athens on 27 April and Crete fell a month later.

Soviet influence in the Balkans was virtually at an end, with Hitler firmly in control now, but the winter campaigns had compelled the postponement of the German invasion of the Soviet Union by four to six weeks. Stalin was forced onto the defensive. After the military success of the Wehrmacht in the Balkans and the rising expectation of an imminent attack, the Soviets significantly increased the volume of their raw material deliveries to Germany to the point where once again, as in the summer of 1940, it was not possible for the Germans to cope with everything that was arriving on their borders. This time it was exacerbated by the German railway network being completely overloaded with troop movements as part of preparations for operation Barbarossa.

The huge quantities of materials coming into Germany from the Soviet Union included over half a million tons of grain shipped in just ten weeks up to June. New contracts were being signed for oil, nickel, zinc and copper with remarkably little Soviet haggling over prices. By this time, German exports had dwindled to a trickle either deliberately or as a result also of the very limited commercial rail traffic. In a further bid to mollify Hitler, Stalin had agreed for Molotov to sign the Soviet-Japanese Neutrality Pact with the Japanese Foreign Minister Yosuke Matsuoka in Moscow on 13 April. This was designed to appeal to Hitler by allowing Japan to concentrate all its forces against the United States in the Pacific and make it less likely to enter the European war on the side of Britain. Intelligence reports coming into the Kremlin made all such moves of vital importance. Over 100 German divisions were massing on the Soviet border with another fifty in Yugoslavia signalling that if Hitler chose to attack, he was well placed to do so. Stalin may have hoped against hope that the invasion would not come before another 12 months and he may have done everything he could think of to strengthen the position of Schnurre and the Foreign Office hoping that they could exert pressure on Hitler to hold back, but the signs were there and he couldn't ignore them.

He drafted a communiqué on 14 June to be carried in all the Soviet media in which he said, 'rumours of the intention of Germany to break with the [Molotov-Ribbentrop] Pact and to launch an attack against the Soviet Union are completely without foundation'.[6] He may well have hoped for a public acknowledgement from Berlin that they concurred, but he waited in vain. On 16 June information from the Soviet Schuze-Boysen spy ring inside the Luftwaffe indicated that a date for the attack had been issued but Stalin refused to face up to reality and denounced the report as 'disinformation'. When General Zhukov asked for permission to put the Soviet troops on the western frontier on 'full military readiness' two days later, Stalin was deep into denial and attacked the messenger with threats of shooting him. 'Germany on her own will never fight Russia!' he declared and refused permission to move troops to the border to avoid provoking the Germans.

By 20 June, the staff at Moscow's German embassy had packed up and gone but von der Schulenburg was still in Moscow and the following day arranged to meet Molotov in the Kremlin where he read out to him a telegram just arrived from Berlin. 'It is with the deepest regret', he began, 'that the German government felt obliged to take certain military measures in view of the Soviet military build-up on the border.' He added that his own efforts to preserve peace and friendship had failed. Molotov protested at this 'breach of confidence unprecedented in history' but von der Schulenburg had done his duty by reading out the message and was not able to do more. In Berlin, Ribbentrop called in the Soviet ambassador. Dekanozov thought Ribbentrop's appearance suggested that he was drunk but he was sober enough to accuse the Soviet Union of border violations and inform the ambassador that German troops had crossed into the Soviet Union. He was unable, however, to resist coming after Dekanozov as he left the building and professing his own deep regret at the decision and urged him to tell Moscow that he, personally, had tried to dissuade Hitler.

Just why Stalin refused to believe the huge volume of intelligence pointing to a German invasion had been debated at length. Stalin's seems to have been unduly influenced by his intelligence chief Golikov who had submitted a report on 20 March 1941 which concluded that an attack on the Soviet Union would not take place before a German victory over Britain and that all rumours to the contrary should be regarded as British propaganda and German disinformation.

Dr Geoffrey Roberts gives six reasons for Stalin's complacency.

1. He believed that an attack would not come before 1942.
2. He believed that the Soviet Union was well prepared to defend itself.
3. He believed any attack would be preceded by an ultimatum.
4. He believed that Hitler was bluffing.
5. His views were supported by large sections of the Politburo.
6. He was desperate to believe he had not made a mistake by misreading the situation.

In reference to the second point it is true that the Red Army was superior in numbers to the Germans along the border in June 1941. The mistake was in anticipating what kind of war it would be and that the third point above would give him time to call up reserves. He had been completely fooled by the German deception measures taken in the days before an attack, as were the bulk of international observers.

Just before dawn on 22 June 1941 the codeword 'Dortmund' went out to all German units on the border and at 03.15, all along the 1,300km border with the Soviet Union from the Black Sea to the Baltic, three million German troops and nearly 700,000 more from other Axis countries, together with thousands of tanks and aircraft, crossed the border into the Soviet Union. Barbarossa had begun. Army Group North under General Leeb with the 4th Panzer Group stormed all across the Baltic States towards Leningrad. Army Group Centre under General Bock with the 2nd and 3rd Panzer Groups headed for Moscow while Army Group South under Rundstedt with the First Panzer group drove into Ukraine.

NOTES

Introduction

1. John W. Wheeler-Bennett, 'Twenty Years of Russo-German Relations: 1919-1939', *Foreign Affairs* Vol. 25, No. 1 (1946).

Chapter 1: The Bolshevik Revolution

1. John Erickson, *The Soviet High Command 1918-1941* (Macmillan & Co Ltd, 1962), p. 13.
2. John W. Wheeler-Bennett, 'The Meaning of Brest-Litovsk Today', *Foreign Affairs* Vol. 17, No. 1 (1938), p. 137.
3. Ibid., p. 139.
4. Mark Davis Kuss, *Collective Security or World Domination: the Soviet Union and Germany, 1917-1939*, LSU Doctoral Dissertations (2012), p. 30.
5. Ibid., p. 36.
6. Wheeler-Bennett, 'The Meaning of Brest-Litovsk Today', p. 145.
7. Ian Johnson, *The Secret School of War: The Soviet-German Tank Academy at Kama*, thesis, The Ohio State University (2012), p. 8.
8. Erickson, p. 22.
9. Ibid., p. 26.
10. E.H. Carr, *The Bolshevik Revolution* (Baltimore: Penguin, 1953), Vol. 3, p. 366.
11. Erickson, p. 145.
12. Matthias Strohn, 'Hans Von Seeckt and His Vision of a Modern Army', *War in History* Vol. 12, No. 3 (2005), p. 319.
13. George W.F. Hallgarten, 'General Hans von Seeckt and Russia, 1920-1922', *The Journal of Modern History* Vol. 21, No. 1 (1949), p. 29.
14. Arthur L. Smith, 'General Von Seeckt and the Weimar Republic', *The Review of Politics*, Vol. 20, No. 3 (1958), p. 125.
15. Kuss, p. 39.
16. Erickson, p. 58.

17. M.V. Glenny, 'The Anglo-Soviet Trade Agreement, March 1921', *Journal of Contemporary History* Vol. 5, No. 2 (1970), p. 72.
18. Eric Waldman, *The Spartacist Uprising of 1919* (Marquette University, Milwaukee 1958), p. 176.

Chapter 2: The Russo-Polish War
1. Jun Okami, *Von Seeckt 1920-1926: A Study of Military Management*, thesis, University of Surrey (1988), p. 148.
2. Erickson, p. 147.
3. Phillippe Sands, *East West Street* (Weidenfeld & Nicolson, 2016), p. 149.
4. Okami, p. 36.
5. Ibid., p. 152.
6. Robert Himmer, 'Soviet Policy Toward Germany during the Russo-Polish War, 1920', *Slavic Review* Vol. 35, No. 4 (1976), p. 150.
7. Okami, p. 156.
8. Wheeler-Bennett, 'Twenty Years of Russo-German Relations: 1919-1939', p. 26.
9. Okami, p. 186.
10. Himmer, 'Soviet Policy Toward Germany during the Russo-Polish War, 1920', p. 673.
11. Ibid.
12. Ibid., p. 676.
13. Glenny, p. 75.

Chapter 3: Early Tank Warfare Doctrine
1. Mary R. Habek, *Storm of Steel: The Development of Armor Doctrine in Germany and the Soviet Union,1919–1939* (Cornell University Press 2003), p. 27.

Chapter 4: The Genoa Conference and Rapallo
1. Kuss, p. 68.
2. Robert Himmer, 'Rathenau, Russia, and Rapallo', *Central European History* Vol. 9, No. 2 (1976), p. 171.
3. Ibid., p. 156.
4. Ibid., p.178.
5. Harvey Daniel Munshaw, *Extra! Extra! Read all about it: The British and American Press coverage of German-Soviet Collaboration 1917-1928*, thesis, University of Central Missouri (2008), p. 37.
6. Okami, p. 182.
7. Kuss, p. 70.
8. Munshaw, p. 38.

9. Ibid., p. 39.
10. Kuss, p. 72.
11. Munshaw, p. 44.
12. Hallgarten, p. 32.
13. Wheeler-Bennett, 'The Meaning of Brest-Litovsk Today', p. 152.
14. Munshaw, p. 50.
15. Robert A. Kilmarx, *A History of Soviet Air Power* (Faber and Faber, 1962), p. 64.
16. Heinz W. Gatzke, 'Russo-German Military Collaboration During the Weimar Republic', *The American Historical Review* Vol. LXIII, No. 3 (1958), p. 568.
17. Ibid., p. 570.
18. Hallgarten, p. 32.
19. Gatzke, p. 572.
20. Okami, p. 244.
21. Munshaw, p. 46.
22. Gatzke, p. 575.
23. Ibid., p. 576.
24. Ibid., p. 577.
25. Kuss, p. 74.
26. Erickson, p. 169.
27. Kilmarx, p. 66.
28. Gatzke, p. 579.

Chapter 5: The Locarno Treaties

1. Kuss, p. 77.
2. Hugh Ragsdale, *The Soviets, the Munich Crisis, and the Coming of World War II* (Cambridge University Press, 2004), p. 53.
3. 'The USSR System of Neutrality and Non-Aggression', *Bulletin of International News* (1928), p. 589.
4. Gatzke, p. 582.
5. John P. Sontag, 'The Soviet War Scare of 1926-27', *The Russian Review* Vol. 34, No. 1 (1975), p. 67.
6. Ibid.,p. 69.
7. Erickson, p. 285.
8. Sontag, p. 70.

Chapter 6: Lipetsk, Tomka and Kazan

1. Habek, p. 73.
2. Anthony Rimmington, *Stalin's Secret Weapon: The Origins of Soviet Biological Warfare* (Oxford University Press, 2018), p. 90.
3. Ibid., p. 91.

4. Munshaw, p. 64.
5. Johnson, p. 17.
6. Erickson, p. 201.
7. Johnson, p. 23.
8. Munshaw, p. 52.
9. Ibid., p. 74.
10. Gatzke, p. 585.
11. Ibid., p. 586.
12. Ibid., p. 587.
13. Ibid., p. 588.
14. Erickson, p. 266.
15. Ibid., p. 264.
16. Okami, p. 235.

Chapter 7: The Middle Years

1. Kurt Rosenbaum, 'The German Involvement in the Shakhty Trial', *The Russian Review* Vol. 21, No. 3 (1962), p. 239.
2. Ibid., p. 241.
3. Ibid., p. 243.
4. Ibid., p. 249.
5. Ibid.,p. 252.
6. Gabriel Gorodetsky, *Soviet Foreign Policy, 1917-1991: A Retrospective* (Cummings Centre Series 1994), p. 56.
7. Kuss, p. 81.
8. Erickson, p. 272.
9. Habek, p. 94.
10. Ibid., p. 127.
11. Ibid., p. 131.
12. Ibid., p. 135.
13. Ibid., p. 142.
14. Ibid., p. 165.
15. Erickson, p. 326.

Chapter 8: The Rise of Nazism

1. Erickson, p. 330.
2. Ibid., p. 333.
3. Ibid.
4. Nevin Gussack, *When Brown Meets Red: Nazi-Communist Collaboration 1919-1945* (Createspace Independent Publishing Platform, 2015), pp. 4–6.

5. Davis William Daycock, *The KPD and the NSDAP: A Study of the relationship between political extremes in Weimar Germany, 1923-1933*, University of London, 1980, p. 172.
6. Ibid., p. 181.
7. James J. Ward, *Smash the Fascists: German Communist Efforts to Counter the Nazis, 1930-31* (Cambridge University Press, 1981), p. 38.
8. Daycock, p. 224.
9. Ibid., p. 240.
10. Timothy S. Brown, 'Richard Scheringer, the KPD and the Politics of Class and Nation in Germany, 1922-1969', *Contemporary European History* 14, no. 3 (2005), p. 324.
11. Ibid., p. 331.
12. Gussack, p. 10.
13. Daycock, p. 256.
14. Ward, p. 47.
15. Daycock, p. 261.
16. Geoffrey Roberts, *The Soviet Union and the Origins of the Second World War: Russo-German Relations and the Road to War 1933-1941* (Macmillan, 1995), p. 10.
17. George H. Stein, 'Russo-German Military Collaboration: The Last Phase, 1933', *Political Science Quarterly* Vol. 77, No. 1 (1962), p. 58.
18. Ibid., p. 61.

Chapter 9: The End of Collaboration

1. Teddy J. Uldricks, 'Stalin and Nazi Germany', *Slavic Review* Vol. 36, No. 4 (1977), p. 600.
2. Documents on German Foreign Policy 1918-1945: Jan.-Oct. 1933, p. 857.
3. Erickson, p. 347.
4. Ibid., p. 348.
5. Stein, p. 54.
6. Roberts, *The Soviet Union and the Origins of the Second World War: Russo-German Relations and the Road to War 1933-1941*, p. 15.
7. Wheeler-Bennett, 'Twenty Years of Russo-German Relations: 1919-1939', p. 32.
8. Nuremberg Military Tribunals, 1953, Vol VII, p. 416.
9. Erickson, p. 383.
10. Ibid., p. 378.
11. Ibid., p. 396.
12. Gussack, p. 17.
13. Gorodetsky, p. 67.

14. Wheeler-Bennett, 'Twenty Years of Russo-German Relations: 1919-1939', p. 34.
15. Ragsdale, p. 58.
16. Ibid., p. 59.
17. Erickson, p. 416.
18. Roberts, *The Soviet Union and the Origins of the Second World War: Russo-German Relations and the Road to War 1933-1941* p. 26.
19. Ibid., p. 35.

Chapter 10: The Spanish Civil War
1. John McCannon, 'Soviet Intervention in the Spanish Civil War, 1936-39', *Russian History* Vol. 22, No. 2 (1995), p. 157.
2. Gerald Howson, *Arms for Spain: The Untold Story of the Spanish Civil War* (John Murray, 1998), p. 126.

Chapter 11: The Molotov-Ribbentrop Pact
1. Wheeler-Bennett, 'Twenty Years of Russo-German Relations: 1919-1939', p. 37.
2. Ragsdale, p. 119.
3. Ibid., p. 124.
4. Ibid., p. 120.
5. Ibid., p. 127.
6. Ibid., p. 129.
7. Ibid., p. 114.
8. Roger Moorehouse, *The Devil's Alliance: Hitler's Pact with Stalin 1939-1941* (Vintage, 2014), p. 174.
9. Anna Marie Cienciala, 'The Nazi-Soviet Pact of August 23 1939: When Did Stalin Decide to Align with Hitler and Was Poland the Culprit?', in M.B.B. Biscupski, *Ideology, Politics and Diplomacy in East Central Europe* (University of Rochester Press, 2003), p.150.
10. Samantha Carl, *The Buildup of the German War Economy: The Importance of the Nazi-Soviet Economic Trade Agreements of 1939 and 1940* (Millersville.edu), p. 4.
11. Cienciala, p. 153.
12. Ibid., p. 162.
13. Gabriel Gorodetsky, *Soviet Foreign Policy, 1917-1991: A Retrospective* (Cummings Center Series, 1994), p. 68.
14. Ibid., p. 161.
15. Moorehouse, *The Devil's Alliance*, p. 23.
16. Cienciala, p. 168.
17. Ragsdale, p.173.

18. Gorodetsky, *Soviet Foreign Policy, 1917-1991: A Retrospective*, p. 72.
19. Ibid., p. 58.
20. Cienciala, p. 156.
21. Geoffrey Roberts, 'Infamous Encounter? The Merekalov-Weizsäcker Meeting of 17 April 1939', *The Historical Journal* Vol. 35, No. 4 (1992), p. 921.
22. Grover Furr, *Leon Trotsky's Collaboration with Germany and Japan* (Erythros Press, 2017), p. 91.
23. Ibid., p. 13.
24. Ibid.
25. Alexander Bittelmann, *Trotsky the Traitor* (1937). PRISM: Political & Rights Issues & Social Movements, p. 6.
26. Michael Jabara Carley, 'End of the "Low, Dishonest Decade": Failure of the Anglo-Franco-Soviet Alliance in 1939', *Europe-Asia Studies* Vol. 45, No. 2 (1993), p. 322.
27. Cienciala. p. 172.
28. Ibid.
29. Ibid., p. 179.
30. Roberts, *The Soviet Union and the Origins of the Second World War*, p. 80.
31. Cienciala, p. 187.
32. Ibid.
33. Carley, p. 305.
34. Ibid., p. 313.
35. Ibid.
36. Ibid., p. 328,
37. Roberts, *The Soviet Union and the Origins of the Second World War*, p. 82.
38. Carley, p. 326.
39. Cienciala, p. 192.
40. Ibid., p. 194.
41. Ragsdale, p. 179.
42. Cienciala, p. 196.
43. Ibid.
44. Moorehouse, *The Devil's Alliance*, p. 33.
45. Ibid., p. 35.
46. Cienciala, p. 148.
47. Carley, p. 330.
48. Erickson, p. 530.
49. Moorehouse, *The Devil's Alliance*, p. 39.
50. Cienciala, p. 202.

51. Ibid., p. 211.
52. H.W. Koch, 'Hitler's "Programme" and the Genesis of Operation "Barbarossa"', *The Historical Journal* Vol. 24, No. 4 (1983), p. 893.
53. Roberts, *The Soviet Union and the Origins of the Second World War*, p. 94.
54. Ibid., p. 96.
55. Ibid., p. 99.
56. Keith Sword, 'British Reactions to the Soviet Occupation of Eastern Poland in September 1939', *The Slavonic and East European Review* Vol. 69, No. 1 (1991), p. 88.
57. Moorehouse, *The Devil's Alliance*, p. 186.
58. Ibid., p. 196.
59. Koch, p. 914.
60. Ibid., p. 918.

Chapter 12: Barbarossa

1. Koch, p. 920.
2. Moorehouse, *The Devil's Alliance*, p. 227.
3. Ibid., p. 232.
4. *The German Campaign in Russia* (Department of the Army Pamphlet 20-261a, 1955), p. 22.
5. Ernst L. Presseisen, 'Prelude to "Barbarossa": Germany and the Balkans, 1940-1941', *The Journal of Modern History* Vol. 32, No. 4 (1960), p. 368.
6. Moorehouse, *The Devil's Alliance*, p. 256.

SOURCES

Alpert, Michael, *Franco and the Condor Legion: The Spanish Civil War in the Air* (Bloomsbury Academic, 2019).

Bittelmann, Alexander, *Trotsky the Traitor* (1937). PRISM: Political & Rights Issues & Social Movements.

Bolianovskyi, Andrii, *Cooperation between the German Military of the Weimar Republic and the Ukrainian Military Organisation, 1923-1928* (Harvard Ukrainian Studies, 1999).

Brown, Timothy S., 'Richard Scheringer, the KPD and the Politics of Class and Nation in Germany, 1922-1969', *Contemporary European History* 14, No. 3 (2005).

Campbell, Kenneth, 'Colonel General Hans von Seeckt', *American Intelligence Journal* Vol. 22 (2004).

Candil, Anthony J., *Tank Combat in Spain: Armoured Warfare During the Spanish Civil War 1936-1939* (Casemate, 2021).

Carl, Samantha, *The Buildup of the German War Economy: The Importance of the Nazi-Soviet Economic Trade Agreements of 1939 and 1940* (Millersville. edu).

Carley, Michael Jabara, 'End of the "Low, Dishonest Decade": Failure of the Anglo-Franco-Soviet Alliance in 1939', *Europe-Asia Studies* Vol. 45, No.2 (1993).

_____, 'Fiasco: The Anglo-Franco-Soviet Alliance that never was and the unpublished British White paper 1939-1940', *The International History Review* 41:4 (2018).

Carr, E.H., *The Bolshevik Revolution* (Baltimore: Penguin, 1953).

Cienciala, Anna Marie, 'The Nazi-Soviet Pact of August 23 1939: When Did Stalin Decide to Align with Hitler and Was Poland the Culprit?', in

Biscupski, M.B.B., *Ideology, Politics and Diplomacy in East Central Europe* (University of Rochester Press, 2003).

Corum, James S., *The Luftwaffe: Creating the Operational Air War 1918-1940* (University Press of Kansas, 1997).

Daycock, Davis William, *The KPD and the NSDAP: A Study of the relationship between political extremes in Weimar Germany, 1923-1933*, PhD thesis, University of London, 1980.

Deets, Michael Joseph, *German-Soviet Relations and the International System*, thesis, College of William & Mary - Arts & Sciences, 1994.

Dukes, Paul and Hiden, John W., 'Towards an Historical Comparison of Nazi Germany and Soviet Russia in the 1930s', *New Zealand Slavonic Journal* No. 1 (1979).

Erickson, John, *The Soviet High Command 1918-1941* (Macmillan & Co Ltd, 1962).

Furr, Grover, *Leon Trotsky's Collaboration with Germany and Japan* (Erythros Press, 2017).

Gatzke, Heinz W., 'Russo-German Military Collaboration During the Weimar Republic', *The American Historical Review* Vol. LXIII, No. 3 (1958).

Glenny, M.V., 'The Anglo-Soviet Trade Agreement, March 1921', *Journal of Contemporary History* Vol. 5, No. 2 (1970).

Gorodetsky, Gabriel, 'The Impact of the Molotov-Ribbentrop Pact on the Course of Soviet Foreign Policy', *Cahiers Du Monde Russe Et Soviétique* Vol. 31, No. 1 (1990).

_____, *Soviet Foreign Policy, 1917-1991: A Retrospective* (Cummings Center Series, 1994).

Gussack, Nevin, *When Brown Meets Red: Nazi-Communist Collaboration 1919-1945* (Createspace Independen Publishing Platform, 2015).

Habek, Mary R., *Storm of Steel: The Development of Armor Doctrine in Germany and the Soviet Union,1919–1939* (Cornell University Press, 2003).

Hallgarten, George W.F., 'General Hans von Seeckt and Russia, 1920-1922', *The Journal of Modern History* Vol. 21, No. 1 (1949).

Higham, Robin and Kipp, Jacob W., *Soviet Aviation and Air Power: A Historical View* (Westview Press, 1977).

Himmer, Robert, 'Rathenau, Russia, and Rapallo', *Central European History* Vol. 9, No. 2 (1976).

_____, 'Soviet Policy Toward Germany during the Russo-Polish War, 1920', *Slavic Review* Vol. 35, No. 4 (1976).

Hooton, E.R., *Phoenix Triumphant: The Rise and Rise of the Luftwaffe* (Brockhampton Press, 1994).

Howson, Gerald, *Arms for Spain: The Untold Story of the Spanish Civil War* (John Murray, 1998).

Johnson, Ian, *The Secret School of War: The Soviet-German Tank Academy at Kama*, thesis, The Ohio State University (2012).

Jukes, G., 'The Red Army and the Munich Crisis', *Journal of Contemporary History* Vol. 26, No. 2 (1991).

Kilmarx, Robert A., *A History of Soviet Air Power* (Faber and Faber, 1962).

Koch, H. W., 'Hitler's "Programme" and the Genesis of Operation "Barbarossa"', *The Historical Journal* Vol. 24, No. 4 (1983).

Kocho-Williams, Alastair, *Engaging the World: Soviet Diplomacy and Foreign Propaganda in the 1920s*, University of the West of England (2007).

Kuss, Mark Davis, *Collective Security or World Domination: the Soviet Union and Germany, 1917-1939*, LSU Doctoral Dissertations (2012).

Larrazabal, Jesus Salas, *Air War over Spain* (Ian Allan, 1974).

Low, Alfred D., 'The Soviet Union, the Austrian Communist Party, and the *Anschluss* Question, 1918-1938', *Slavic Review* Vol. 39, No. 1 (1980).

McCannon, John, 'Soviet Intervention in the Spanish Civil War, 1936-39', *Russian History* Vol. 22, No. 2 (1995).

Moorehouse, Roger, *The Devil's Alliance: Hitler's Pact with Stalin 1939-1941* (Vintage, 2014).

_____, *Poland 1939: The Outbreak of World War II* (Basic Books, 2020).

Munshaw, Harvey Daniel, *Extra! Extra! Read all about it: The British and American Press coverage of German-Soviet Collaboration 1917-1928*, thesis, University of Central Missouri (2008).

Okami, Jun, *Von Seeckt 1920-1926: A Study of Military Management*, thesis, University of Surrey (1988).

Presseisen, Ernst L., 'Prelude to "Barbarossa": Germany and the Balkans, 1940-1941', *The Journal of Modern History* Vol. 32, No. 4 (1960).

Proctor, Raymond L., *Hitler's Luftwaffe in the Spanish Civil War* (Greenwood Press, 1983).

Radomska, Sofiya, *Soviet-German Relations in the Inter-War Period*, thesis, Södertörns högskola University College (2006).

Ragsdale, Hugh, *The Soviets, the Munich Crisis, and the Coming of World War II* (Cambridge University Press, 2004).

Rimmington, Anthony, *Stalin's Secret Weapon: The Origins of Soviet Biological Warfare* (Oxford University Press, 2018).

Roberts, Geoffrey, 'Infamous Encounter? The Merekalov-Weizsäcker Meeting of 17 April 1939', *The Historical Journal* Vol. 35, No. 4 (1992).

_____, *The Soviet Union and the Origins of the Second World War: Russo-German Relations and the Road to War 1933-1941* (Macmillan, 1995).

Rosenbaum, Kurt, 'The German Involvement in the Shakhty Trial', *The Russian Review* Vol. 21, No. 3 (1962).

Sands, Phillippe, *East West Street* (Weidenfeld & Nicolson, 2016).

Schwendemann, Heinrich, 'German-Soviet economic relations at the time of the Hitler-Stalin pact, 1939-1941', *Cahiers Du Monde Russe* Vol. 36, No. 1/2 (1995).

Smith, Arthur L., 'The German General Staff and Russia, 1919-1926', *Soviet Studies* Vol. 8, Issue 2 (1956).

_____, 'General Von Seeckt and the Weimar Republic', *The Review of Politics* Vol. 20, No. 3 (1958).

Sontag, John P., 'The Soviet War Scare of 1926-27', *The Russian Review* Vol. 34, No. 1 (1975).

Stein, George H., 'Russo-German Military Collaboration: The Last Phase, 1933', *Political Science Quarterly* Vol. 77, No. 1 (1962).

Strohn, Matthias, 'Hans Von Seeckt and His Vision of a Modern Army', *War in History* Vol. 12, No. 3 (2005).

Sword, Keith, 'British Reactions to the Soviet Occupation of Eastern Poland in September 1939', *The Slavonic and East European Review*, Vol. 69, No. 1 (1991).

Temin, Peter, 'Soviet and Nazi Economic Planning in the 1930s', *The Economic History Review* Vol. 44, No. 4 (1991).

Tucker, Robert C., 'The Emergence of Stalin's Foreign Policy', *Slavic Review* Vol. 36, No. 4 (1977).

Uldricks, Teddy J., 'Stalin and Nazi Germany', *Slavic Review* Vol. 36, No. 4 (1977).

Waldman, Eric, *The Spartacist Uprising of 1919* (Marquette University, Milwaukee, 1958).

Ward, James J., *Smash the Fascists: German Communist Efforts to Counter the Nazis, 1930-31* (Cambridge University Press, 1981).

Watson, Derek, 'Molotov's Apprenticeship in Foreign Policy: The Triple Alliance Negotiations in 1939', *Europe-Asia Studies* Vol. 52, Issue 4 (2000).

Weitz, John, *Hitler's Diplomat: Joachim von Ribbentrop* (Phoenix, 1997).

Wheeler-Bennett, John W., 'Twenty Years of Russo-German Relations: 1919-1939', *Foreign Affairs* Vol. 25, No. 1 (1946).

_____, 'The Meaning of Brest-Litovsk Today', *Foreign Affairs* Vol. 17, No. 1 (1938).

Wulff, Petter, 'Sweden and Clandestine German Rearmament Technology', *Icon* Vol. 11 (2005).

Zaloga, Steven J., *Spanish Civil War Tanks: The Proving Ground for Blitzkrieg* (Osprey Publishing 2010).

Documents

Anon., 'Russia & Germany: Political and Military Reflections', *Foreign Affairs* Vol. 20, No. 2 (1938).

Secret Supplementary Protocols of the Molotov-Ribbentrop Non-Aggression Pact, 1939 (digitalarchive.wilsoncenter.org)

'The USSR System of Neutrality and Non-Aggression', *Bulletin of International News* (1928).

'The Franco-Soviet Pact of Mutual Assistance', *Bulletin of International News* (1935).

The German Campaign in Russia (US Department of the Army Pamphlet 20-261a, 1955).

'France-USSR: Treaty of Mutual Assistance', *The American Journal of International Law* (1936).

Documents on German Foreign Policy 1918-1945: Jan.-Oct. 1933.

Nuernberg Military Tribunals, 1953, Vol VII.

INDEX